PATH

TO

PUBERTY

THE ULTIMATE RESOURCE GUIDE FOR MOMS OF DAUGHTERS

TATIANA BERINDEI

Path to Puberty: The Ultimate Resource Guide for Moms of Daughters
Copyright © 2024 by Tatiana Berindei

Published by **Voice of the Womb Publications**

Disclaimer:
The information provided in this book is for educational and informational purposes only. It is not intended to be a substitute for professional medical advice, diagnosis, or treatment. Always seek the advice of your physician or other qualified health provider with any questions you may have regarding a medical condition. Please do not disregard professional medical advice or delay in seeking it because of something you have read in this book.

The author and publisher make no representations or warranties with respect to the accuracy, applicability, fitness, or completeness of the contents of this book. They disclaim any warranties (expressed or implied), merchantability, or fitness for any particular purpose. The author and publisher shall in no event be held liable for any loss or other damages, including but not limited to special, incidental, consequential, or other damages.

Trademark names and registered names mentioned in this book are the property of their respective owners and are used for identification purposes only. The use of such names in this book does not imply any affiliation with or endorsement by the trademark or registered trademark owner.

ISBN: 979-8-9906054-0-4

Cover design by Tatiana Berindei
Images by Maria Ramirez Giraldo (DEL)
Printed in the United States of America
First Edition: 2024

This book is dedicated to my daughters - my sun and my moon.
May you walk in beauty, and always know yourselves as sacred.

This book is a multimedia experience. Which means that it comes with a boatload of cool stuff! To redeem your additional files and resources, go to pathtopuberty.com/bookowners. This page will continue to be updated with the latest info and offerings, just for you!

TABLE OF CONTENTS

HOW TO USE THIS BOOK

To be honest, I kind of hate the part in books that tells you how to read them. I find it a bit infantilizing. You are a grown-ass adult and will read this book however the hell you want to. There is a chapter list, so you can see what we're going to be covering. Just read the book! I put the chapters in an order that made sense to me, but that is not necessarily the order you have to read them in. I usually read books in the order in which they were written, but you do you!

The only thing I will suggest you do for sure is read this book *before* your daughter hits puberty. Read it when she's 6, 7, 8 years old - or even younger! And then read it again when she's in the thick of it. And then share your experience with friends. Give them the book, too!

That doesn't mean that if you are picking this up for the first time and your daughter is 11 or 12 or 13, you won't get something out of it. You just also might have some "damn, I wish I had read this sooner" kinds of moments.

I expect this book to become a reference for you that you return to again and again. You could even start a reading group with other moms of daughters! That would honestly be a fabulous way to read this book, as you will then also be cultivating an in-person community, without which the kind of radical culture shift encouraged here is really difficult to create.

This book has exercises in it. Not, like, gym exercises. Personal growth exercises, I guess you could call them? Expansive exploratory exercises.

(Triple E?) I don't know what to call them. I just hope you do those exercises. (Another great reason to read this with others - for the support, accountability, and exercise buddies). I will be honest and say that I rarely do exercises in books, so I won't be heartbroken if you don't do them. (I also, clearly, won't know). But they're pretty good, I think, and they are designed to give you a more 3D, in-depth experience with this material.

I swear sometimes in these pages. (See above. And below). I grew up in the Boston area in the 80s and 90s. It is what it is. This is written in my voice, which is sometimes funny and light, and sometimes very deep. It's also a voice that is sourced from many years in ceremony and deep, earth-based, spiritual practice. So, I'm going to bring things forth from that perspective.

You might know some of the things in here already. Some things or perspectives might be entirely new to you. I wrote this as if it was new to you, so if you find a part and you're like "I know this stuff already," well, then that's cool. And - who knows! Maybe even if you know it already there will be something new in it, or a different way of looking at it, for you too. Or maybe you know more than I do about it and can message me and be like "actually, you were wrong about this part", or "you missed some key info", or "if you said it this way, more people might understand it." And maybe I'll even change it in some future edition! You never know. Unless you are a total asshole about how you present the information. Then probably not.

Like most people, I think I'm right about the things I have conviction about. Which is pretty much the whole book. Unlike most people, I am also willing to have critical conversation and debate (just not on social media) and *sometimes* I even let new information change my perspective and understanding. (Being right does feel really, really good, though, doesn't it?)

Please don't use anything in this book to beat yourself up, or as an example of how you are failing as a parent. Our isolated western culture is what has failed us as parents, and what is failing our children. We are all doing the best we can within that broken structure. The last thing I want is for this book to perpetuate the myth of perfectionism, or the idea that you are somehow doing it wrong. Sure, we can always do better, and I don't think that striving to be better versions of ourselves than we were yesterday is in and of itself a bad thing. It is also just so, so, so important to recognize the things that are working, and that we are doing well, every day.

There is no perfect way to do this life thing. There is cause and effect, things that yield certain results and other things that yield different results. So sometimes we have to play around with what works, and sometimes what worked before doesn't work anymore and we have to adjust course. Your child is unique, as are you, so some things in here just might not apply to you. That's totally okay. There is A LOT in here. If you find just one nugget of gold and apply it, that's amazing. Hopefully, you will find many.

The way I talk about things might not always fit into your worldview. I have not necessarily tried to make this book inclusive. On the whole, I don't actually know if I believe inclusivity as far as ideas are concerned is possible, or if attempts at it are even an entirely positive thing, as I have seen how we often censor what is deep and true in us in the process of trying to caretake other people's feelings under the guise of "inclusivity." At least, that's what I do sometimes. That whole "burned at the stake" memory runs deep in our collective female body. And if it's not censoring ourselves, then we are going around judging one another's words and output to see if it matches up with a certain inclusivity narrative. How are we supposed to have diversity that way, if people are afraid to say anything but what they are "supposed" to say, for fear of being called out or canceled? It just doesn't make sense to me. So I gave up trying to be "inclusive" in this writing and I am just going to speak from my heart and

3

my source of truth. If you don't feel you have the capacity to read this without scanning for the current party line, then it might be best if we just part ways here. I'm not asking you to love everything that I say in here, or even agree with me all the time. But it is my prayer that you can take the info presented here, find the kernel of truth, and mold it into the belief system that makes the most sense to you.

Speaking of belief systems….As I see it, the systems that hold up the majority of organized religion - Christianity, Judaism, Islam, and even Buddhism - are historically based in and have benefited from the suppression of women. I take issue with the global systematic oppression of women and the attempt to wipe out the divine feminine that has been driven by organized religion and empirical expansion, and that still persists to this day. I'm not quiet about that. That's a wound that has seeped into the fabric of our culture and colored our world. We need to face how that has shaped our collective treatment of women, babies, and women's bodies before we can truly move forward. We actually can't talk about reclaiming a way to honor our female bodies, our young daughter's periods, and coming of age without addressing our collective female history. So we will.

At the same time, I also think there is a tremendous amount of crossover in embodied spiritual practice and the core religious teachings from all lineages, so if you are committed to finding value in here, no matter what your background, then you will. But you also might be triggered sometimes. I believe in kindness and giving people grace. Know that about me. I promise I'm not trying to be offensive - but I am from Boston, remember? Also, my dad was from Eastern Europe. I speak bluntly and sometimes with a lot of passion and conviction.

I see that there is great beauty (and total similarity) in the core teachings of all of the major religions that also matches up perfectly with the spiritual teachings I have gathered in my years spent with Indigenous elders from around the world. I celebrate that and have done my best to bring forward the most profound pieces I have gleaned in my spiritual studies.

Sometimes in this book, I will reference a specific Indigenous teacher or teaching. When I do this, it is because I have been given the express permission to do so by that person and have checked in with them to make sure that the way I am delivering the information is accurate. (Unless they are no longer alive, in which case I have done my best to honor them and make a request from the spiritual dimensions, or have directly asked permission from their descendants.) Much harm has been done by white people taking information and resources that don't belong to them and, without permission, reappropriating it for their own benefit. The kindness and inherent giving nature of Indigenous cultures does not excuse that kind of behavior.

As a way of expressing my profound gratitude for the positive impacts that Indigenous wisdom has had on my life path, 10% of the quarterly profits of this book over its lifetime will be returned to these cultures in 4 ways: There are two grandmothers that I have direct and long-standing relationships with, Grandmother Nancy Andry and Nana Vilma Cholac Chicol, who will benefit from a portion of the proceeds of this book so that they can continue to travel, teach, and do their sacred medicine work in the world. Some funds will go to support the Medicine Wheel Ride (https://www.medicinewheelride.org/), a group founded in response to the atrocities that are happening today against women on reservations across the US and Canada that Grandmother Nancy is a strong supporter of. The rest will go to support the Nateema Jee Shuar Cultural Center in the Amazon, started by one of my elders, Natem Anank Nunkai, and continued in his memory by his wife and son. So, know that by purchasing this book, and sharing it widely, you are contributing to these causes as well. Thank you.

Lastly, if you have picked this up and you are a dad: first of all, I commend you for caring enough about your daughter to enter into territory that is clearly foreign to you. This book was not written for you - the language is directed specifically at women and mothers - but that doesn't mean you won't be able to glean valuable information that you can use to help your daughter become the fullest version of herself. I'm assuming that if you are reading this as a dad, it's because your daughter's mother is unavailable, no longer alive or absent for some other reason. If that is the case, please know that my heart is with you - and thank you again for caring enough to read something like this. We need more men like you.

If you're a dad just reading it because you're interested and curious, that's cool too! We need more men like you, also. There are gifts in the design of a woman's body that we discuss that will obviously be out of reach for you. But I have also seen some incredible men do really good work at accessing their inner softness through being willing to implement some of the tools and concepts in this book. If you have not already done so, I strongly encourage you to find a female mentor for your daughter as she walks through these coming years, and share this book with that woman. Even when your heart is in the right place (which, if you're reading this, I am sure it is) there will be situations when there is just no substitute for a safe and loving female role model.

Okay, I think that's it. Enjoy! Let me know how it goes!

WHY THIS BOOK

A Woman is a Whole Universe[1]

In these pages, you will find topics that might seem unnecessary to include in a book on puberty. They are in here because the world of women, and what it means to be in a woman's body, is an entire universe.

We have been conditioned to see the natural functioning of our bodies as an inconvenience at best, or as sinful and dirty and something to be done away with at worst. This conditioning runs deep. It is at the core of many religions. It is in the very fabric of obstetrics and gynecology, in women's health care, and a distortion of it even exists at the core of the modern-day feminist movement.

The foundations of our contemporary feminist, liberal, western society are built upon this premise: that as women we are no different from men and can do everything that men can do and more. Taken at face value, heck yes! I'm not saying that we should limit what we deem women as capable of by any means. Women are fucking amazing! But if we look a bit deeper, there is something else going on underneath here, something that still has its origin in the misogynist idea of our bodies as sinful or somehow wrong.

---

[1] In my Radical Birthkeeper training with Emilee Saldayya and Yolande Norris Clark, there was one day when Emilee related a story to us in class of the moment when she realized that she had only been looking at one side of an early birth client of hers, but the woman was, in fact "a whole universe." This phrase stuck, cause, yeah. She is.

7

We don't often think of it this way, but the core of political feminism as it's currently practiced is rooted in the false narrative that our biological processes are to be done away with and manipulated as much as possible so that we can level the playing field with men. Menstruation and motherhood are considered to be lesser aspects of womanhood, second to a career, and they really don't have much of a place in a productive, go-go-go, success-oriented society. In response to a culture completely built and designed by men and for the 24hr male clock, this makes sense.

But what if it's not our bodies and biological processes that need changing? What if it's the playing field? What if we are actually being called to restructure how our culture works? I think it's pretty safe to say at this point that the pace and flow of our culture isn't working very well for anybody anymore - men included.

I have such gratitude and respect for the generations of women before me who paved the way to make a more inclusive place in our society for women to hold positions of power and influence. I cannot imagine living in a world where I would be simply deemed someone else's property, would need my father's, brother's, or husband's permission to do just about anything, and couldn't open my own bank account - not to mention vote.

But in the early days, there were actually two feminist movements: one that placed the emphasis on denying our biology and focusing on the equality of our mental brilliance so that we could be toe-to-toe with the men, and one that, in addition to honoring our mental brilliance and equality, placed more emphasis on the amazing wonder of the female body and learning deeply about it in order to harness its wisdom and free ourselves from the shackles of the authoritative healthcare system that is especially damaging to women. The first camp is the one that eventually overtook the feminist movement and is at the core of what we now know as feminism. This book picks up where the second camp left off.

While I respect the feminist movement in many ways, I cannot help but wonder - what has been the cumulative cost of denying our biology? What is the impact on our health - physically, spiritually, and emotionally - and therefore the future of our society? Could it be possible that in denying or trying to override our unique female biology in order to be societally equivalent to men, we have actually created a larger handicap for ourselves and cut ourselves off from the deepest well of power that only those born in women's bodies have access to?

I believe the key to true equality and justice is to celebrate what makes us unique and different, and to own it wholly and completely, without needing to change or modify ourselves to fit some standard set by someone else. This *includes* our biology. It means restructuring the world to include the inherent wisdom in women and the children born from them, not squashing ourselves into a truncated version so we can fit into the world designed by and for men. It means re-structuring our culture, and our world, to honor the pacing of the bodies of women, because the body of a woman is the body of the earth, and the earth is sacred. Without her, humanity cannot exist. This is what my elders have taught me and what I know to be true in my bones.

The truth is - we ARE different from men. And different is not bad. It does not make us weaker. If we learn how to harness the power inherent in our constantly changing bodies, it actually can give us a tremendous advantage. This is the secret and the power that nobody talks about, the root of the patriarchal stronghold, and much of what we will explore together in these pages. And what a gift that we get to start our girls out in this way.

You can take your womb health into your own hands, and you can teach your daughter to do the same. In fact, in most cases, as you will see in the pages of this book, once you have honed it, your intuition and sense of what is happening in your own body is going to be far more accurate than any medical professional's opinion that you will come across in your journey of women's health.

Our health is in our hands. Our health is in our wounds - that's right, in our dark and scary and hurting places. Our health is in our hearts. Why do we have to outsource our agency to someone else? It is quite literally up to us to take back our health, and it starts with making friends with our femaleness. All of the diets, exercise, and self-love affirmations aren't going to do much if, deep down, you have been taught to hate your body and its monthly functions.

We are moving out of a time when we have long been identified as victims of our physical experience. This victim story is the biggest lie we were ever sold. The gifts of a woman's body are vast and innumerable. The power available to us when we choose to fully inhabit ourselves is indescribable. The subjugation of women throughout history stems from a desire to dominate and control this power. Yes, we are working with thousands of years of programming, so turning it around in one generation is unlikely. However, I have not completely written it off. What if it is possible? What if our generation teaching our daughters what is in this book is the tipping point? We still have a long way to go and a lot of work to do, but it starts now, in this moment. It starts with a willingness to befriend our bodies, love our wombs, take a breath, and pause in gratitude for the experience of being born female. It is not a curse. It is our greatest wealth.

We are at a time in history unlike any other that we have ever seen. For the first time, women in many places have access to roles and positions of political power we never dreamed possible before. Through the brilliance of her mind, a woman truly can become whatever she decides she wants to be in life (at least in many countries). At the same time, in very different circles, ancient wisdom is being resurrected about how to be in a healthy relationship with the sacred vessel that is a woman's body. I believe that we are seeing, possibly for the first time ever, a time when both truths get to coexist. One does not have to be at the expense of another. It is my hope that within these pages we will weave these two worlds together: the worlds of intellect and intuition, of mind and body, of success in the outer world and a feeling of wholeness within.

My Story

When my oldest daughter, Sunna, was born in 2012, I had already been on my spiritual journey for over 10 years. While not fully launched into my career path yet, I definitely had gathered a life education unlike anything you could ever find in school, in addition to my years of college.

I had survived a psychically and emotionally abusive, yet very informative, relationship with a Cherokee medicine man. With him, I learned the ins and outs of abusive relationship power dynamics (as well as a ton of medicinal and food plants, and wilderness survival skills). I escaped this relationship with the help of my mother, who bought me a one-way ticket to the big island of Hawaii where her friend ran a Dharma retreat center.

In Hawaii, I reclaimed my sovereignty and sexual power, learned how to transmute anger into gardens, and connected with my blood, doing self-guided rituals to honor my moontime and my womb. Hawaii was where I built my first moonlodge, with the grace of my teacher, Rashani, and where I wrote "the list" that helped me manifest the man who would later become my husband. At this time, I also started learning about somatic process work, diving deep into Peter Levine's trauma work, Arnold Mindell's Dreambody process work, and Byron Katie's The Work, as well as the teachings of many great spiritual leaders.

By the time Sunna was born, I had taught for years in preschools and Waldorf schools, and worked two thirds of my life as a nanny. This work and the study that accompanied it was foundational in my understanding of child development, and has informed much of my parenting journey.

I had also been thrown into the study of death and the afterlife by the deaths of my father and brother, both occurring shortly after my wedding and within three months of each other. To help me process their deaths and my immense grief, I became a Sundancer in the Ghost Sundance that was started by Sam Little Owl on the Fort Berthold Reservation in North Dakota. It was there that I also learned a tremendous amount about the ceremony of menstruation. For years, every time I set foot on the Sundance grounds, I would bleed. Much instruction, from both the human and spirit realms, was given to me during that time.

As my peers finished school and started their careers, I followed my deep longing for an education that I knew I would not be able to find within the walls of academia. I spent years traveling the country, going to ceremony after ceremony, and working gig jobs just long enough to save up enough to go to the next ceremony. When Sunna was born, I had already recorded an album with my husband of entirely original songs grounded in the spiritual truths I was uncovering on my journey. I had begun my study with the medicine Natem with a dear Uwishin (or traditional healer in the Shuar language) from the jungles of Ecuador. I was a year into my 2-year ministry training at the Center for Sacred Studies. I had begun my study of homebirth midwifery and was actively attending births, both as a midwifery student in people's homes and as a doula in the hospital. I was pretty deep into my study of "women's empowerment" and thought I knew a thing or two. I was kind of arrogant about it, if I'm honest.

And then came Sunna.

After a grueling and unexpected hospital induction, I lay there with a warm, squirmy, slimy little person on my chest, both of us completely and utterly stunned and shocked by the unfolding of the last 24 hrs. I thought I would be doing this at home. I had chosen to forgo ultrasounds in my pregnancy, so the sex of the baby was a surprise. I had been totally convinced in my pregnancy that I was carrying a boy. (True of my second pregnancy too. I was wrong both times). The moment I realized that not only did I now have a tiny person to take care of but that tiny person was *female*, I heard a voice say loud and clear, "Now the REAL WORK begins." In that moment, it was clear to me that everything I thought I knew about the power of women was just a scratch on the surface and that this child was going to be my greatest teacher yet.

This has proven to be unequivocally true - of both her and her sister. But Sunna is the one who inspired this book because she is the one whom I have successfully brought through 12 years of life at the time of this writing, and who was not only completely prepared for and anticipating her first menses, but is a shining, mostly happy and confident 12-year-old girl. She comes to me with all her questions about her body and her feelings, and she trusts me as the best resource for information about these things.

This is MUCH more than I could say for myself at her age. When I was 12, I was shy and depressed, overweight, and several years into a compulsive eating disorder that I still struggle with sometimes to this day. I had little clue about periods and what to expect, but already had stretch marks on my thighs that my mother vigorously rubbed aloe lotion on in an attempt to make them go away because, as it was very clearly hammered into me, having stretch marks, especially at my young age, was NOT okay. My body, as it was, was not okay. The lotion gave me an allergic reaction (my mother's anguish probably did too), and my mother gave up in exasperation, clearly horrified by how my body was evolving.

When I finally did start my period that year, I knew that something magical and very special had just happened. But I seemed to be the only one who felt that way. Everyone else held it in the "things we don't talk about" category, and I was quickly conditioned to identify this time of the month as a grave inconvenience and something to regularly complain about with my peers.

By the time I was Sunna's current age, I "knew everything there was to know about sex" because my "well-educated" peers had taught me. I started having descriptive and in-depth conversations with my friends about sex when I was 8, and my play with my best friend at the time would often consist of imaginary scenarios where we would be "making out" with our boyfriends against the wall. Yup, 8 years old. By the time my parents tried to have "the talk" with me when I was 10, I had already practiced giving a banana a blow job and was MORTIFIED at the thought of having any conversation about sex with my parents. They handed me a book, which saved all of us the embarrassment of actually having to discuss the topic in person, to my deep disadvantage.

If there was one thing that drove me to do things differently with my own child, it was this fact. Of course, there were many factors that drove this, as I'm sure there are for you in picking up this book, but this was one of the most motivating, as I hope to spare her the years I spent hating and degrading myself and giving away my sexual energy and power to boys and men who definitely did not deserve it.

Getting Comfortable with Being Uncomfortable

We think our children are innocent in ways that they might not actually be. Our children are curious and inquisitive, starting really young. They want to know where babies come from. They want to know about their bodies and other people's bodies. *There is absolutely nothing wrong with this.* It is the most normal thing in the world. And if *we* don't proactively teach them about it, **they will find the information somewhere else.**

In today's digital age, where the world's compiled information is at our fingertips (along with a whole lotta porn and sexual predation), that terrifies the heck out of me. But it also motivates me to provide something different. Something holistic and rooted in ancient esoteric wisdom. Something to remind our girls of the inherent power that they were born with, simply by being born into the brilliance of a woman's body.

We don't want to think of our children as sexual beings, with good reason. The sexual objectification of children is one of the most abhorrent things I can conceive of, and it makes me sick to my stomach to know that this happens around the planet every single day. But our children are human, which means that if they grow to maturity, as we all hope they will, they will be faced with sex. Just like we teach them to dress themselves, put their things away, brush their teeth, eat with utensils, count, and read and write, it is also our responsibility to teach and prepare them for the world of sex and sexuality. And just like the above-mentioned actions, it is important to teach them about it in a gradual and evolving way that meets them where they are in their development and readiness.

We don't like having conversations about sex and bodies with our kids because it makes us uncomfortable. We have no roadmap, and we feel totally awkward. For most of us, we did not have parents that explained things to us in a way that worked for us or actually educated us about what was happening in our bodies, what was normal and what wasn't.

I have one friend whose mother never told her about her period and what it was. She simply woke up one morning in a pool of blood and understandably thought she was dying. I sadly have heard a similar story from many women along my journey. Maybe you are even one of them.

For most of us, we still have complicated relationships with our own bodies and sexuality, even as sexually active adults with children. We feel unprepared for the conversations when the questions arise. They catch us off-guard, and so we punt them down the road for later. We avoid, we change the subject, we make up cute words that aren't real to describe body parts (more on this and why it is so detrimental later), or we just straight up lie.

This isn't a book primarily about talking to your girls about sex, but sex is a topic well-covered here because, as we go into detail about later, you cannot separate sex from the puberty conversation, as much as you might want to. The biological purpose of puberty is to prepare our bodies for sex. So, we'll talk about biology.

But there is also a deeply spiritual side to holding a womb inside of our bodies. This womb work has been at the core of my spiritual instruction and maturation these past 20 years. Woven into these pages, you will find much of what I have gleaned from my work not only with my own womb, but with countless other women in ceremonial and healing spaces.

Restoring Birth and the Mother-Baby Matrix

While this is primarily about puberty, I would be remiss if I didn't mention birth here, because the world of birth as it is today is what initially led me to sovereign birth work, and then to writing a book about puberty. My views on birth are radically different from most of what you will find out there, but they are informed by my deep work with the womb, my own journey, and what I am hearing in stories from around the world as women take birth back into their own hands.

When we work with the womb, we work with blood, we work with birth, and we work with death. These are all the realms of the women's mysteries. What we have today in the developed world in terms of birth practices, *especially* in the US, is nothing short of barbaric. In modern American birth practices, the women's mysteries have been usurped and distorted, with devastating results. In the United States, maternal mortality rates are steadily *rising* despite (and likely because of) increased technological interference. This maternal death rate is even worse among black and Hispanic populations.[2] Cesareans now constitute a third of all births in the United States - a statistic formerly unheard of as recently as 40 years ago (though not nearly as bad as in my father's home country of Romania, where I recently learned that the cesarean rate is around 90% because most doctors there no longer know how to support a vaginal birth).[3]

Most obstetricians globally have never witnessed a normal, physiological birth in its undisturbed, brilliant unfolding. Therefore, they have no idea

---

[2] https://www.cdc.gov/nchs/data/hestat/maternal-mortality/2021/maternal-mortality-rates-2021.htm
[3] From a lecture given on March 7th at the 2024 WALC conference by Kajsa Brimdyr PhD, CLC

how to support a woman's body to do what it is designed to do. This is mostly because supporting that process requires them to get out of the way almost entirely. How terribly humbling. The result is that the inherited mammalian wisdom that has been passed on to us in our DNA through hundreds of thousands of years of successfully birthing babies undisturbed and outside of hospitals is being systematically thwarted. Our bodies are not suddenly more broken now than our ancestors' were, we've just entrusted them into the wrong hands. If birth didn't work, and work exceptionally well on its own, human beings would not still be here.

Nowhere else have women so outsourced their agency and power than in the world of birth. What would be considered rape and abuse in any other context is somehow considered normal in the world of obstetrics, so much so that women don't even question the routine practice of cervical checks, electronic fetal monitoring, routine IVs, ultrasounds, or giving mother and baby narcotics such as fentanyl in the form of epidurals, which are sold to women as a mostly harmless and benign procedure when nothing could be further from the truth. The drugs we receive while in labor not only pass into the baby and influence their first hours and days of life, but they also influence the baby's tastes and desired flavor preferences in the future.[4] This means that when we give birth drugged, we quite literally give our children a taste for drugs. But no one tells us this. This normalization of violence and abuse towards women and babies is what pains me the most about our current birth culture.

We have *so many* cultural myths to unpack around what is considered "normal" in a human birth. When you start to dive into the world of physiological birth, at first it can seem overwhelming. Birth has almost

---

[4] From a lecture given on March 7th at the 2024 WALC conference by Kajsa Brimdyr PhD, CLC

everything to do with energy and VERY little, if anything, to do with "science." We have it so backwards. And our maternal mortality rate is evidence of that. Babies die sometimes. More often than mothers do (or are supposed to). That is a sad, and also true, part of the natural cycle of life, of which death is an inextricable part. From the perspective of the natural world, it makes far more sense for a baby to die than for a mother. The natural fact of it doesn't make it any less devastating. And, in nature, mothers die sometimes, too. Death is - and will always be - a part of birth.

When babies die in a hospital we don't hear anything about it. Because the baby was in the hospital, the cultural assumption is that everything that could have been done to save the baby's life was done. We don't question if anything could possibly have been done to endanger it in the first place. So it becomes a non-thing. Not for the families of course, but for the rest of us. We just don't really hear about it.

But if a baby dies at home, it makes all the media outlets. Someone has to be found at fault. Someone had to have done something wrong. It is so hard for us to be with the excruciating pain of loss, that we have to find someone to blame. We have so much cultural cognitive dissonance around the fact that sometimes babies die. And the inconvenient truth around it is that sometimes it just happens - and it isn't anyone's fault. It's just part of life.

I'm not trying to be cavalier about this immensely sensitive and devastating topic. In some ways, it isn't even my place to discuss it, as both of my children were born alive, and stayed that way. And yet - I have given birth. Twice. And to give birth - especially outside of the hospital or medical midwifery model as I did with my last baby - is to contend with and face the possibility of death, of both yourself, and of your baby. There is no way around it. The truth is that none of us will get out of here alive. And some of us don't ever make it past the portal of birth.

The number one myth - that all of our other birth myths stem from - is that we have the power to control life and death. And that we can take death out of the birth equation. And the immense irony is that the more we try to take death out of the birth equation, the more maternal death, trauma and abuse ensues. If we were to truly stop trying to take death out of the birth equation, we'd likely see far less trauma and maternal death.

I am in no way saying that we should never try to save a life if we are able to do so. And I am very grateful for the advances in modern medicine, especially when it comes to emergencies. What I am saying is that our immense fear of the reality of death in birth has caused us to see problems and pathology in the birth process where there are none.

It is because of this fear that we have almost entirely forgotten what birth is originally designed to be, in its most natural state. It is my most fervent prayer, for the sake of our future generations and for the health of mothers, that we remember.

Birth in its original design is meant to be a tremendous rite of passage for a woman. It is when she faces death to give life to the future. When left to operate as intended; that is, when she surrenders to divine forces larger than her small self, childbirth shows her how powerful she is. It prepares her to believe in herself so strongly that she is well-equipped to mother her new baby and all of the unknown that comes with that. The natural hormonal elixir, that is only fully released when birth and postpartum are undisturbed, imprints both the mother and baby with the neural pathways necessary to access a deep connection to the divine.[5]

---

[5] Portal: The Art of Choosing Orgasmic, Pain-Free, Blissful Birth by Yolande Norris-Clark

Oxytocin has been dubbed the "love hormone," and at no other time in a human's life is the level of this hormone more elevated than in the first hour after birth - *when that hour is undisturbed.* When we arrive here, we are meant to be imprinted with love. If you take away all the dogma and all the story, LOVE is what is at the center of all of the world's religious and spiritual teachings. This sacred and irreplaceable original imprinting is what we are sacrificing at the altar of modern obstetrics. Yes, we will still love our babies even if our births are disturbed, but will we love them with an intensity and unquenchable fire that consumes every fiber and every cell in our being simultaneously, permeates to the core, and radiates outward towards infinity? Maybe not. BULLSHIT

The sovereign birth world led me to writing a book about puberty because it is once we start to bleed that the depth of negative programming around womanhood really starts to sink in. Our first blood is our introduction into the women's mysteries. If our introduction into those mysteries is shrouded in shame, disgust, and a distancing of ourselves from our bodies and their natural processes, then outsourcing our moment-to-moment decision-making power to someone who "knows more than we do" when it becomes our time to birth is an easy and natural next step for our cultural initiation.

No one knows more than you do about your body or your baby. No one else inhabits your body 24/7. Why have we been led to believe that someone else can know us better than we can know ourselves? Being supported and giving away our power are two entirely different things. There is no power for a woman in birthing outside of her home, her sacred territory. This is true whether we are with an obstetrician or with a midwife. When she enters a hospital, she has entered a battlefield and will likely have to fight hard for the right of her body to make its own intuitive choices, for her right to refuse interventions and to escape being gaslit, coerced, ignored, patronized, drugged, abused, and lied to by those she has entrusted with her and her baby's care. Either that or she will rest fully into it, believing the lie that she is making the safest choice for her and her baby, when in truth, over 98% of births would occur more safely and without any need for medical assistance or intervention if trusted and left alone.[6]

If she feels an inner hollowness that she can't explain afterwards, there is usually no one to turn to who won't just tell her how wonderful it is that she has a healthy baby. Worst is when she has been successfully convinced that her or her baby's life truly was in danger, and that the place and the people that likely caused the near-death experience were, in fact, instrumental to her and/or her baby's survival. This is the story she carries and shares with others, even if somewhere, buried way deep down, she knows it isn't actually true. This is how the myth of the safety of the hospital birth is perpetuated. Her body knows the truth, but she has been repeatedly conditioned over her years as a menstruating woman to disregard that inner wisdom. Her trust in herself and her ability to mother has been damaged by it all, and she continues to seek outside of herself for guidance on how best to care for her new infant. And on it goes in a vicious cycle.

I am deeply and profoundly sorry if some of this is part of your birthing story. Know that **it is not your fault**. The cultural, fear-based narrative and programming around birth is so amazingly strong and pervasive that its current can be very, very hard to buck. And even then, it is only possible to do so if you know that it is necessary. Most women never even know or believe that birthing outside of this maniacal system is an option for them. But it is. More and more women around the world every day are choosing

---

[6] Spiritual Midwifery by Ina May Gaskin

the path of sovereign birth, as evidenced by the vast and ever-growing library of stories on the Freebirth Society podcast. Learning this after we have already birthed our babies can bring up some very real and very deep grief, and that is okay and normal. There are tools, stories, and exercises in these pages that can help you start to soothe and heal some of the pain that might come up for you after reading this. I've got you, Mama. We are in this together. You are not alone.

We can do better than this. We will. The way we view and talk to our daughters about birth matters so very much - just as much as everything else in here, if not more so. I hope that this book can be a part of shifting the way we raise future women to know themselves. It starts with our birth. And then it starts with first menses. And then it starts with pregnancy, birth, and postpartum. And then it starts with menopause. And then it starts with death. And then it starts again with birth. It is not a line, but a circle. So, knowing where to start was tricky for me at first. But starting here - by reclaiming this blood rite of passage for our young girls - was for me, at this time, with my eldest daughter about to cross the threshold, the next logical step.

Reclaiming Ancient Tradition, or Something New?

It is easy, and quite common, to romanticize ancient traditions and times of yore. Indigenous peoples around the world often find themselves the object of fascination and projection by those (primarily anglo) people who grew up without a clear sense of spiritual connection or lineage. Ultimately, though, we are all just fallible human beings, no matter what our lineage.

I believe that a strong connection to larger spiritual truths is a human need. However, in our quest for a sense of belonging to something larger, outside of formal religion, it is easy to glom onto ancient traditions that belong to other cultures - both on our soil and elsewhere. This is almost always going to get you into trouble (speaking from direct experience here - and lots of it!), and if it doesn't get you into trouble, it most certainly makes you kind of an unconscious ass.

Every single one of us on this planet can trace our roots back to Indigenous cultures from someplace. Most of us at this point are mixtures of cultures and tribes and colonizers from all over. Every culture had something valuable to offer before it was colonized - an original wisdom that still exists to this day, in our very DNA.

While I do carry some practices from lineages that I was not born into that have been handed directly to me, I do so *because they have been handed directly to me* by an Indigenous person who requests that I carry it and has given me extensive direction behind it. To just take a teaching because I like how it looks or sounds or the concepts and ideas behind it, without any direct encouragement, instruction, permission, or acknowledgment of where it comes from is what constitutes cultural appropriation. Being given something and taking something are two totally different things.

When it comes to traditional Native American cultures, lumping them all into one "Native American" group is problematic. Every tribe had and has their own way of doing things, and many disagree/d with one another's ways. Some were/are even diametrically opposed in their approaches. In my spiritual journey through ceremonies with a variety of different tribal elders, I have come across a broad spectrum of approaches to menstruation that vary from tribe to tribe and person to person. One of the things I struggled with the most, especially at first, is the segregation of menstruating women from the majority of tribal ceremonies. This is something that challenges most non-native women I know who were raised with deeply feminist values. This segregation, however, was also the doorway for me into learning everything I currently know about the spiritual aspects of menstruation.

Sometimes in this book I refer to menstruation as "moontime." This is mostly because some of the indigenous cultures that I have worked with call it that, and it has stuck in my vernacular. Using the word moontime is also an acknowledgement of our inherent connection with the ocean, and the influence on the tides of our inner waters that the moon can have.

The sweat lodge is a ceremony that exists across many different tribes and goes by different names - inipi, temezcal, etc. What is pretty universal, with some exceptions based on the person pouring the lodge, is the protocol of women on their moontime not going into the lodge along with everyone else. When I first encountered this protocol, I was outraged. I saw it merely as a form of subjugation and oppression of women, and I would fume when not allowed in because of my menses. But as I calmed down enough to ask questions and open myself to learning *why*, I was often met with some beautiful responses (AND sometimes misogyny and confirmation of my original outrage).

In its highest, most respected form, it is understood by many cultures that one of the reasons a woman on her moon does not attend a ceremony with everyone else is that she is already in ceremony, simply by being on her moon. When given the space and solitude (or company of a few other women in a similar state), without being required to care for everyone else's needs, moontime is a ceremony. Period. (I just couldn't help myself...)

Having a special, beautiful space prepared for mooning women to go, to be in prayer outside of the main ceremony, helps hold the reminder to women that they and this time are sacred - and a lot of ceremonial spaces do not have this. (I could write a whole book just about this one piece, and maybe someday I will). When menstrual segregation becomes a problem is when a woman does not know how to pray, or has never been taught how to be in ceremony with herself or communion with something larger than herself - Mother Earth, God, Universe, Source, Creator, what-have-you. Without the physical space to anchor in that reminder and support her to learn this in herself, it can feel punitive. This is part of why it lands so hard for many anglo women when they come into these spaces in an attempt to remember just that - how to pray. When a baseline practice of prayer is not in place, then this "rule" of sitting out ceremony does feel like some kind of punishment, rooted in a lack of trust of the woman to be able to hold herself in respect and integrity.

Moontime energy can be strong, and it deserves to be respected as such. But that doesn't mean it needs to be feared or shunned. Sam Little Owl, the Mandan medicine man who founded the Ghost Sundance in North Dakota, taught the rule of CSR - that if a woman on her moon is holding herself with 1) Care for the people 2) Sincerity in her prayers, and 3) Respect for all present, then she can do no harm. She can only help amplify the prayers of the people. This is a beautiful teaching to start inhabiting in your own life and to pass on to your daughter, and is shared here with the blessing of Sam's daughter, Joni Little Owl.

Every person who runs ceremony does so in their own way. Some are very traditional and adhere to strict protocol that has been handed down to them. When strict protocol is in place, it can be helpful to give ceremonial leaders/holders the benefit of the doubt and receive it as being out of deep respect for you, your primal connection to spirit, and the timing of your personal ceremony. So much collective healing is happening right now, and honoring our moontime as the personal ceremony that it is, especially in ceremonial spaces, is part of that healing. If you find yourself on the pathway to attending traditional indigenous ceremonies, make sure you ask about and adhere to their protocol around moontime. Whether we agree wholeheartedly with the way someone does something or not, it is important to be respectful in how we show up. This is especially true of white people being invited into Native space, but really it's just also true all the time.

For *years*, nearly always when it was time to go into ceremony, I would get my moon - even if it wasn't quite time yet, and even if I had been planning and preparing for the ceremony for months. It didn't matter what kind of ceremony it was, either - sweat lodge, Sundance, retreat of some kind, medicine ceremony - my body didn't seem to care. In fact, it seemed to want me to learn about the ceremony of moontime by being in and around ceremony during this time. For it was in these years that my moon, more than anything, taught me what I share in this book and live in my life.

I want it to be made very clear that I have nothing but gratitude, love, and respect for the First Nations elders and teachers that I have had, and still have, on my spiritual journey. I have been humbled a million times over (I'm sure that part isn't done yet!), brought to tears of gratitude and joy, laughed harder than I ever have in my life, found a life-long community, and found my way into union with divine creation and the Creator. I learned how to pray. No amount of money could ever come close to valuing what I have received and continue to receive from these ancient lineages and teachings.

And yet many of the things I am sharing with you, unless cited, for the most part are information that was given directly to me by a higher intelligence that spoke to me during my menses. While that information was, I'm sure, informed by the spaces I was in and the people I was around, unless I directly state the person or tribe I received the information from, it was from this source. And if I share something that was shared with me by another, it is only done with the express consent of that person or their descendants.

In my years of study, I had many elders continually encourage me to seek my own indigenous European roots. So much was lost of ancient European knowledge during the times of the Inquisition and the colonization of Europe by the Roman and Ottoman empires (before it was even officially Europe). When I did go searching for it, I finally realized that much of the ancient knowledge from my own cultural heritage in Russia and Romania was preserved within the rituals of the Orthodox Church. This was made clear upon my father's death, when I intimately encountered the Romanian Orthodox rituals around honoring the dead. It makes sense if you think about it. If you have to capitulate or die, you find a way to bring the traditions in with you.

No one owns the earth. No one owns the plants, the wind, the water, or the fire. When we learn how to come into right relationship with ourselves, we learn how to come into right relationship with these elements as well. This relationship with the elements, more than anything else, is the most valuable thing I have learned in my years and years of ceremonial life. And that communication with the elements is something no tribe can claim. In my experience with a diversity of tribes, it is the one thing that unites them all. It is a birthright given to every human being and known by every traditional culture around the world.

I believe we are in a time of creating something new. The elders are even saying it is time to make new ceremonies. It is not a time to appropriate ancient wisdom from cultures that aren't ours. There are ancient technologies that some cultures are holding that are very helpful to know in these times, and that some elders are still willing to teach if asked in a respectful way. But even then, we need to learn the best ways to apply them to the world as it is now. I think this is especially true when it comes to moontime and our daughters. I think we are in a time when we are creating new rituals, new ceremonies, and new culture around what it means to bleed and what it means to be a woman. This is exciting - and can sometimes be challenging too. We like having things spelled out for us. We like maps. We like to know where we are going. And with these kinds of rites of passage, outside of rare guidance we might receive from cultures that still know how to do this well, there really isn't a clear map. Even with that guidance, we still have to take it and mold it to work for the generations that are here crossing this threshold now.

Throughout the course of this book, you will gain valuable tools you can use to start creating *your* version of the map, but the creating itself you will have to do on your own and in your community. The map is inside us. The map is our wombs. The map is the constellation of who we are in community with and everything they bring with them. It will be different for each one of you. It will not be a one-size-fits-all approach. And that is so incredibly wonderful!

For Her, Through You

If it's not already clear, this book is not aimed at children. This book is written for you, Mama, as a woman who was raised in a world with *insane* conditioning around what it means to be a woman, from all sides. I wrote this not only as a roadmap to help you support your daughter in blossoming into a self-assured young woman, prepared to deal with her changing body and the world at large. I also wrote it as a guide for you to start embodying some of these principles and teachings in your own life (if you aren't already), and to either start or continue to heal your relationship with your own womb and her stories.

When you have conscious awareness and the tools to navigate it, getting sideswiped by your own past and conditioning is much more manageable. It will still happen, but you'll be better prepared and equipped to deal with it when it does. It is my desire and intention that the exercises and perspectives I am sharing can help you to untangle some of that conditioning and set the framework to bring forward what you truly want for your daughter.

Like it or not, the best and primary education we give our children is the lives we lead right in front of their eyes. This is the hardest truth about parenting, and the greatest lesson that my daughters continue to give me. They will not do what I say, or take any advice from me, unless I am modeling that advice in my own life and behavior. Oof! And even then sometimes not, because they are their own people and need to find their own path in the world. It can be a tough pill to swallow. This parenting shit is hard sometimes! But the sooner we get this and start doing the work on ourselves in our own lives, the better off we, and our children, will be.

So let's dive in!

CHAPTER 1

WARNING: YOUR DAUGHTER'S PUBERTY WILL BRING UP ALL YOUR SHIT FROM MIDDLE SCHOOL

It's true. I'm sorry if I am the first person to tell you this.

I was honestly kind of terrified of my daughter reaching this age. For me, middle school was THE WORST three years of my life and you could not pay me any amount of money to go back and do that all over again in exactly the same way. It was so bad.

When she turned 9, I started having mini panic moments. I would suddenly be gripped by fear that she would have to face some of the monsters I dealt with in my youth. And the same monsters started to haunt me again. Memories of getting kicked out of my 7th grade lunch table would resurface, fresh as if it just happened yesterday. My own body image stuff started to get more pronounced than ever.

I felt entirely unprepared for what lay ahead. In certain moments, I would freeze and be *extra* careful about what came out of my mouth, so as not to perpetuate the harm that was caused to me by my mother's words when I was that age. Sometimes the best route for me has just been to shut my mouth entirely and focus on my breathing - or walk away. It has not always been an easy path. But I am so grateful that I've had tools and resources to lean into as my daughter and I have traveled this journey together.

While we are mainly focusing on the microcosm of your family, your daughter, and your internal experience as a mother in this work, I don't believe that we can separate the individual from the collective experience and context within which we find ourselves. Those middle school horror stories didn't just happen out of nowhere. So, because of that, we're going to dive into a *very* brief and extremely truncated version of the history of colonization and the impact that it has had on our collective female experience. This is for the purpose of exploring some of the deeply held, and usually unconscious, beliefs that we may be holding, and therefore inadvertently passing on to our daughters.

Most of these limiting beliefs were acquired through childhood experience, passed to us by our communities and "Mother Culture," and are perpetuated to this day by some of our cultural narrative. But where did these beliefs come from *originally*? Why are "mean girls" a thing? I am someone dedicated to finding the root cause of things, because as any good gardener knows, if you don't pull the weeds out at the root, they are bound to return. If we truly want to create cultural and global change that lasts (which I DO), we need to be willing to examine the depths and the source of that which keeps us stuck, limited, and sick in our own little microcosm.

We're going to zoom pretty far out to gather the context, and then back in to see how this applies to you and your daughter now. I hope you don't get too dizzy. It's going to be a ride for a minute! Here we go.

Common Beliefs and Their Historical Context

I am someone who zooms out to the bird's-eye view frequently. I find that an expanded perspective allows me to draw parallels, recognize patterns, and see how things fit together on a global and collective level. It does mean that sometimes nuance and specific detail gets lost in the process, as is natural when we zoom far enough out. For the purpose of this section, and to keep it brief, I will stay at the bird's-eye view level, acknowledging that there is much detail and nuance that will be lost or overlooked.

I am not a history scholar, but I am a genuinely curious person who has read a lot of books, traveled around the world, and found myself in places and spaces many don't even know exist, and some only dare to dream about. All of this has informed my understanding of our collective history as women and the resulting impact on our world as it is structured today.

I am also most familiar with the Christian and Indigenous worldviews, including some traditional African and ancient European spirituality. This is due to being of European heritage, having grown up in a country founded on Christian values but operating on colonized Indigenous land, and having studied deeply with Indigenous people from many different continents.

So, I recognize that my perspective is limited and focused mainly through those lenses. Consider this a sweeping brushstroke. I am not trying to be comprehensive in this examination, but am focusing specifically on a few key historical events that I find particularly interesting, for the purpose of examining their effect on our internalized narrative as women and what we can do to change it.

A Small Slice of Women's History

It is not lost on me that with the advent of empiricism and colonialism came the gradual destruction and devastation of the earth and her natural resources. The subjugation of the power of women's inborn connection to the natural world, alongside a targeted decimation of people the entire globe over who have lived in closest relationship to the earth, have been specific tools used in the building of global empires. It is this parallel that leads me to believe that education around the innate natural rhythms of a woman's body and women's mysteries, along with elevating the enduring wisdom of Indigenous cultures post-colonization, is what will serve as a roadmap out of this destructive era back into a harmonious relationship with the natural world.

There was a time on the earth when matriarchal and matrifocal societies were commonplace. Often when we hear about matrilineal and matrifocal cultures of old, we hear references to ancient Mesopotamian and Babylonian cultures, the remnants of which we can only experience as dead relics in museums. But there are still people alive today whose cultural origin stories speak to matriarchal beginnings.

According to a talk I attended by Chief Glenn Drapeau of the Elk Dreamers clan, Dakota nation, the Dakota origin story states that in the beginning there were only women on earth. (Quite a switch from the Adam and Eve narrative, isn't it?) Men were sent down to earth from the star nation as a response to the women's request for a different form of companionship. Their role was to be someone who listened, who held the women with respect, honoring, and reverence, and provided that ultimate companionship for her. Their purpose here was inseparable from the presence of women. And so, women's place was inseparable from the earth, as she was the direct reflection of that original form and the original inhabitant. Her ways were the ways of Earth.

The Dakota origin story is not the only one I have heard that reflects this placement of women as having been here first, and therefore being intimately knowledgeable about the ways of the earth in a different way. Though I don't believe they came from nowhere or that they are mere legends, the cosmic origins of stories like these (as well as the details of them) are well beyond both the scope of this writing and my place as a person outside of these lineages to expand on. What they do reveal, however, is a completely different worldview and acknowledgement of women and their innate connection to the earth (as well as an acknowledgement that our planet is not the only place in the universe).

In Rhiane Eisler's groundbreaking feminist treatise The Chalice and the Blade, she walked us through our current-day understanding of history and how misunderstood so much of it is. Viewed through a male lens, the world looks very different than when broadened to include the place of women - including the potential that women's place was at one time very different than it has been for the past 25,000 years.

The refusal to recognize and honor the power of women was at the core of colonization and the building of global empires, beginning with the Roman and Ottoman empires. The patriarchal stronghold was already deeply in place during the time of Christ, and fed the creation of an organized religion. In the gospel of Mary Magdalene, it is clearly spelled out that after Jesus' final ascension, Mary spoke in council with the apostles and shared that, in fact, it was she who had been given the complete ascension roadmap by Christ. Unable to cope with the fact that Jesus had shared the deepest teachings not with the male apostles, but with the only woman, Mary Magdalene was silenced and dismissed in that meeting. What has since proliferated around the globe, under the name of Christianity, has its roots in that original refusal to acknowledge that a woman could possibly be holding the ultimate keys to liberation.

With the rise and dominance of Christianity in Europe came the attempt to eradicate all empowered women, who knew the ways of the earth and didn't fit the expected mold of chaste and demure femininity, via the witch hunts. This eradication was based in the foundational beliefs that the body itself is sinful, and sex is the ultimate sin. Herbalists and midwives, or any women who knew the ancient ways of the divine feminine, were some of the key targets, as were particularly ugly or particularly seductive and attractive women. Women were therefore often turned against one another in an "eat-or-be-eaten" kind of atmosphere. In some villages in the middle ages, all but one woman in the village would be killed in an attempt to eradicate the world of "witchcraft." All this bloodshed and ignorance transpired in the name of Christ, who would likely have been utterly horrified at what unfolded.

That focus of stamping out Earth-based traditions was then taken overseas. Some stories tell that when European men arrived in North America, as would be expected, tribes that were matriarchal sent their female leaders to speak with these new arrivals. But the European men insisted on talking only to other men, disregarding the women's rightful roles in facilitating conversations. Imagine being sent to talk to the President and refusing to speak with anyone but the local senator. They simply could not fathom women as holding positions of leadership. Later, as the United States became a country, American women would look to the positions of power held by women in certain Native tribes in the Iroquois Confederacy as inspiration for the early suffragist and feminist movements.

The Native people, whose culture was informed by women's connection to the earth, the cycles and rhythms of nature, and a cosmic connection with a Creator not at all unlike the "God" referenced by Jesus, were slaughtered by the thousands. The land they inhabited and believed themselves to belong to was stolen from under their feet. The creation of new countries was then established in the wake of mass genocide across continents and islands. Some tribes were eradicated entirely; others were enslaved or forced to assimilate into other tribes or the church in order to survive. "Boarding schools" were established in North America by the Catholic church to dismantle the Native American family unit and systematically wipe out their culture and language. All of the Native people I know, regardless of tribe, understandably share a deep traumatic wound dating back to this initial attempt at extinction, as well as a resounding and well-deserved honor in their ability to maintain their cultural ceremonies, language, and threads in spite of it all.

A Cosmic Understanding of Physical Atrocity

According to one of my spiritual elders, Mayan grandmother Nana Vilma Cholac Chicol, the Mayan calendar has some insight into this global past, as well as the current energetic shift we are in. According to the Mayan calendar, in 2012, we exited a 25,000-year cosmic cycle of domination by a masculine energetic.

Okay, pause for a minute, because 25,000 years is kind of a lot to wrap the modern mind around. That's, like, a VERY long time. This expanded timeline is something that I appreciate so much about many of the Indigenous elders I have had the good fortune to learn from. I have heard, for instance, that the Kaggaba, or Kogi, nation considers the impact of their decisions on the next 3,000 years. 3,000 years! That goes way beyond 7 generations. And definitely far further than most people in our modern world dare to consider.

But back to Nana Vilma. According to Mayan wisdom, we are going from 25,000 years of masculine domination into a new 25,000-year cycle of a more feminine way of being. This does not mean that women are now going to be "on top" as so many men fear - because that is not the feminine way. The feminine way is not a hierarchy, but a circle. Nana says we are in this precarious time of the women needing to lead the way back into a circle.

37

It means our models of leadership need to shift because, even as women, we have internalized misogyny and patriarchy working through us as a result of being brought up in Western culture. So, we need to examine where those old models are still living inside of us and weed them out. Competition is not the way. It is only through collaboration that we can create the new world, and that takes some serious willingness to self-examine, stand confidently while also humbling ourselves, admit when we are wrong, and listen deeply to the needs and expressions of others - including those who cannot speak words, like the water, plants, animals, and babies.

It also means that anything that is built and rooted in the old patriarchal structures and energetics will no longer be able to sustain itself without that cosmic energetic support. And we are clearly seeing the crumbling of systems and structures happening all around us right now. It means that we are figuring this out because we are in a new era and we don't really have a roadmap for what comes next. We have ancient technologies that have been preserved by a long line of courageous Indigenous elders who have known that this time is coming. But exactly what to do with those technologies and how to employ them is being created as we speak.

Again, I believe so strongly that part of the map that will get us out of this modern-day mess, into something life-sustaining and led by a feminine energy, lies inside of women. It exists in the gifts and wisdom of the female body and the inherent connection to the natural world that its intelligent design offers us. So for me, this book is more than just a guide to help you prepare your daughter for her menses. If we can get this one dialed in, together, we have the potential to change a culture rooted in death and destruction. Menstruation is one aspect of this, and is most of what we will focus the conversation around. But as we have already seen, this re-membering applies also to the world of sex, birth, and the wise-women years of menopause and cronehood. How we do all of it matters - and it matters more than we might realize.

The Impact on the Female Narrative

What has been the collective cost on the female psyche when we look out at a world brutally made by and for male dominance? There is no doubt of the consistent historical global persecution of women, or that it still exists today. The reminders are around us everywhere - in our medicine (which is based mostly off of studies of male physiology), in our legislature here in the US, in pay discrepancy that *still* exists in 2024 where men get paid more than women to do the same job, in villages around the world where women are expected to perform certain roles and have no other options, in the over-sexualization of women's (and now children's) bodies, etc.

We are subjected to intense scrutiny as far as our appearance goes, and we subtly and sometimes overtly pass this scrutiny on to the women around us. The ubiquitousness of this judgment of the appearance of our female peers never ceases to amaze me. It has gotten to the point where this narrative has become so inculturated that we don't even realize that a) it is a narrative that has been supplanted to separate us from one another, and b) we are complicit in the perpetuating of it. But the only way out of a maze is to first recognize that you are in one.

So here are some of the most common lies I have seen that we as women have internalized as a result of our collective history:
Being in a woman's body is not safe.
Nothing I do matters or has impact.
I am not enough.
I am not worthy.
I am oppressed.

I am a helpless victim.

I am too fat, too thin, too ugly, too much, too wild, too _____.

My worth is determined by my appearance.

My body is not okay as it is - I need to change it.

My period is: dirty, shameful, annoying, a curse.

My fertility is dangerous.

If I celebrate my body, I am being arrogant.

If I accept myself as I am and do nothing to change, I am being arrogant.

I can trust doctors more than I can trust my own intuition about my health.

I need someone else to know more about my body than I do.

Birth is inherently dangerous and belongs in a hospital.

Trusting other women is dangerous.

If she succeeds, I cannot succeed - there is only room for one of us.

My perceived sex appeal and my value are directly linked.

Sex is something I should just know how to do.

I should look like the women in porn.

I should have sex like the people in porn ...

And on and on. Obviously, there is more. This is by no means an exhaustive list. It is exhausting to read though! And even more exhausting to have running quietly in the background. We don't have to look far to find valid 'evidence' in our lives and the culture at large to support almost every one of these lies. But that doesn't make them true.

It should be somewhat obvious, after our very truncated historical overview, of where some of these beliefs have come from historically. Of course, there are vast swaths of history and cultural influences that I left out which also contribute to the origin of some of these beliefs. The question now becomes: what do we do when we find these beliefs operating in us? How do we turn this ship around?

Self Awareness and Healing

Abraham Hicks, a spiritual medium whose teachings I have followed for several years, defines a belief simply as "a thought you keep thinking." Using that definition, we can see that a belief is not a fixed, unchangeable thing, even if it has been passed on to us from previous generations. But it is true that before we can change our self-limiting beliefs, we first have to acknowledge that they are in operation. This is often the trickiest part, as self-limiting beliefs love to hang out in the deepest shadows of our psyche. These beliefs don't want to be discovered, as discovery often means death.

Self-awareness is such a valuable tool. Noticing when I have one of these lies running allows me to energetically cut it off, rewrite it, or simply turn my back on it and refuse it entry into my psychic space. Asking ourselves how and why a less-than-desirable situation might actually be there for our own growth and healing opens up a doorway to otherwise inaccessible realms. There are some fabulous tools out there to help us rewrite our beliefs and stories, and I have included some of my favorites in the resources and recommended reading sections, as well as in the exercises at the end of each chapter.

Sometimes, however, addressing these beliefs at the purely mental level is not enough. We are vibrational beings. We hold tremendous memory in our DNA, in our cells, and in our bodies. It is becoming more and more recognized that trauma can be handed down generationally. Traumatic events, if not adequately metabolized, can quite literally alter how our cells function. Eckart Tolle, in his book *A New Earth: Awakening to Your Life's Purpose*, speaks about our collective "pain body" when we look at issues related to groups of people. As a group, women certainly have a substantial pain body that we have acquired throughout the past 25,000 years of abuse and subjugation. Having tools and ancient technologies that we can utilize

41

to support our physical and energetic bodies in the transmutation of this collective pain body is essential. Learning how to vibrate differently on a cellular level is the ultimate key to living our lives outside of the limitations of generational trauma and persistent negative beliefs. Does it start in the body? Does it start in the mind? Wherever it starts, there is no denying that there is a definite feedback loop.

Working with our wombs as women is a gateway into a healing realm beyond words. If you work with the concepts and exercises in this book, they can be a doorway into some of the work of dismantling this negative programming. However, please don't believe that all your work will be done, even if you do all the exercises. Our wounding did not take place in a vacuum, and so our healing cannot, either.

The true test of healing is relational, and it happens daily. That is where the rubber meets the road. We can work diligently on our meditation cushions and yoga mats all day long, but if afterwards we cannot go out into the world and show up in full presence, self-honesty, vulnerability, joy, and clarity with our families and communities, what is the point?

Our excuses don't become us. But over time, we will become our excuses. Regardless of how much pain and trauma we have walked through and witnessed, I do believe it is possible to move forward and live amazing lives in spite of it. I'm not saying it is easy, but it is possible. We just have to want the healing more than we want the identification with the pain and struggle. I have so much compassion for the part of me that is terrified to grow, heal, and change. Healing can be really scary sometimes, but so can living a life stuck in the smallness of our wounding. Because of this, even when it's hard, I eventually choose the healing over and over again.

I have personally known people who have walked through atrocities most of us could never fathom, who are shining and vibrant human beings leading remarkable lives and helping other people do the same. Suffering can become an identity if we wear it long enough. When it does, it is much harder to break away from. But it doesn't have to be that way. We can heal and repair and we can work through mountains of pain and trauma. We can kintsugi ourselves.[7]

At this moment in history, we are all working on transmuting generations of pain and suffering, and learning to metabolize and own our joy in the face of it. Kahlil Gibran said, "The greater the well carved by sorrow, the deeper the joy that can be contained therein", and I totally believe this is so. Sometimes when we look out at the suffering in the world, it can seem like it isn't okay to be joyful. I can't remember who said it recently, but it struck my soul: it is our responsibility, if we are not the ones in the midst of crisis (or even if we are…), to celebrate and experience our joy fully. Let yourself feel your joy and your pleasure, as well as your pain. Our pleasure is sacred and is our birthright. Expanding our capacity to feel pleasure and joy is a most worthy endeavor.

The vastness of the bounds of the world of healing are way outside of the purview of this writing. I've given you some beginning tools to either start you on your journey or to augment what you've already got going on. I encourage you to pursue this lifestyle outside of this reading though. Because it is a lifestyle. And it's so, so worth it.

But we are here to talk about our daughters! And periods! And sex! So let's go!

---

[7] https://www.bbc.com/travel/article/20210107-kintsugi-japans-ancient-art-of-embracing-imperfection#

We are NOT the Victims of Our Bodies

I was raised with very little conversation around my monthly cycle, if any. If there was conversation, it was usually with peers, and it was usually of a negative and complaining nature. It was clear that what happened to us every month was a terrible affliction to be kept quiet about and to be ashamed of, unless you were in the company of others who suffered the same affliction. We were victims of our female experience, with our monthly cycle being the exclamation point at the end of the sentence.

The Victim Role and The Drama Triangle

I was first introduced to the drama triangle and ways to transcend and elevate it in my ministry program at the Center for Sacred Studies. It was then brought into my life again in my study at the Radical Birthkeeper training through the Freebirth Society. All in all, I find it an invaluable tool - and annoyingly accurate.

Commonly referenced in psychology, and also making its way into the personal development world, the Karpman Drama Triangle (first identified by Stephen B. Karpman) outlines a common dynamic found in most interpersonal relationships. This dynamic involves the playing out of three distinct roles or identities - that of the villain/perpetrator, that of the victim, and that of the hero/rescuer. Usually when people reference the drama triangle, they are thinking of it being enacted amongst two or three different people. However, this triangle dynamic can also be applied to our relationship to aspects of ourselves, modes of coping or habit behaviors, and the cultural milieu which we inhabit.

To be clear - no one is immune to the triangle. We all bounce around it multiple times a day. It really doesn't matter how spiritual you are or how much work you've done on yourself, you will inevitably end up on the drama triangle. Almost daily. This is just part of life. The key is to recognize when you are on it and what role you're identified with in the moment, and then choose to make a shift.

I have had layers of exploration with the drama triangle. When I first started working with it, it was solely in the realm of interpersonal relationships. While it was (and continues to be) absolutely revelatory in that arena, recently, I have found an even greater expansion and more aha moments when I apply it to how I interact with my life and environments at large.

While we will definitely traverse the triangle and find ourselves playing out each role in different situations, we all have a default role we tend to fall back on. My default role (and I think the default for many women based on historical evidence, cultural conditioning, and programming) tends to be the victim. I am SOOO good at this role, having a lifetime of practice identifying as a victim in all sorts of scenarios. I could get an Oscar for that shit.

It is one thing to acknowledge the very real disparities that exist for women in the world as it has been and exists today. It is quite another to choose to limit ourselves due to those disparities. When the victim becomes an identity that we unconsciously assume, it filters into everyday life in ways that have no bearing on or relationship to how that identity may have originally been supplanted. Taking on that role does nothing for our ability to create something new and different. In fact, it prevents it. This is true on the macro cultural level that we have been exploring, but also in the mundane everyday moments like the following illustration.

Here's a typical, everyday example of how the triangle can often play itself out in my household: the perpetrator is the messy kitchen/ whomever I am blaming at the moment for the messy kitchen (generally my spouse, or my children, or both). I am the victim because poor me, I am the only one who cleans up after myself and now I either have to clean up a mess that's probably not even mine, or just live with the mess and complain about it (or complain about it as I clean it).

The rescuing happens either through angrily cleaning it and hating the process, or ignoring it entirely but still complaining about it. Sometimes I choose to escape the environment and take myself out for coffee or something. Usually, I rescue myself with sweet things. Eating something, of course, does nothing for the messy kitchen and makes no rational sense as a response to stress (it might even just add to the mess and/or work of cleaning), but it's one of my age-old coping mechanisms anyway.

Sound familiar at all?

For you, it might not be the messy kitchen, but we all have some place (or many places) where this dynamic shows up in our lives. It shows up in the micro moments throughout our day, as well as in big deal, big moment scenarios in life.

Life Off the Triangle

Beginning to explore these roles and how we play them out in our day-to-day experience can be totally eye-opening and life changing. As we begin to identify the behaviors and choose to step off of the drama triangle entirely, we experience the world with new eyes. Easy to say and sometimes *very* difficult to do, this step outside the triangle dynamic is a daily life's work in and of itself, but one which I can say is totally worth it. Life off the triangle is just a whole lot more fun and enjoyable.

So what does life off the drama triangle look like? Let's take the above example of the messy kitchen. If I approach my messy kitchen and I am

NOT on the triangle, either a) I don't even notice the mess because I'm too focused on something that lights me up, OR b) I have this kind of internal conversation with myself: "Oh, look, dishes again. Do I have time to do them right now?" If yes, I throw on some music or a podcast and do them, enjoying the process, the feel of warm water on my skin, and the transformation of the kitchen afterwards. I might even be inspired to sweep the floor and wipe down all the counters and cabinets, loving making my kitchen beautiful again. If my kids are around, I joyfully encourage them to help out, especially the little one, as she loves to help and is learning how to be a future adult. I let her flow in and out of the work, and eventually it all gets done.

If the answer is "no, I don't have time right now", I say thank you for the fullness of life, give gratitude that we have so much food that we can make so many dirty dishes, and accept that mess as part of the ebb and flow of life. Then I move on with my day. Sometimes I am even pleasantly surprised to find that someone else has done the dishes the next time I come into the kitchen!

We generally slide through these roles quite fluidly - finding ourselves the victim in one dynamic, the hero/rescuer in another, and in yet another situation taking on the role of perpetrator or villain. Or, we can also choose to occupy one role in several different scenarios. As I mentioned above, I am very well-versed at playing the victim role. I recognize that the concept of choice when it comes to these roles might be triggering for some to consider. How is that different from victim blaming? Most of the time, these roles are played out completely unconsciously, so is there really any choice at play? And yet, from my experience, choice is the most accurate and powerful word - because if we can choose to identify as the victim, the hero, or the perpetrator, *we can also choose not to.*

The drama triangle dynamic playing itself out is very different from having a shared sense of humanity and displaying love and care for one another. If your child falls and skins their knee and comes to you crying, is it an act of heroism to provide a bandage for them? Of course not - unless, in the process, you are condemning the pavement, telling them how horrible it is that this happened, and aren't they such a poor little one, and either subtly or overtly reinforcing that it is *only through your help and protection* that they can heal from this experience or prevent it from happening again.

While on the outside the actions taken can often be similar - lovingly cleaning the wound and giving the child a bandage - it is the attitude with which the action is taken, the charge around our inner landscape, and the role that becomes an identity in the process that makes the difference as to whether the situation is "on or off the triangle."

I am in no way denying that there are very real situations in life and in the world where people do horrible things to one another. Nor am I suggesting that these atrocious activities are somehow sanctioned or okay. Abusers and true criminals need to be held accountable for their actions, though I believe how that accountability currently happens needs a complete restructure. What I am pointing to more is a state of mind and an identity that we take on after certain events happen in our lives. Human beings are amazingly resilient, and we can live through outrageous and horrible things. Who we choose to identify as afterwards, though, is entirely up to us.

When I am in the victim role, my inner monologue usually involves some thoughts along the lines of "the universe has it in for me", "everyone and everything is out to get me", "this specific person hates me", etc. When I choose to shift and ask the questions "what is here for my learning?" and "how is this experience here for my growth, healing, and development as a person?", everything changes. When we are willing to ask ourselves these kinds of questions, to hold the world this way, and to deeply take in the inquiry and allow answers to come forward, we re-pattern our relationship with the reality around us. We are vibrational beings, remember? We also live in a vibrational universe. So when we ask these kinds of questions, we don't only shift out of the drama triangle, but the world around us and what becomes possible starts to reconstruct itself in response to that shift. Something that wasn't even on our radar screen a moment ago is now suddenly within reach.

For me, this has been the number one mindset shift that has given me back my agency and a sense of choice in life after numerous traumatic events. These events included rape, psychic abuse, birth trauma and sociopathic manipulation that resulted in spending seven years building a business, from which I finally departed without legal ownership of any of my work. These events seemed entirely out of my control, and each one has been a time where I could have easily lived in identification as a victim of my experience, and sometimes did for a time. But choosing to step off the triangle in regards to each and every one of these scenarios, and recognize the part I played, has been the main key in my liberation and my ability to move forward with my life with complete freedom and agency. Has it been easy? No. In some of these cases, it's taken me years. But in each experience there has been amazing growth and education for me, but only when I refrain from villainizing, victimizing, or heroing myself or others in the process.

I can observe how I participated in the creation of an event that did not feel good at all, while still holding deep compassion, love, and grace for myself. This allows me to harvest the gold and the lessons for me in whatever transpired. This is profoundly different from blaming myself or taking responsibility for the actions of others. I am still very clear that there are things that occurred that were not my fault or my responsibility, nor would they be okay in any way to replicate. But I am not holding on to an identity as a victim of my life experiences. I can truly give thanks for these experiences and the growth they have fostered in me, even though it has been fucking excruciating at times.

This work of stepping off the triangle is not easy when we have a lifetime of practice making our rounds through identification with the different roles. Like mastering anything, it takes intention, desire, willingness, and practice. The willingness question was one we investigated deeply in the Radical Birthkeeper training, and is really crucial to this process working - because if some part of us is not yet willing to let go and get off the triangle, then no matter how hard we try, we won't. We have to be willing, and you cannot force willingness. To be willing is a state of grace that has to be invited in. It has its own timing and needs to be respected.

I am more than a year out from my 7-year toxic business relationship, and there are still sometimes places where I am just not yet willing to shift off the triangle. So, I meet that resistance, gently and softly. It's no different from meeting resistance in our bodies on the yoga mat. If we barrel through it, we hurt ourselves. But if we meet it gently, softly, with presence, time, and consistency, it slowly starts to shift on its own. Someday, I believe that willingness around the entirety of this situation will arrive and I will be able to truly see all the ways that every aspect of that whole experience was for me. I am inviting it in. And until willingness has fully arrived, I spend time off the subject as much as possible. I check in from time to time. Has it softened at all? Can I go deeper? And then I move on.

It takes tools that go beyond just the mind to include the body and the spirit in making the shift and the integration. It is a whole being, whole heart experience and expansion. It is downright terrifying sometimes.

Often, it means we are working on an ancestral level, transmuting patterns and stories that were never ours to begin with, but were either passed on to us through the generations or are part of our collective female pain body experience - or both. Often, we actually will benefit from having other people to do this work with, as the sensations and feelings that can arise can be too much for one nervous system to process. We need other nervous systems to help us regulate.

The good news is, not only are there a plethora of tools to help us with this, we also have help from the unseen realms in this work, if we remember to call on it. This inner work is not easy, but it is absolutely possible. And the freedom, love, and joy on the other side are entirely worth it.

I Repeat - We are NOT the Victims of Our Bodies

Women's bodies are a landscape which has been painted for us by society as one fraught with adversity. We are faced with the shame and pain of menstruation, the discomfort of pregnancy, the issue of abortion, the debilitating pain and trauma of birth, and the disaster of aging and menopause. Our bodies are objectified and sexualized. They are subject to scrutiny in the world and the workplace in a way that is almost non-existent for men. Our beauty is both a requirement for entry into certain levels of privilege and prestige, and also a curse, forcing us to bear the brunt of unwanted visual, audible, and physical attention and abuse.

Much religious dogma exists that underlies this degrading false narrative and keeps us stuck in the victim role, simply for being born women. Whether we were raised with it or believe it or not is irrelevant, as this dogma has shaped the unfolding and creation of the majority of our cultural and societal operations. But, it is one of the biggest lies of the past 25,000 years because when we dig deeper into the feminine mysteries, we discover that not only is this identity of victim for being born female a lie, the inverse is actually true. Those of us born with wombs have access to immense spiritual power, simply because we are born as women. The womb is a gift, a portal to the divine that we have the incredible honor to carry and benefit from, if we choose to.

What does womanhood, and menstruation in particular, outside of the victim role look like? What if, instead of looking at menstruation as something that happens *to* us, we were to look at it as something that happens *for* us? Menstruation is a portal into ourselves and a huge signifier of our health. Menstruation not only serves the physical process of cleaning out our wombs every month that we are without child, it offers us access into unseen realms and a connection with a deeper dream life from which magical creations can spring forth.

If we let it, it also encourages us to take a much-needed rest period. This rest is especially valuable and needed if we live in the masculine model of a go-go-go, do-or-die culture of productivity and perfectionism. Menstruation also gives us a time to energetically clean out anything from the past that is no longer serving us. We cry more easily, we feel things more deeply, and this all serves a very important and sacred purpose.

When we take our menses off the drama triangle, we allow ourselves access to the deeper gifts that it has to offer us. Instead of being the victims of the perpetration of our natural bodily functions that then need to be rescued by doctors providing pharmaceutical intervention, we can tap into the innate power and cleansing that menstruation provides. This is why I feel so passionate about this work. I want this for my daughters, for your daughters - to know how sacred and special this time can be.

As moms, we want to be close enough with our daughters and have them feel safe and comfortable enough to talk to us about what is happening with their bodies, because a healthy woman should have a relatively easy, regular menstruation. If that is not the case, there is likely something else going on that needs support. If we don't address this early on, it can snowball into something that afflicts them throughout their young life, into their adulthood, and impacts their overall well-being, sense of self, ability to bear children, etc - all because we approached menstrual pain and suffering as "that's just the way it is."

Because, in fact, that is NOT just the way it is supposed to be. Many, many women who have suffered from excruciating conditions such as PCOS, endometriosis, or fibroids have expressed that their conditions could be traced back to the earliest years of their bleed. Believe it or not, there are many doctors who work in women's health who operate under the "that's just the way it is" narrative of menstrual pain and irregularity. When I was a teenager, I was prescribed a certain birth control, which ultimately resulted in a 9-day bout of excruciating hemorrhagic bleeding followed by months of irregular periods. I will share more about this story later on, but when it happened, this is the line I was given by several doctors, almost verbatim: "There is nothing wrong with you. That's just the way it is." Pardon my French, but FUCK THAT.

There is another way. There is a way to be IN LOVE with our bodies, with menstruation, with giving birth, with aging, with death. These are the women's mysteries that we are here to explore together.

Exercise - Unpacking Beliefs

In order to re-write beliefs and deprogram ourselves from self-limiting and harmful thinking, we first have to know what beliefs we have been unconsciously harboring. This exercise is intended to help you examine some of your previously held beliefs so that you have more choice in how you operate in relation to them.

Step 1:
Find a comfortable place where you can be undisturbed for at least 30 to 60 minutes. This is something that deserves some uninterrupted attention and can take a moment to really drop into. Have paper and pen or pencil with you, and a place where you can write comfortably.

Remember that these beliefs generally don't want to be discovered, as they lose their power when they are named, so be gentle and easy with yourself if nothing is coming at first, or if you find a bunch of reasons why you can't do this exercise.

Step 2:
Close your eyes and take a few deep breaths to center yourself here and now. Feel where your body makes contact with the surface you are sitting on. Feel your feet. Feel your breath as it moves in and out. Let yourself drop into your body.

Step 3:
Answer the following questions. Allow yourself to write freely, whether what is coming out makes logical "sense" or not. Put your discerning mind aside for this exercise - let it know that it can return to assess and edit after you are done. No editing as you go! Keep your pen or pencil moving.

Be as honest as you can. This is for you and no one else. The more honest you can be with negative attitudes and beliefs you may be holding onto, the easier it will be to let them go. There need be no shame about anything that comes out. This is for gathering information. None of these beliefs is who you are anyways.

Questions:
What beliefs did you absorb about menstruation growing up?

Where did they come from?

Who was the primary female role model in your life? What was your perception of her relationship to her body, menses, and sexuality?

What was your experience of your first blood?

How do you feel about your own menses now?

What is your relationship to your femininity, body, and sexuality?

What would you like your daughter's experience of her menstruation and her relationship to her body to be?

What fears are you holding onto regarding your daughter?

If there was one thing you could go back and tell your 8-year-old self about her path to womanhood, what would it be?

Step 4:
Now ask yourself: if there are still negative beliefs circulating, are you willing to shift any of these beliefs? Be really honest with yourself. Scan the

list - which one seems like the easiest, most ready to shift? Which one jumps out at you?

Notice how that belief makes you feel in your body. Where is there tension? Which part of your body is holding on to this story? What is the emotion attached to it? Fear? Anger? Sadness? Grief?

Step 5:

Once you have located the emotion, *allow yourself to feel it fully*. Don't censor your expression of the feeling, just let it move through you. Make whatever sounds you need to make, and move your body however you want to move it. Feel your feelings!

Step 6:

Rest in the quiet stillness after the release. What new, generative, positive story wants to come to replace the negative belief that was in operation? What is an empowering statement that you can try on instead that rings just as true, if not truer, than this old belief? Write it down!

Exercise - Building Trust with Your Body Wisdom

There is a lot of material in life that we need to make decisions about on a regular basis. There is no paucity of people and influencers in the world telling us their opinions and versions of truth - if anything, the pool is just growing larger and louder. Tuning out the noise to hear ourselves can be challenging sometimes.

Finding *our* truth vs what someone else suggests for us is crucial in making decisions in our lives that feel aligned and in integrity with what we say we want for ourselves and our children. This means being able to wade through the conditioning, programming, and suggestions that are rampant everywhere we look.

My favorite tool for ascertaining my truth is the body, so I offer this exercise to you as a way to tune into the wisdom in your body for what is true for you NOW. I emphasize the now because what is true for us can change from day to day, moment to moment. There is nothing wrong or weak about this - as much as the current political landscape suggests that we have to have one opinion on things forever and ever that never changes, or else we are somehow fraudulent. This is just not how life works, though. We are constantly evolving creatures who are designed to shift, change, and grow according to different inputs and stimuli. It is a *good* thing to be able to take in new information and shift and change our perspective accordingly.

This exercise can help you to hone the internal resource, trust, and flexibility to respond to decisions from a place of inner truth and wisdom instead of reaction and pre-conditioned response. I particularly like to practice this exercise when there are two or three different choices before me and I am having trouble deciding which direction to go in. I have used this simple but very effective tool with my clients in my coaching practice for years, with much success. You can use it for small decisions, like the example given below, or to gauge your truth on larger issues.

If you are new to practices that lead you into your body, you will want to find a moment of quiet and solitude to practice this at first. As you get more adept and practiced, you will be able to do this anytime and anywhere.

Let's give an easy hypothetical scenario to use for this exercise:

You have been invited to an event during a week that is already pretty packed for you. Logically, you can find reasons both to go and not to go, but you are having trouble deciding. How will you choose?

Step 1:
Find your seat. Close your eyes and take a few deep, grounding breaths. Feel the place where your body meets the ground or support beneath it (chair, bed, etc.). Breathe.

Approach the next step with curiosity, as a researcher might gather information.

Step 2:
Think about going to the event. Notice how your body responds. Is there any place that tenses up? Is there an opening somewhere? A feeling of lightness or density? Just notice and take in the information.

Breathe and release that option.

Step 3:

Think about not going to the event. Notice how your body responds. Is there a relaxing or tensing somewhere? Density or lightness? A feeling in the pit of your stomach? Nothing? Notice and take in the information.

Step 4:

Now that you have gathered this information, you get to choose what to do with it. Which choice gave you a feeling of more ease? Sometimes we won't get a really clear sense either way. In these moments I like to ask: is there a third option? And then notice what happens in my body.

Not everyone experiences lightness as good and density as bad. For me, I have learned that when I feel an internal sense of lift and expansion, that is a yes for me. I have had clients, however, for whom a feeling of density is actually incredibly grounding and what denotes a yes for them. You will know because whichever one it is, *it will feel good to you.*

Sometimes my body will also noticeably lean forward when something is a total yes. Similarly, I have experienced a backwards leaning with a no, as if being physically repelled. This can be subtle or sometimes surprisingly strong.

We may not always know why we receive a yes or a no from our body. Sometimes we get the opposite of what our logic would suggest is the right thing. The important thing is to start building trust with your body wisdom. Follow through with the answer you have been given, even if you could rationalize yourself into the other side. Hold the matter lightly. Yes, maybe there will be someone there you are supposed to meet, and if you didn't follow your unexpected yes, you would miss a golden opportunity, even though logic dictates that your plate is too full. You also just might have some much needed fun. If the opportunity is truly meant for you, it will come around again in another form.

Maybe you got a no, even though your mind told you that going would be really good, you don't want to let someone down, you have FOMO, etc. If you honor that no, perhaps you will rest instead and keep yourself from an illness you would have manifested had you gone, or maybe you'll have that really important conversation you've been needing to have with your spouse, or you are making space for something else that is even more important and aligned to enter in. The possibilities of why things occur or don't occur are endless, and impossible for our minds to predict, no matter how many scenarios it can play out, but the wisdom in our body most often just knows.

Watch that you don't steamroll over the wisdom of your body with logic after you have completed this exercise. That is the real work. You have gathered the information - now it's time to put it into practice. You have received your yes or no; now commit fully to it! Put it in your calendar (either the event or the block of space). Watch what happens.

Exercise: Womb/Belly Practices

This rich series of exercises is an offering from my friend Devorah Bry MA, CHT. She is a somatic therapist and founder of the HoneyRoot experience - a several day somatic experiencing gathering for womb holders - which was originally conceived in the Nevada City area of Northern California. She now lives with her daughter on the coast of Maine. This exercise is from her guide "Women's Embodiment Circles: A Handbook of Group Values and Empowering Embodiment Exercises based on the HoneyRoot experience," which is linked in the resources section.

Pick one of these and really dive into it. Start with one, but try them all, taking your time to be with each practice as its own experience. Which one is your favorite? Which one will you return to again?

Womb/Belly Practices ~

1. Rest with your body face-down on the ground. Open your belly to feel the warmth, as though you're lying on the warm body of mother earth herself. Invite your belly to feel and be nourished by this warm, stable presence. Rest here for a while, and then begin drawing this earth energy in through your belly button. Re-umbilicalize yourself with the earth.

2. Roll around on the floor. Use gravity to allow your body to move in whatever way it wants to move. With or without music, do a partner dance -- the ground being your partner!

3. Waddling. Find a nice, wide, bent-knee stance, like that of a third-trimester pregnant woman. Relax your upper body and wiggle your spine a bit to welcome fluidity. Using an exhale, release any

muscles around and within your anus and yoni.[8] Take yourself for a 15-20 minute waddle walk in nature (or even just down the street). Allow your weight to really shift right and left as you take your steps. Breathe into your belly and place your hands there, if that feels okay for you. Feel (or imagine) fluid sloshing around in your belly as you walk. Drop your tail and allow your sacrum to be heavy. Find a pace that feels honoring of your current pregnancy. When you return home from your walk, take a moment to notice what (if anything) has changed in your mind, your felt sense of your body, your creativity, and your relationship to your power.

4. Womb Massage. A nice way to begin is by lying on the ground, belly side down. Take several deep breaths in this position, building pressure in your womb space as you inhale, releasing pressure as you exhale. Next, turn over onto your back (or sit up if you prefer), and begin massaging your uterus. Stay curious and loving while you rub, palpate, and shake. Keep steady pressure on any points that call your attention. Listen in as you massage. Do this for 5 to 10 minutes. Afterwards, lie in stillness for a few minutes and notice what is moving through you - sensations, images, emotions, thoughts.

5. Sculpting Your Womb. This is a practice to be done with clay, Play-Doh, or some other malleable substance. Move towards the soft sculpting material and begin to shape your womb. Allow this to come from the inside out. Even if you no longer have a uterus, this is a wonderful exercise to do. Let your arms and hands be the

---

[8] Yoni is the Sanskrit term that connotes the female sexual organs, but also is interpreted to mean "origin, abode or source." It is a term that many use nowadays to refer to female genitalia as a way of showing respect to the organ of creation

messengers for your womb space. It does not matter how the final product looks. This exercise is a practice in listening deeply, and an exercise in expressing creativity from the inside out. Enjoy the process.

CHAPTER 2

SCIENCE CLASS: PUBERTY AND MENARCHE - WHAT. EXACTLY. IS HAPPENING?

Body Sovereignty and the Medical System

Before we dive into all the science of hormones, anatomy, what is happening in the body during puberty, and the different phases of our cycle, I want to discuss why this is so relevant and important for us as women to familiarize ourselves with.

In Pursuit of Non-Pathological Care

Women (and young women) knowing and being intimate with the terrain of their own bodies is something I feel insanely passionate about. We live in a culture where we have normalized outsourcing our self care to medical professionals, and entrusting someone else to know more about what is going on inside our bodies than we do. In our for-profit model of healthcare, looking for, finding, and treating illness in people is a lucrative business and is what all medical doctors are trained in. They are not trained to look for and support foundational health and vitality. When we look at it from the perspective of the drama triangle, the medical establishment is the ultimate hero, which always necessitates a victim.

What this has led to is an insane amount of costly and unnecessary "care" that often does more harm than good, especially to women, and especially in the US. (If you want an in-depth exposé of the situation in the United States as far as women's health goes, read *Everything Below the Waist* by Jennifer Block. Be prepared to be horrified). I am not anti-science - in fact, I researched quite a number of scientific studies to write this book. But "science as God" is a very lacking, myopic approach to life. There is so much that just hasn't been studied, can't really effectively be studied using proper scientific methods (this is especially true of the social sciences), and rightfully belongs in the hands of the Great Mystery. I'm not saying you should never see a doctor or that in some cases intensive medical treatment isn't warranted. Emergency medicine and comprehensive disease care when it comes to critical illness and injury is something I am very grateful exists.

For all their bad rap and overuse, and while I am very discerning in their use (and will resort to herbal varieties first and foremost), I'm actually grateful that antibiotics exist, because it means that things that used to be really horrifically terrible and deadly aren't anymore. I'm grateful to have that option. I'm also not saying that doctors are horrible people. In fact, I believe that the majority of people who are motivated to make a career out of medicine are downright exceptional and outstanding human beings who care very much for other humans. The problem lies, for me, primarily in the training and the way the system is designed to function.

In most people most of the time, *especially* women, the majority of chronic issues that are prescribed medical interventions as treatment would be better off addressed in natural ways - a change in diet, lifestyle, and/or emotional support. Oftentimes in womb-related issues, physical manipulation is warranted, as in Mayan Abdominal Massage, Holistic Pelvic Care, or the Arvigo method. Sometimes the sickness is on a spiritual level. Our lifestyles based on the nuclear family model have created a deep soul sickness for many people, particularly mothers. But there is no quick fix, money, or research dollars in these modalities or lines of inquiry, so they are not what is taught, even though, in the majority of cases, they are what would be most effective.

When you look at the current state of the majority of people's knowledge of themselves, I guess this makes sense. What do we expect to happen when we let someone else hold the reins to our health? But it doesn't have to be that way. When it comes to self-knowledge and care for ourselves, and passing this knowledge on to our daughters, knowing the ins and outs of not only what "typical" female anatomy is, but our own unique anatomy, is crucial. When we go deeply into this path, we come out knowing more than most doctors about the holistic reality of womb health.

There is nothing wrong or shameful about knowing what your vulva looks like and exactly how your body works. In fact, how better can you know if there are changes that occur that might be serious and actually warrant a change in diet or lifestyle, or the help of a professional? For our young girls, encouraging them to look at themselves down there and really get to know their bodies as they grow and change is a huge gift we can give them on the path to true, holistic, and all-inclusive self-love. We just have to get over our preconditioned shame about owning our own bodies. The generations of women being considered nothing more than property still has a lingering ghost in the way we have given authority of our bodies over to western medicine.

It's kind of sad to think that many people would be more uncomfortable if I told them I encouraged my child to look at her own genitals with a mirror than if I told them I took her to see the gynecologist. Isn't it bizarre when you think about it? Men can inspect their genitalia multiple times a day without thinking about it. Just because we have innies instead of outies doesn't mean there is anything wrong with looking at ourselves. We have made it *more* normal to have some stranger in a white coat, often a man, observe, poke, and prod our genitals than to investigate our bodies on our own. If that isn't oppression, I don't know what is!

Women who intimately know themselves are threatening to the medical institutions as they currently exist. In *Taking Charge of Your Fertility* by Toni Weschler, she explains a scenario in which one of her FAM (Fertility Awareness Method) clients was part of a study on ovulation. This client would go into her appointments announcing when she had just ovulated, which was then confirmed by the study *but was questioned and disbelieved by the practitioner when announced by the woman herself before-hand.* Why is it so hard for the majority of medical professionals to wrap their minds around the possibility that a woman might actually know more than they do about what is happening in her own body?

The truth is, for all their education, there is still so much lacking in terms of comprehensive knowledge of the female body in the western medical paradigm. It is more than a little scary if you think of how much power over our bodies we have given them, considering this. It wasn't until the 1990's that the National Institutes of Health even created an official Office of Research on Women's Health[9] (and, according to Block's research, that office receives limited funding). Until the publication of *Our Bodies, Ourselves* in 1971, images of the clitoris could only be found in archived medical drawings from the 1800s and before. The clitoris had been entirely eliminated from images and discussion in medical textbooks, never

---

[9] Everything Below the Waist: Why healthcare needs a feminist revolution by Jennifer Block

mind high school anatomy class, and there are still sadly a majority of people completely unaware of the actual entire anatomy of a clitoris. (No, it is not just the little spot in the front.)

I have had medical practitioners look at me with mistrustful scrutiny and dismay when I tell them I threw my back out in labor and I am pretty sure it's because I slightly tore the ligament that connects my uterus to my lower spine due to unnaturally strong uterine contractions brought on by pitocin. Women aren't supposed to know that much about their own bodies. I've even met practitioners who didn't even know there are ligaments that connect the uterus to the spine. (It "wasn't their specialty".)

Historically, there has also been zero acknowledgement in the medical community of how emotional experience and trauma impact the health of the physical body. The tides seem to be turning on this one somewhat, but you will still be hard pressed to find a doctor who will plainly admit to it. This correlation between emotions and physical health is true regardless of what body you're in, but even more so for women, as we are hormonally designed to be more dynamically feeling creatures. Ask any alternative practitioner who deals with the womb and she will share countless stories of witnessing the direct correlation between a woman's emotional world and the state of her uterus. In the medical paradigm, there is no acknowledgement of this phenomenon (outside of gaslighting), as there are no research dollars to study it, and no money to be made off of such a finding.

Is this the lion's den of "women's healthcare" you want to throw your daughter into? Or would you rather prepare her to know herself and her body intimately, inside and out, and teach her how to care for her sacred and precious form primarily herself? In order to do this effectively, we need to teach our daughters *accurate* information about their anatomy, as well as affirm their moments of intuitive knowing. When we claim intimate knowledge of our bodies and ourselves, we can finally reject the notion that our biology, and everything that comes with it, is grounds for social inequality. Accepting this narrative of being the victims of our bodies (which can often lead to trying to override our biology to act just like men), is at the root of us submitting to an overuse of medical technology that is, overall, harming us more than helping us.

Fortunately, there are more and more practitioners that are well-versed in modalities like Holistic Pelvic Care, Arvigo Therapy, Breast Massage, and Mayan Abdominal Massage that are based in a true understanding of the holistic ecosystem that is a woman's body. Taking your daughters to these practitioners if they are available where you live is, in my opinion, a viable option and alternative to the usually humiliating, often traumatizing, and sometimes even rape-like standard gynecological visits. We can also, if we are motivated and educated, teach them most of what they will need to know ourselves.

I know that there is more education and wisdom spreading in the medical world of how to adequately care for women's bodies. I am so grateful to people like A'magine Nation and the crew who created the film *At Your Cervix* and are actively working to change legislation and pelvic exam practice in the United States. The problem is, you don't know until you go who has what kind of bedside manner. While we can hope this would be the case, it is not a given that just because a GYN is a woman, she will be better or kinder than a male. She received the same training, after all, and she likely had to work harder than her male counterparts for the same recognition, which can harden some women considerably. And unfortunately, in the US, it is still legal in many states for OB/GYN training to include learning how to do pelvic exams on unconscious, anesthetized patients who have not given, and are not able to give, consent. What kind of subconscious message does that give to rising doctors about how to treat their patients? Never mind *not* teaching them what is and isn't routinely painful for women, because someone who is unconscious can't give feedback.

For a young woman on the cusp of a budding sexual life, these experiences in a doctor's office can be downright traumatic and humiliating. Personally, I am not willing to subject my daughter to that. I trust in her innate wellbeing and her knowledge of herself, and my own intuitive sense, enough to know that if something is seriously wrong and would warrant medical care, we will know. Beyond that, in our household, we take care of ourselves differently.

The healthiest people I know in my life are the people who, if they use other practitioners, use Acupuncturists, Chinese Medicine practitioners, Somatic practitioners, Homeopaths, Naturopaths, Massage Therapists, Herbalists, Arvigo practitioners, Craniosacral therapists, Yoga instructors, Functional and Integrative medical practitioners, Reiki practitioners, Traditional Indigenous healers, etc. That's because these modalities focus on wellness, and inviting and maintaining the wellbeing that is our inherent birthright. They do not focus on disease, but on eliminating or metabolizing that which is in the way of wellness. And so wellness is, more often than not, the end result. More progressive countries than the United States recognize this and incorporate many of these modalities into their standard of medical practice. The fact that in the US you have to pay out of pocket for most of these is more indicative of the politics of our healthcare system than the effectiveness of the practices themselves.

Like any modality, the quality of the practitioner, their training, and their willingness to step outside the drama triangle is critical to the success of the methodology. The hero role is so seductive, because let's be honest, it feels really, really good to help someone else. The problem is when we build an identity around it, and practitioners in any arena are not immune to this identification as the hero. Most of these practitioners, if they are good, will direct you to applying the techniques and wisdom they carry into your own daily life and practices. They will encourage self-responsibility. We cannot just outsource our agency to alternative practitioners, either. That said, in my experience, these "alternative" modalities are far more effective at healing the root cause of a thing than the western medical paradigm - especially in the realm of women's health.

An extreme degree of fear and outrage often accompanies the suggestion that one can care for one's own health and body. This is evidenced by the fact that I and everyone else writing about alternative modes of being and self-care have to put disclaimers on their work. Most people have been so conditioned as to become virtually unable to successfully claim responsibility for their lives. Stepping outside of the medical paradigm has become the modern-day form of heresy. Nowhere is this more true than in the world of birth. The grip of our death-phobic culture is immense. Death is sad, and losing people we love is hard, but death is not the ultimate failure, as our modern savior-based medical paradigm would have us believe. Am I grateful that we have certain life-saving measures available to us through modern medicine? Yes. Do I think we take the whole thing a little over-board most of the time? Also yes. We will never beat death, no matter how hard we try. We cannot control death, just like we cannot control nature. No one comes out of this game alive. What if we all started to acknowledge that a bit more? What would that do to our worldview, the way we take care of ourselves, what we prioritize, and the way we live our lives?

In chapter 8 of *Becoming Supernatural*, Dr. Joe Dispenza does a phenomenal job of dissecting the programming that the global populous has been subjected to by the pharmaceutical industry. Through his analysis of several pharmaceutical commercials for the shingles vaccine, he shows us how there has been a collective hypnosis at work on the global population. The rest of his book is dedicated to proving that we as humans have the capacity and the power to learn how to heal ourselves. His research that he has done in conjunction with the Heartmath Institute is compelling and fascinating and if you have not looked into it, it is something that I urge you to do. The narrative that we need the medical system as it currently exists to save us from our feeble and failing bodies is an abject lie.

I can understand a doctor's concern with the idea of someone not coming to see them and get regular labs done when that person is neglectful of themselves. It is true that early detection for things like certain cancers is what indicates overall treatment success and survival rates. I can see how having someone who is already very progressed in their illness come to see a doctor for help could be frustrating for that doctor, as there is less that they might be able to do to actually help that person succeed in their health goals. But we have to be willing to start trusting one another and trusting ourselves when it comes to our own health. We have to be willing to step off the drama triangle and not need to be able to fix, heal, or save people in order to feel like valid human beings. Also, if a person is unable to access shelter, real food and clean water, that will greatly impact their ability to care for themselves effectively. Wouldn't it be nice if all the money we spent on non-essential "healthcare" went to ensure that everyone had access to those things?

This calls for a complete overhaul of our current medical system, which is long-overdue and insanely complicated to suggest within the current model. The system is not actually broken - it is functioning exactly as it was intended to. For that reason, I don't actually believe that we will find success in trying to change what is, but in creating something new entirely. Which is why we are going to go to science class now.

Ready?

The Endocrine System and Hormones

Ahh, hormones - those little messengers in the body we've all grown to know and love - or be a bit wary of. It never ceases to amaze me how such tiny, microscopic players have such a humongous impact on our energy levels, relationships, weight, appetite, fertility, mood, skin, behavior, and even access to a sense of oneness with all life. We like to think we are so big and mighty, but really these hormones are running far more of the show than we realize. So before we dive into all the "which hormones do what in the body" stuff, I just want to take a moment and say thank you to our brilliant endocrine system and all it does for us.

In that spirit of thanks, I invite us into this exploration of the endocrine system and hormones. Not just to figure out with our minds what they do in our bodies and why they are important to respect, but also to explore more ways that we can offer that respect in action in our daily lives. If there is one system in the body that you can focus on that will have the largest overall impact on your health and wellbeing, I believe it is the endocrine system.

Also - let's just take a moment and acknowledge that while it serves our cognitive reasoning to sort things out into boxes and categories, the human body doesn't function that way. As you will see in a moment, all of the "systems" in our body are interrelated and designed to function in harmony with one another. Our hormones are involved in every single process of the body. Instead of just a science class, let's view the purpose of this exploration as being about bringing our full presence and gratitude to the brilliance of how our bodies function, so that we can provide them with the inputs and environment they need to perform optimally.

I like knowing where these master endocrine glands are because when we are aware of where things are located in our bodies, our ability to tune into and communicate with those parts of our bodies increases. The positive impact this can have on our ability to regulate ourselves, or know when something is off and therefore work to correct it, is immeasurable. We do not need x-ray scans and ultrasounds to look inside of our bodies. I first knew I was pregnant with my first baby because I "saw" the zygote in my uterus in meditation. A cultivated felt-sense awareness can tell us so much about what is happening inside of us, and can support us in seeking help if, indeed, the message is that we need that.

So with that, let's explore a little bit of our endocrine system and all that it does for us as women.

The Endocrine Glands

Hypothalamus: The hypothalamus is an almond-sized part of the brain located kind of right in the middle of your head. If you were to draw a line from the top of your head down into the direct middle of your brain, and another line into your head from the top of the bridge of your nose, where the two intersect is approximately where you would find your hypothalamus. And as far as your hormones are concerned, it's kind of the command center. Its job is to read and respond to all of the incoming messages in the body in order to keep your body in a stable state of homeostasis and keep all systems functioning properly.

Pituitary: The hypothalamus communicates directly with the pituitary gland, a little round gland found just below it. It is the pituitary gland's job to receive the messages from the hypothalamus and then communicate with all the other glands and organs involved in the production of hormones throughout your body - kind of like the Greek god Hermes of the brain.

Pineal: Also an essential part of the endocrine system (and kind of magical in its acknowledgement by many ancient spiritual texts) is the pineal gland - a tiny pinecone-shaped gland located slightly above and behind the hypothalamus, adjacent to the thalamus. If you were to draw a line directly back into your brain from the center of your eyes and then up from where your spinal column inserts, the intersection of those lines is where you'll find the pineal gland. Its primary job is to regulate melatonin, which impacts our sleep/wake cycles and can also have a big influence on our menstrual cycles.

Thyroid: The thyroid is a butterfly-shaped gland located in the middle of your neck, kind of straddling your throat on either side. The thyroid is very important in regulating metabolism, energy levels, weight regulation, and internal body temperature.

Parathyroid: The parathyroid glands are little pea-sized glands on the back side of the thyroid gland, and are essentially part of the thyroid. They regulate the amounts of calcium, phosphorus, and magnesium in the bones and blood. So, they are also pretty important.

Thymus: The thymus is located on the upper part of the chest, kind of behind and slightly to the left of your sternum. A key player in proper immune functioning, the thymus produces white blood cells and helps to destroy abnormal cells in the body. Thank you, Thymus!

Adrenals: Located on top of each kidney, the adrenals are the main distributor of stress hormones. They are in charge of regulating our blood pressure, and also play a key role in metabolism. Busy moms know these glands well, as ours are often pretty taxed. (I have had adrenal fatigue that was so bad, I could actually feel the strain as a slight ache on my kidneys. I do not recommend letting yourself get to this point.)

Pancreas: Involved in the production of insulin and glucagon, which are key in regulating blood sugar, the pancreas is located in the back of the abdomen, behind the stomach. The pancreas is also involved in the process of digestion.

Ovaries: And last, but most definitely not least, we have the ovaries. The ovaries live on either side of the uterus, connected by the beautiful uterine tubes. Not only are these powerhouses where every egg we will ever have in our lives and the original source of our babies live, they are also the main producers of estrogen and progesterone, whom we will meet now.

The Primary Female Hormones

Estrogen: There are actually three main types of estrogen (and over thirty estrogen-related hormones in the body), which is why the estrogen conversation can get confusing sometimes. For our purposes, and to keep it simple, we're just going to talk about them all as one main group - estrogen.

The main star of the female show, estrogen is produced primarily by the ovaries. (Men also have some estrogen, but in much lower levels and produced by the adrenals and fat cells.) She is the key player in the regulation of the menstrual cycle. When estrogen levels rise, it signals the thickening of the uterine lining in anticipation of ovulation, and therefore potential pregnancy.

Estrogen is also involved in: the maturation and stimulation of the ovaries, the development of the breasts and support of their feeding function, memory function and libido, cholesterol production, regulation and protection of the heart and liver, skin elasticity, and bone strength and density. She's a powerhouse!!!

Progesterone: Known primarily as the one responsible for maintaining a pregnancy until the placenta takes over, progesterone also influences sleep, relaxation, and mood stability. Progesterone helps keep estrogen in check, and also has an impact on breast development and breastfeeding.

Pregnenolone and DHEA: Often referred to as a "precursor" hormone, in women, pregnenolone is made from cholesterol in the brain, adrenals, and ovaries. Pregnenolone then makes DHEA, which then makes estrogen, progesterone, and testosterone, as well as other adrenal hormones (hence the "precursor" label). Pregnenolone has been shown to have anti-inflammatory properties, especially in the brain. It also has antidepressant properties and is involved in memory and cognitive functioning.

Testosterone: Yes, women have testosterone, too - just in much lower levels. Testosterone is produced in the ovaries and adrenals and is involved in sex drive. Its main job in the female body is to make you feel like having sex right around the time of ovulation.

Luteinizing Hormone (LH): Released at ovulation by the pituitary gland, LH stimulates the release of a mature egg from the ovary.

Follicle Stimulating Hormone (FSH): Also produced by the pituitary, FSH controls the production of estrogen and triggers the maturation of ovarian follicles. As we age, the rise of FSH signals the ovary to stop releasing eggs altogether, resulting in menopause. Both FSH and LH are critical to the healthy growth and development of the ovaries in puberty.

Gonadotropin-Releasing Hormone (GnRH): Made and released by the hypothalamus, GnRH is kind of like a signaling hormone and has a direct feedback with specific sex hormones - namely FSH, LH, estrogen, and progesterone in females. At the onset of puberty, GnRH is used by the pituitary gland to signal the release of FSH and LH to begin the maturation of the ovaries. So in puberty, GnRH is a key player. If the levels are too high, early onset of puberty is likely. Levels that are too low are responsible for late or delayed puberty. Once hormone levels have matured and been established, GnRH takes more of a back seat and is controlled by the levels of testosterone, estrogen, and progesterone, peaking at ovulation.

Insulin: Produced in the pancreas, insulin is involved in the metabolism of proteins, glucose, and fat. Insulin helps to maintain blood sugar by making sure that the glucose stores in the body make their way into the cells so that they can be used as fuel.

Cortisol: Everyone's favorite stress hormone! Released by the adrenals but controlled by the hypothalamus and pituitary gland, cortisol does actually have a really important role in the body - in small doses. In small doses, cortisol suppresses inflammation, helps regulate blood sugar and blood pressure, helps regulate your body's stress response, contributes to a healthy sleep/wake cycle, and positively impacts your metabolism. Too much though, and all those systems go haywire.

Melatonin: Generally thought of as the sleep hormone, melatonin is released in the pineal gland in response to darkness. Melatonin levels have also been found to rise along with progesterone, peaking in the late luteal phase. Melatonin decreases with age, and is currently being researched in its implications for postmenopausal bone loss and sleep disorders.

Leptin: The main signal of satiety, or a feeling of fullness after eating, leptin is directly correlated with levels of adipose, or fat, tissue in the body and is made primarily in fat cells. Leptin is also directly related to the onset of puberty and the maintenance of healthy menstrual cycles, as it signals to the body whether or not there are enough fat stores to begin menstruating. It increases LH and estrogen levels and is correlated with progesterone levels. There is still more research that needs to be done on the exact ways that leptin communicates with other sex hormones in the body, but the fact that communication is happening, and leptin is part of it, is clear.

How These Hormones Work Together

We love piecing things out in our culture, separating things into their different parts and components, and analyzing them individually. But, as we've mentioned, that is not how the body or the natural world works in reality. Harmony, or different parts working symbiotically together, is a key component to the appropriate functioning of the natural world. In our bodies, all of these individual hormones work together and in rapid-fire order.

What I find fascinating is that the primary way that the hypothalamus sends messages is via oscillation. This means that it is actually vibrations that are responsible for our body's ability to function optimally. So much for hippy spiritual theory being a bunch of crap! It is actually vibrational frequencies that run most of the show in our endocrine system. As a singer who loves the vibrational locked-in feeling that harmonizing with others gives, this fact makes me happy to no end. Our hormones, when functioning optimally, are basically a singing choir, vibrating in harmony together. (Must be why singing with others is so good for your health!)

The way these different hormones and glands are connected are through what are called axes, or pathways. The three main pathways that we will discuss here, and how they get initiated, are the hypothalamic-pituitary-adrenal axis, the hypothalamic-pituitary-gonadal axis, and the hypothalamic-pituitary-thyroid axis. Don't let the big words scare you! It sounds way more complicated than it actually is. These long names are basically just very uncreative code for the order of operations in the body. So, the hypothalamic-pituitary-adrenal axis is the hypothalamus signaling to the pituitary gland and then to the adrenal glands. Same for the others: the hypothalamic-pituitary-gonadal axis is where the hypothalamus communicates with the pituitary gland and then with the gonads (in our case, the ovaries) and the hypothalamic-pituitary-thyroid axis is where the hypothalamus communicates with the pituitary gland and then the thyroid. When you break it down this way, you can see the beauty and simplicity of the design. It's really not as complicated as everyone would have us believe.

What I find absolutely fascinating about these axes is what kickstarts or initiates their proper functioning. It is again a simple thing, but something that we have become pretty divorced from in our trend of mostly indoor, on-screen lifestyles over the past 50 years. We can look to our food and water and exercise as sources of health, which they definitely are, but when it comes to hormones, we are missing the main piece that triggers all healthy hormonal functioning when we do so.

That piece is light.

As part of the hypothalamus, we have what is called the suprachiasmatic nucleus, or SCN. The SCN is basically what controls our circadian rhythm, or internal clock. Carrie Bennett, who teaches at the Institute of Applied Quantum Biology, refers to the SCN as akin to the conductor in a symphony. Its job is to keep all the signals firing at the right time and in smooth concert with one another. The SCN operates in response to signals that are sent to the hypothalamus from the light receptors in the back of our eyes. More specifically, blue light receptors. It is the perception of blue light and the signals that it then triggers (via the retinohypothalamic track that - you guessed it! - sends the signal from the retina to the hypothalamus) that helps us to tell internal time. Once it receives the blue light signals, the SCN then oscillates in a pattern that signals to the mitochondria in all of the cells in the body what time it is.

Our biological processes are designed to function in certain ways at certain times. For example, the presence of blue light signals to our adrenals, via the hypothalamic-pituitary-adrenal axis, that it's time to make cortisol to keep us awake and alert for the day. That is part of cortisol's job in the body. The hypothalamic-pituitary-gonadal axis is also kick-started by the presence of blue light. This is when pregnenolone production gets initiated, which then gets used to make all the other sex hormones in the body. As the lack of blue light gets detected towards the end of the day, the pineal gland is then activated to produce melatonin, and our body is signaled that it is time to get ready to sleep.

In the natural world (off-screen and outside), the presence of blue light begins with the arrival of the dawn. As the sun rises, the level of blue light in the sky increases until the sun is at its highest peak (often referred to as solar noon). An hour or so after sunrise, UVA light then starts to present. UVA light is part of what triggers the optimal functioning of the hypothalamic-pituitary-thyroid axis, even though that axis is also initiated with the presence of blue light. UVB light, which is required for conversion into vitamin D3, happens within a few hours before and after solar noon and fluctuates in intensity based on location and time of year. After solar noon, blue light starts to gradually decrease, until sunset when it signals to our brain that the day is coming to a close and it's time to turn off certain hormonal functions and turn on other ones.

When we are constantly barraged with artificial light in the form of bright light bulbs and screens, especially after sunset, it messes with our hormonal signaling. As Carrie Bennett says, every time we look at our phone, we are basically telling our brain that it is the middle of the day. The blue light from screens and artificial lighting is so strong that our brains register it as solar noon. So if first thing in the morning we reach for our phones, we are interrupting our hormonal cascade for the rest of the day. Same if, once the sun goes down, we get comfy and scroll our phones for hours.

Putting it into Practice

I think it's safe to say that the majority of people in North America nowadays are dealing with some sort of hormonal imbalance. And when you look at the actual science of how our bodies are designed to function and contrast that with how most people live their lives, it starts to make a lot of sense. We can diet and exercise our hearts out, but if we aren't getting the right light signals into our brains, it is not going to matter.

Unless you had your daughter when you were very young, it is likely that you might be entering perimenopause at the same time that she is starting puberty. Perimenopause can last 10-15 years (!) and generally starts between 35-40 years of age. Perimenopause is really a symptom of out-of-whack hormones, and can affect our mood, our libido, our ability to concentrate, our sleep, and can cause headaches, night sweats, vaginal dryness and hot flashes. If you had your daughter when you were in your 40s, the chances that you will be in or through menopause when she gets her first bleed are pretty high. So while knowing how hormones function optimally is crucial to starting your daughter off with strong hormonal health, it can also benefit you tremendously. Modeling care for yourself this way will trickle down to your daughter.

We can navigate our hormonal changes with grace and ease. We do not have to buy the lie that menopause needs to be a time when we go absolutely crazy, or treat it like some kind of horrific death sentence. Not at all - if we understand our hormones and how they work.

So, how do we take this information and make it useful for us in our lives? It doesn't have to be complicated, and it doesn't mean that we have to throw away our computers and phones and permanently move outdoors. (Although, I mean, you do you. I won't discourage you from it if that's what you want to do! The science is proving the hippies were right, after all...)

As you can see above, the main trigger that controls the majority of our hormonal processes is blue light. That means we want to focus on managing our intake of blue light.

The biggest thing is to block artificial light when the sun is not out. If we wake up before sunrise, we want to make sure that we aren't exposing ourselves to a bunch of artificial light right away via our phones or bright lights. Wearing blue blocker glasses or using candles or hoogalite bulbs instead of incandescents until we can get outside for sunrise is an easy switch. (My favorite blue blockers and light bulbs are in the resources section.) If we must look at our phones before we have taken in the sun, we can either use our blue blocking glasses or make our phone screens red to eliminate the blue light. You can find videos on youtube that show you how to do this. (I have my phone screen on red most of the time, but especially during hours when the sun is not out.)

Ideally, we want to be outside (not looking through a window or glasses) for a few minutes within the first 20 mins of sunrise, regardless of the weather. We don't have to look at the sky or the sunrise, we just have to be outside to receive the light. This is what will give the appropriate signal to the SCN that the day has begun. Just 3-5 minutes of sunrise light outside in your eyes is sufficient time to get the signal across.

There is a great free app called Circadian (also linked in resources) that will tell you, based on the location information you give it, when sunrise, sunset, UVA, and UVB times are for you. UVA rise is another time that we want to be catching the light, as the signaling of the hypothalamic-pituitary-thyroid access is triggered specifically by UVA. Getting a 20-minute walk in at UVA time is ideal, if we can swing it. But even just a few minutes is great.

While it's not technically a hormone, D3 is involved in a lot of hormonal functions, and for proper D3 conversion, we want to get some exposed-skin midday UVB if we can. And then, finally, it is ideal to peek at the sunset for a few minutes as well, to let our brain know that it's time to wind down the day. All of this light exposure needs to happen outside, without glasses or sunglasses on, in order to have the most impact. Through a window just won't cut it (unless it's open), as there are essential frequencies of light that the glass filters out.

Something I am incorporating into my routine as much as possible are "light breaks." This is just me going outside for a few minutes at different points of the day, without glasses or sunglasses on, just to put my face towards the sun (if there is any) or get the proper light signals in my eyes. In the winter, this obviously takes a bit more work and intention, but it is absolutely worth it.

Again, once the sun goes down, it is a crucial time period for blocking artificial light. This is probably the hardest one, as many of us (myself included) have a habit of unwinding with screen-time at the end of the day. Here, again, we can employ our blue blocker glasses, or switch our light bulbs out for ones that don't have blue in the light frequency (or use candles a la the Amish. No, but seriously, candlelight is awesome). Any artificial light after sundown can spike a cortisol surge, erroneously signaling to our bodies that it is the middle of the day.

All of this circadian stuff, however, is based on the adult circadian rhythm. In adolescents, as critical parts of their brain are taken off-line for development during puberty, their circadian rhythm is delayed. The circadian delay has been shown to start at the onset of puberty and has been found to be greater in males than in females, though in both it peaks between the ages of 15-21.[10] Due to a resistance to what scientists refer to as "sleep pressure" (which, in the study I have referenced, they did hypothesize could be exacerbated by increased exposure to artificial light) combined with a delayed circadian rhythm, teens are drawn to stay up late in the evenings and sleep in later in the day.

There have not been enough studies done on the specific circadian changes in the brain and how they are affected by puberty in humans, but in rats the growth and development of the SCN was shown to be directly impacted by the hormonal changes of puberty.[11] So, this circadian phase delay is likely involved in the proper development of the SCN and subsequent appropriate circadian responses in adulthood.

In traditional cultures, around 13-15 is the age when specifically the boys would start to be responsible for tending the fires all night. There are

---

[10] https://www.ncbi.nlm.nih.gov/pmc/articles/PMC2820578/#:~:text=According%20to%20this%20model%2C%20human,in%20the%20morning%20%5B8%5D.

[11] https://www.ncbi.nlm.nih.gov/pmc/articles/PMC2820578/#:~:text=According%20to%20this%20model%2C%20human,in%20the%20morning%20%5B8%5D.

significant changes in the adolescent brain that make that the perfect role for them. However, this does not mean that it is a good idea to have your tween or teen's room flooded with artificial light in the evenings, or that encouraging excessive screen use after dark is a good idea just because they are adolescents. The light from a fire and the light from a screen are two very, very different kinds of light, and blue light at the wrong times will still have a detrimental impact on them. But they will be more inclined to stay up later, regardless (though, again, this drive is typically less extreme in females). And it does mean that once they are a teenager, letting them sleep in in the morning is a healthy thing to do, considering the vast amount of synthesis, growth, and restructuring that their brain is doing during this phase.

Puberty and Menarche

Okay! So, we all know of menarche as a girl's first period, but what exactly is going on leading up to this momentous event?

Menarche refers specifically to the first period. But there is so much else happening before - and after - that moment. Puberty generally refers to the timeframe of maturation leading up to and through menarche. And the variations of normal are pretty wide.

The average age range of menarche is between 11 and 15. The first ovulation, however, is not always at the same time. It *can* be, but it can also be as late as a few months or *2 years* after a girl's first period. It is rare (and devastating to think about for a number of reasons), but there have also been cases of young girls becoming pregnant before the onset of menarche - meaning they ovulated before their first period and were likely raped during that time. Ugh.

87

For most girls, though, ovulation won't start for at least a couple of months *after* her first bleed; sometimes not for a couple of years. This means that she could have irregular or missed periods for a little while at first, *which is completely normal.*

Puberty generally begins 3-4 years before menarche, and some scientists say that first bleed marks the end of puberty. I disagree with this line of thought because, clearly, the emotional and social factors we generally associate with puberty, as well as the continuation of physical growth and development, extend well into the teenage years and beyond the initial onset of the menstrual cycle.

Hormonally, at the onset of puberty, A LOT gets initiated, which can explain why, seemingly overnight, our daughters seem to change. Here's what is happening microscopically: the hypothalamus releases the hormone GnRH, which tells the pituitary gland to signal the increase of FSH and LH in the ovaries. As FSH and LH levels rise, the ovaries begin to grow and mature and start making estrogen and progesterone.

Interestingly enough, GnRH and its relationship with FSH and LH is actually present in embryonic development. It is also active immediately after birth, where it continues the development of the gonads and sex organs until the age of about 3-4 years in girls, at which time the brain hits the pause button. This time period between birth and age 3-4 is referred to as "minipuberty." I think this explains a lot as to where the "threenager" comes from, and why the hormonal onset of puberty can remind us so much of those three-year-old temper tantrum days, when hormonal fluctuations were happening but essentially in reverse order.

Puberty in girls officially starts when this hormonal communication between GnRH, FSH and LH (called the hypothalamic-pituitary-gonadal axis) gets turned on again, usually somewhere between the ages of 8 and 12 years old. What exactly initiates the flipping on of this switch still lives, even for scientists, in the realm of mystery. (Win for the mystery!) But these are the primary hormones that we are contending with when the beast in our daughters is suddenly unleashed.

While all this is happening, there are also very clear visual cues that are taking place. They grow - fast! This is when you'll start spending a fortune, and tons of time, acquiring new clothes and shoes that they then outgrow in a few months time. They get taller and they start amassing more healthy fat around their hips, buttocks, thighs, and belly. Thelarche, a fancy name for the early stage of puberty when the breasts begin to grow, will begin. Once the breasts have started developing - sometimes a whole year or two later - the adrenal glands start releasing androgens, and pubic hair in the armpits and on the labia majora will start to appear (called pubarche).

The sebaceous (sweat) glands develop - and with them, the smells! And sometimes the zits, too. Acne, in my opinion, is the ultimate *worst* reason to prescribe a child going through normal puberty birth control. That is not the answer. I strongly believe that acne can mostly be addressed with good skin care and dietary changes (specifically in the kinds of fats that are being ingested, as well as proper amounts of dietary fiber so that the liver can process and release stored fats and hormones), and I also know that there will be some people who struggle more with this than others due to their genetics.

What is Normal?

It's easy to forget what our first cycles were like, especially if we've been having a regular cycle every month for over 20 years, interrupted only by pregnancy and postpartum. I for sure do not remember the regularity, consistency, frequency, color, or feelings associated with the first few times I bled. And what my daughter's body does might be completely different from what mine did then or does now anyway!

So here's a quick guide for "ranges of normal" for first periods: Bleeding for an hour and then stopping, bleeding a whole lot for a week and then not bleeding again for a couple of months, spotting blood for a couple of cycles and then bleeding a lot more, bouts of weeping and complaining about mild cramps and the unfairness of it all, is all within the range of normal and should not be cause for concern.

Outside of normal would be EXTREME amounts of blood (I'm talking fill-up-more-than-a-thick-pad-an-hour, can't-wear-pants-there-is-so-much-blood levels of blood), tremendous pain, bleeding before the age of 9, or not bleeding until after the age of 16. Painful periods are something to keep an eye on, because as we've touched on in other parts of this book, periods in a healthy body really should not be painful. Some occasional dull cramping, sure - this can be dealt with easily by resting, relaxing, and maybe taking some cramp bark tincture. But outside of that, we should not be experiencing pain with our periods. If we are, there is something out of balance that is wanting some attention.

We do this thing where we want everything to be textbook and follow a precise and prescribed pattern of behavior. But with the female body in particular - menstruation, pregnancy, birth and menopause - there is no such thing. There are patterns that are common and patterns that are less common, and patterns that could be something to pay closer attention to as they might signal some kind of disorder that needs greater support. There are patterns that are less common but not concerning at all. The variations of normal across women's bodies are vast and innumerable. So as women and mothers of daughters, it is our job to get good at reading patterns and getting to know our unique patterns and the unique patterns of our daughters. Because there is no textbook right answer (even though there are plenty of textbooks). There is no one right way. There are many, many variations of normal. And there are a few exceptions.

The thing about pattern recognition is that we have to widen and broaden our view. It means we are looking at things and how they play out over time - across several months and cycles, maybe even over the course of a year. A general rule of thumb, though: if something is consistently happening that feels off to you, it probably is. Women are wise, and our intuition is valid. Don't brush off a nagging sense that something isn't functioning the way it should just because it isn't in the ranges of extreme that I outlined above. Trust your gut, and if you think you should take your daughter to see someone, do so.

Smells and Hygiene

The other day, I walked into my older daughter's room to grab something and was hit with a wall of stench. She was not in the room. The smell was like a combination of fresh armpits, sweat, and old socks, and it was PUNGENT. I was quite literally stopped in my tracks.

Most tweens are not super excited about bathing regularly. They aren't used to having to bathe daily to keep on top of the new smells that are emerging from EVERYWHERE. For some, the smells aren't even noticeable. For others, they can start to be a source of deep embarrassment. Enter moontime and there is a whole other world of scent to throw in the mix!

We live in a culture that likes to cover up and eliminate smells that are reminiscent of the earth, of natural bodies, or of decay. Now, I'm definitely not saying that we should walk around reeking like a bathhouse as an act of cultural subversion. (I mean, you do you, there will just likely be some social fallout). I enjoy the smell of flowers much more than the smell of decay any day. And yet, personally, I would rather smell the natural smells that emanate from a bathroom after use than the carcinogenic and endocrine disrupting chemicals in a glade "air freshener" or that No-Poo spray that seems to pop up everywhere. But does it have to be one or the other?

Our obsession with covering up the smells of nature is one of the major ways that we have divorced ourselves from the natural world. We simply can't handle the scent of the wild anymore. Our disgust at the natural emanations of the body is not actually inherent to our species. It is a conditioned response. Very young children do not register smells as "good" or "bad" - they are simply smells, until the adults around them qualify and teach that certain smells are "bad."

We are designed to be able to nose out decay and putrefaction as a form of protection (especially moms) to ensure that we aren't putting harmful things into our bodies or spending time in places where we can become sick as a result. But the natural smells of our bodies are not that. The smells that emanate from our bodies and the bodies of our children, if we are willing to tune into them, can actually tell us quite a bit about the state of our children's health. They also serve a specific purpose in procreation and the continuation of our species.

There is nothing wrong with strong smells in puberty. They are totally and completely normal and to be expected. However, the social implications of smelling powerfully of a natural process are also to be expected and anticipated, especially in our culture of chemical scent obsession and dependence. So how do we help our girls deal with this in a way that doesn't contribute to body shame, loss of our natural sense of smell, or serious endocrine disruption and potential carcinogens being absorbed on the regular into our skin?

Lucky for us, there are *so many* amazing smells that nature also produces that we have learned, en masse, to capture and bottle in a variety of ways that are not only NOT harmful to our health, but can actually provide us with health benefits to boot! I have included some resources in the back of this book of some of my favorite products, including deodorants, lotions, air fresheners, etc. You can also check out EWG.org for a list of clean personal care products available on the market today (though their list is in no way exhaustive or representative of everything that is out there).

A note about antiperspirants: please don't use these or give them to your child! Our bodies are designed to sweat. This is how the body naturally cleans out toxins on a regular basis. It is GOOD to sweat. If we are heavily physically exerting ourselves, we should be sweating. End of story. Any products designed to block our sweat glands from doing what they are designed to do are contributing to the massive number of cases of breast cancer that we have in this country. The sweat glands (especially in our armpits), our breast tissue, and the lymph are all connected. When we stop our armpits from sweating, we are stopping our body's natural detoxification process. And when we can't rid ourselves of toxins, they build up. Over time, this can lead to devastating issues. I feel so grateful to my mother for alerting me to this fact at the young age of 16. I have only used natural deodorants in my armpits ever since.

The same is true of vaginal douches and washes. The vagina is a self-cleaning organism, with a very sensitive and powerful PH balancing system. It is *so cool* that we have a self-cleaning mechanism this way! When we use heavily scented products and douches to cover up the natural smells of our beautiful vaginas, we are interfering with our body's inherent ability to clean itself. A disrupted vaginal PH can lead to recurrent yeast infections, UTIs, and a whole host of other problems. There is nothing wrong with the natural smell of a vagina! In fact, heterosexual men are hardwired to really like how they smell, completely untampered with. It's part of the intelligent design of nature.

Once again, we come to the power of smell to alert us to the state of our health and whether or not something unfavorable is happening in the body. The vagina has a scent, no doubt. It's supposed to. If that scent is incredibly strong, foul, or pungent, however, that is important information that we would do well not to ignore or just try to cover up! Something is out of balance in our bodies if we are producing smells that are overpowering or highly offensive. Something in our diets, our hygiene (both physical and spiritual), or our stress levels needs to be adjusted. Strong smells can sometimes also be because our body is in a process of detoxification and correcting something that *was* out of balance, or they can be a sign of a serious infection that needs to be addressed.

I'm a big fan of natural deodorants for our smelly tweens and teens. I'm also a big proponent of regular bathing to help mitigate strong natural smells and clear off the toxins our bodies have expelled in the form of sweat. This one can be harder to get the tween on board with (I swear, sometimes it's like pulling teeth with mine, and it's 20 minutes of dragging feet to get there) but is well worth it, for everyone's sake!

And when all else fails, you can always, as I did in my daughter's room on that fatefully smelly day, open the window and let in the fresh air!

Getting to Know Our Pelvic Anatomy and Energetics

While I would be remiss to not cover some female reproductive anatomy in this book, there are some other books that do a far better job than I will be able to do here, and I highly recommend you check them out. I'm sure you've all had an anatomy class before, so some of this will be review. That said, I don't want to make assumptions that your understanding of your own anatomy is complete, either. If I was going solely off of what I learned in high school, my understanding of my own body would be pretty limited. Not to mention that nothing about pelvic energetics is ever taught in school. Don't assume that your daughter's "health" class in school will be enough. It is a sad fact that many women don't fully understand the inner workings of their bodies (which isn't actually surprising, given that western medicine doesn't really, either). And it's pretty hard to teach our daughters how their bodies work when we don't fully understand it ourselves.

I'm just going to go over external soft tissue and organ anatomy here, as well as a toe dip into some energetics. For a deeper dive into our complete pelvic anatomy and how to harness her power, I recommend reading Sheri Winton's *Women's Anatomy of Arousal*, Tami Kent's *Wild Feminine*, and *Healing Love Through the Tao: Cultivating Female Sexual Energy* by Maneewan and Mantak Chia.

At the end of this section is an exercise called The Mirror Exercise, which is a great way to get to know the unique, individual anatomy of our own vulvas. Around the age of 12 or 13, this might be a great exercise to introduce to your daughter, with the gift of a hand mirror. You can also introduce it earlier, if she is one of those children who seems very curious about her own anatomy. Seeing how her body changes over time could be a very beautiful and fascinating thing for her. It doesn't have to be weird at all.

95

External Anatomy

Vulva is the word used to describe all of the external parts of a woman's reproductive anatomy. The mons pubis, labias majora and minora, clitoral head, clitoral hood, vulva vestibule, urethral opening, and vaginal opening all make up what we call the vulva. This, along with the perineum and anus, is what you can see when you look in a hand mirror.

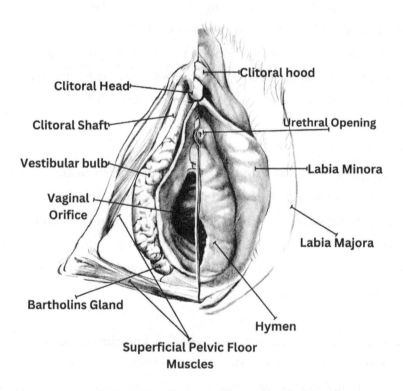

Vulvas come in a variety of shapes, sizes, and irregularities. I am ALL about normalizing this from day 1. Everyone's vulva is as unique as their face. We don't stress about our faces not looking like the models in anatomy textbooks - it should be no different with our vulvas. Here is a beautiful sampling of what normal vulvas can look like. See how different they all are?

Vulva Gallery

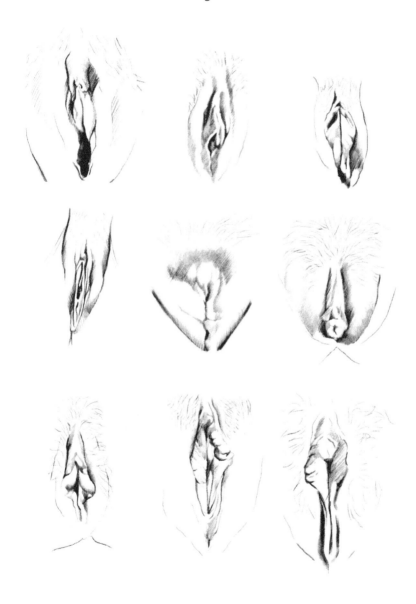

Internal Anatomy

The vagina, cervix, uterus, uterine tubes, ovaries, urethra, vestibular bulbs, urethral sponge, and Bartholin's glands are the internal parts of the female reproductive anatomy.

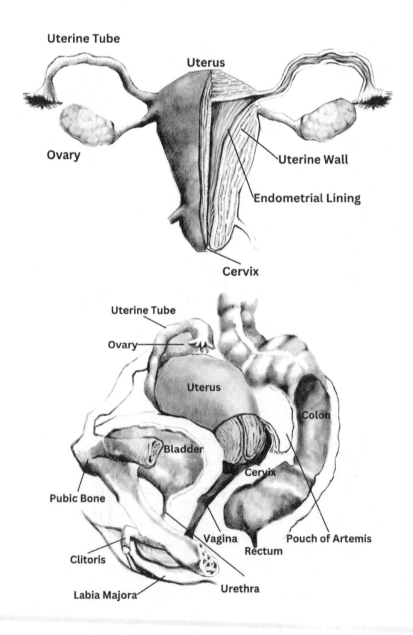

We also have the space between the uterus and colon, which I have lovingly renamed the pouch of Artemis, as I'm kind of over the idea of female body parts being named by the men who "discovered" them (sorry, Douglas). You'll notice that I use the term "uterine tube" instead of "fallopian tube" for the same reason.

The bladder and rectum are in front of and behind the uterus, respectively. As we have babies and age, this proximity becomes more apparent and relevant. It is important to respect the dynamic interplay of how everything fits together. The female pelvis is a powerhouse and houses some very important biological processes. Everything is held together with a complex network of muscles and ligaments that are designed to stretch and flex to accommodate the changes a woman's pelvis has to go through to give birth. Knowing how it all fits together can, again, help us to understand ourselves better.

In Taoist texts, the perineum is referred to as the seat of Chi - the vital energetic life force of the universe. The pelvic bowl, known as the lower tan tien, is the resting place for us to hold the literal power of the universe when we are not circulating it through our bodies. I found this recognition of the pelvic bowl as an energetic storehouse mimicked in the Hawaiian culture's understanding of the pelvis as a "bowl of light." This understanding forms the basis for the Ho'oponopono practice, as it was taught to me by Auntie Nahi, who has since passed, many years ago on the Big Island. The way I was taught, our "bowl" is designed to hold the light of the universe, but as we move through life and encounter strife and conflict, we gather "stones" in our bowl. Thus our bowl becomes filled with stones and there is less space for the light to inhabit. The ho'oponopono practice, while commonly referenced as a forgiveness practice (which it also is) is for the purpose of "emptying the bowl" so that it can once again hold the divine light of the universe.

Many cultures recognize the importance of keeping the pelvic area warm. The practices of vaginal steaming and uterine castor oil packs are ways that we can tend to our pelvic bowl and keep it warm, supple, and nourished. In our current western school of thought, we need to have a "tight" vagina, doing hundreds of Kegels to keep ourselves strong and sexually viable. While there are many problems with this line of thinking, the major one is that it is not actually through tightening and rigidity that we have a strong pelvic bowl, but through movement and relaxation.

Being able to relax and release our pelvic muscles is what allows everything to move freely and have ample blood flow so that it can align perfectly in our ever-changing female bodies. This is what gives us strength and stability. Most of us are over-tightening and over-working our pelvic floor muscles, creating rigidity which can lead to a host of problems, including urinary and fecal incontinence and prolapse. Extended bouts of sitting (like what I am doing to write this book) keep things in our pelvis stuck and stagnant.

The 4 Phases of the Menstrual Cycle

Our menstrual cycle is easily divided into 4 phases. These phases correspond with the seasons of the year, the seasons of a woman's life, the phases in a garden (cultivated and wild), and the seasons of the moon. There is a whole universe to uncover in the phases of our cycle, and I'm just going to give a light brushstroke here of a 'normal' healthy cycle. Obviously, variations of normal are pretty wide, and your body might veer from this general template. This information, however basic and foundational, can still give you a sense of how you can come into greater harmony with your cycle - and teach your daughter to do the same.

I'm not gonna lie, embodying this information takes intention and practice, especially if you were raised by and have had to conform to our modern, linear, masculine culture. But once you've gotten working with this information down, you will know yourself in a whole new way. It is so worth it. Which is part of the gift of teaching this to our girls at such a young age.

Teaching your daughter to track her cycle throughout the month - her discharge, her moods, her energy levels, and her blood - will be one of the most valuable things you can give her when it comes to her body. This is true body autonomy, beyond what anyone can legislate or take away. This can give her agency over her life in a way you may have never had, or may only be starting to come to for yourself.

We want her to know that her menstrual cycle is a vital sign. As women, we have this gift that can tell us even more about our overall health than having a sense of what a normal blood pressure, resting heart rate, and basal temp are for us. I think it's great to know those things too, and the cycle is such a gift in the way it tells us about deeper things that are going on in our bodies. So let's celebrate that gift and honor it by learning how to pay attention to its signs and signals! It takes time and practice to learn, but every woman can, and the benefits to her doing so are tremendous. This is true sovereignty and agency in action.

There is so much more to this than what I am about to share here, and it can really become a lifetime study if we devote ourselves to it that way (which I *highly* recommend). There is also an entire chapter devoted just to our menses later on in the book. Here is the full cycle, broken down into its 4 specific phases.

Menstruation

Season - Winter
Garden phase - Compost, dreaming
Harvesting phase - Bark and roots
Moon phase - New
Goddess phase - Crone/Wise woman

When we are bleeding, this is the winter phase of our cycle, and what most use to reference the beginning of the cycle. In actuality, the cycle is circular so there really is no beginning or end - except for the very clear beginning (which this book is about) and end when we cease to bleed and enter menopause. The rest is circular, or wave-like. Call it what you will, beginning or end, this is when we bleed.

Menstruation is a time to focus on deep nourishment - of the body, mind, and soul. Mineral-rich broths and soups are beneficial to replenish the energy released with the cleansing blood. Think cooked greens, beets, sea vegetables, dark berries, darker legumes, and meats. Rest and gentle movement, along with time for creative expression, and doing nothing, are important ways to take care of ourselves during this time. In the garden, this is the compost phase of things, so asking ourselves what we are releasing, transmuting, and cleansing out are good prompting questions.

Our blood will often range in color. Noting the color can tell us a lot about the state of our uterine health, and this is something you want to talk with your daughter about. You don't have to be inspecting her pads or anything (although doing so with her at least once or twice can help normalize looking at color and make her feel less like this blood is a disgusting thing). But you can also just ask her what color her blood is. Let her know that it can vary - from brown to bright red to deep dark red to light pink and streaky.

Bright red blood is fresh, new blood and a good, healthy sign. Deeper and darker red blood with some clots in it is also normal, especially on our heavier days. The darker color can indicate that it has been in the vagina for longer, and so vaginal steaming and self-massage during the phases where we are not bleeding could be recommended, as this suggests some mild stagnation. Clots are normal - unless they are larger than the size of a quarter. Light pink is also a normal spotting color at the beginning and/or end of your cycle. (If there is light pink blood in the middle of our cycle, not during menstruation, that could be a sign of a serious condition and, if consistent, would warrant some professional attention.)

If our blood is consistently brown, however, that is a signal that there is stagnation, and for some reason, our uterus is having trouble clearing out the built up uterine lining. Brown blood is old blood that has been in there for a while. This could be for a number of reasons. My first go-to, though, would be potential uterine malpositioning, which can be corrected with uterine massage, self-massage, and vaginal steaming during our luteal phase, as well as somatic process work. (What is it that we are not wanting to release, or we are having difficulty releasing fully?) Not getting enough exercise in general can also lead to stagnation of the blood.

In the beginning of your daughter's cycle, her blood is not going to be in a normal pattern. But getting her to start noticing and becoming aware of the color and how she feels is something that you can start right away. You can get her to chart the color and amount of her blood, as well as the timing of her cycle, moods, cravings, etc., just as a healthy habit to start. You will obviously need to help her with this at the beginning. I have found having a nice journal specific to this purpose is helpful.

The reading of the pattern, however, will only be an effective and healthy thing to do once she's been bleeding for about a year or so. Remember that it can take that long or longer for a girl to start ovulating after her first bleed. You, as her mom, will have the responsibility to track and be aware of her cycle alongside her for at least the first couple of years, so that you and she can get to know her baseline together. If you are the one who is teaching her and talking with her about her cycle before it even starts, it will normalize this really early on. It is expected for her to want to feel private at this time, *and* you as her mom are the number one person that it is important she share this info with, for health reasons. My daughter has no issue coming to me and telling me the color, amount, and consistency of her blood because she knows I'm a safe place to bring this stuff to and I don't find it gross. In fact, it seems like she is excited to have someone to discuss it with.

Follicular

Season - Spring
Garden phase - Planning, planting
Harvesting phase - Leaves, shoots, cambium layer
Moon phase - Waxing crescent
Goddess phase - Maiden

After we have shed our blood (and sometimes overlapping the final days of our bleed), we enter into the follicular phase. From a seasonal perspective the follicular phase is the spring. It is often met with a surge of new energy. The follicles in the ovaries are in action, choosing which egg to ripen and release. That release - ovulation - signals the end of the follicular phase. Our basal body temp is lower during the follicular phase and our discharge during this time tends to be dry or sticky, moving to creamier towards the end of the phase. Hormonally, our body is releasing FSH and LH, as well as gradually increasing our estrogen levels.

The follicular phase is a great time for getting in some heavier activity and workouts (getting the blood and lymph moving), trying new things, getting creative with big new ideas, and new adventures. We also might not be as hungry during this time, and our caloric needs are actually fewer (if we are properly nourishing ourselves during our bleeding time). So, eating less - and eating lighter foods during this time like salads, steamed veggies, ferments, sprouts and lean proteins - is supported by the cycle. This would also be a great cycle phase to do a brief fast or cleanse in, if that is what your system is calling for. (I don't recommend fasting for growing tweens/teens, though, unless it is within a religious or ceremonial context.)

Our logical brain is on fire during this time, so project implementation, mapping, and planning are excellent activities to put our focus and attention into. This is the youthful, exuberant phase of the cycle, and we can really work with this energy in a positive and beneficial way. What seeds are we ready to plant? What new growth are we tending? How are we wanting to play and express ourselves?

Ovulatory

Season - Summer
Garden phase - Ripening, fruiting
Harvesting phase - Fruits, berries
Moon phase - Full
Goddess phase - Mother

This is the phase where we are at our most vital, vibrant, and alive. We are feeling passionate, juicy, and ready to celebrate the fullness of life. Our FHS, LH, and estrogen are peaking. An egg has been released into the soft cushion of the uterus and lies in wait. Will germination occur or not?

Our discharge in this phase is often described as "egg white" in texture, which, considering that it signals the release of an egg, seems apt. It is usually copious, and if you take it between your fingers and pull them apart, the discharge will actually stretch as your fingers open. This is the medium that is essential for sperm to be able to swim through, and without this kind of discharge, getting pregnant is pretty challenging.

Estrogen spikes during ovulation, as does our basal temp. Making sure that you have plenty of fiber in the form of veggies and fruits during this phase will help your body metabolize any excess estrogen that might want to accumulate in the liver. We are still drawn to eating on the lighter, fresher side, but incorporating some more lightly cooked foods is also good. It's also an excellent time for dark chocolate.

Our energy is going out at this time. It's a great time for parties, socializing, flirting and outwardly-focused endeavors. It's also when zits tend to pop out! (Interesting fact: the side of your face that zits are more prevalent can often signal which side you ovulated on). This is when we are celebrating our abundance and watching the fruits of our lives ripen.

It is important for your daughter to know about this phase, for obvious reasons. The likelihood of her crush-type feelings being particularly strong during this time (if she has started having those) is high. As she gets older, this is the most likely time that she will want to act on those feelings. This is also when, from a pheromone perspective, we are most desirable to the opposite sex. And I think it goes without saying that if she's going to get pregnant, it's going to be during this window.

This is where opening up a conversation about pleasure can come in really handy as she gets older. If she knows that she can access and request pleasure during this phase, when she will begin to want it the most, you can show her a way around playing with the fire of potential unwanted pregnancy without resorting to hormone disrupting drugs aka birth control. In addition to barrier methods of contraception, knowing about toys, self pleasure, and foreplay can serve her very well in this phase throughout her teenage years and into adulthood. Teaching our daughters about the importance and sacredness of their pleasure also helps to rewrite the toxic narrative going around that the crux of sex is centered around men's orgasm (more on this later).

Luteal

Season - Fall

Garden phase - Harvest, canning/food preservation, putting garden beds to rest

Harvesting phase - Fruits, berries, bark, roots

Moon phase - Waning crescent

Goddess phase - Maga/Witch/Cosmic Creatress

In the luteal phase, our uterus starts to build up a nourishing home for the egg in case germination and implantation want to occur. The uterine lining thickens and grows, and toward the end of this phase, we may find our energy starting to pull a bit more inward. Our temperature will remain elevated until just before menstruation, and our discharge will tend towards a drier, stickier, more crumbly texture. Progesterone levels rise in the first part of this phase, in the event that the egg is fertilized and will need to be nurtured by said hormone until the placenta is developed enough to take over. Just before menstruation, those levels - along with our basal temp - will drop dramatically, signaling that we are about to bleed.

For foods, we want to focus more on foods rich in B vitamins, calcium, and magnesium, such as leafy greens, organ meats, eggs, raw milk, yogurt, beef, shellfish, brewer's yeast, legumes, sesame and sunflower seeds, etc. We also want to keep up a large amount of veggies to continue to help the liver metabolize excess estrogen stores. Baked and roasted veggies are great at this time. Also chocolate.

Interesting facts about cravings: dark chocolate is high in magnesium. If we find that we are often having intense cravings for chocolate, it is likely that we are deficient in magnesium. And as fabulous a way to get magnesium as chocolate is, we might want to consider increasing and diversifying our magnesium sources - including topical or via magnesium flakes in our baths. If we do use chocolate to satisfy the craving, super dark chocolate is the best magnesium source.

Cravings for sweets are often a need for increased protein intake, unless they happen immediately after eating, in which case they are a signal that our body needs enzymes to digest the food we have just eaten. (In nature, sweetness tends to be found primarily in fruits and honey, which are abundant in natural enzymes.) Salt cravings are most often a signal of dehydration, so increasing water and electrolyte intake can help. (I love putting minerals and lemon in my water.) Check out the resources section for where to get some high-quality magnesium and minerals, as well as my favorite digestive enzymes.

Pushing ourselves to do intensive, hardcore workouts or start complicated new ventures at this time will be counterproductive to the natural flow of where our energy wants to be. Intuition is heightened and creative energy is magnified. Where we put our attention and focus will be amplified and even more powerful than normal during this phase. This is a great phase to focus on manifestation (or wombifestation, as I like to call it).

This phase of the menstrual cycle generally lasts around two weeks. This is a time to assess what has been, complete things that were initiated in the follicular phase, and discern if there is anything that needs to change. The creatress phase, where we harvest what we've been cultivating and turn it into something yummy, is a ripe and fecund phase of the cycle. Organization skills also come to the foreground - for me, the luteal phase is when I get a strong urge to deep clean and organize my house, and finish any lingering projects.

The later half of this phase is often when, if there is something out of alignment in our lives or something lingering that we haven't addressed, it will come boldly to the forefront for us to examine. Just like we are called to deep clean our physical homes, our energetic and emotional bodies need it too. If we ignore what this time is bringing up for us, our symptoms of PMS - aggression, irritation, depression - can get louder as a way to signal to us that there is something asking for our attention. People talk about wanting alone time while menstruating, but for me this need for solitude is most pronounced right before I bleed.

Knowing these things about ourselves is so valuable. It helps us to stop pathologizing or ignoring our moods; instead, ask some deep inquiry questions to dive into the root of what might be driving the feelings. I have consciously used this time to clean up lingering things with my husband and friends in my life. Instead of thinking there is something wrong with me or I should just ignore what is coming up and move on, I use the tools I have gathered of conscious communication and address head on what is being presented. The result is generally that I feel much lighter in my being, my relationships improve, and I have more overall energy.

If you need some tools or resources on how to communicate more effectively with those in your life, I have included some resources in the recommended reading section.

A Word About Boobs and Beauty

As we've already discussed, the development of breast buds is one of the first signs that puberty has started. For a young girl of this age, this development is no small thing. It starts to visually set her apart from the boys and other girls in different stages of development, and there can be a lot of concern and comparison with her peers concerning size, shape, etc., of her newly developing breasts and body. How we manage these conversations with our daughters matters a lot in helping them to shape a healthy self-image.

Starting pretty young we are used to people commenting on our appearance - especially as girls. The elusive "beauty" word is thrown around as a value judgment and we have been entrained to equate physical beauty with a sense of accomplishment. This starts incredibly young, when we hyper-focus on children's fashion and comment regularly on their physical appearance. I didn't realize how deeply entrenched this physical commentating was on my own psyche until I started to really dissect the number of times I felt drawn to comment on and compliment my children based on how they looked.

Changing this pattern of speech can be incredibly difficult. I'm not saying there is anything intrinsically wrong with telling a woman or a young girl that she's beautiful - it can feel really good to receive that kind of compliment from time to time. What's problematic is when our appearance is the only or primary thing that gets complimented or commented on. This is what sets the stage for a whole lot of self-consciousness and pathologizing of our physiological differences. When I really started to look at this in myself, I was floored at how often I remarked on another person's clothing. Even if it was positive, I started to notice the bizarre impact this phenomenon had, particularly when I started to do it with children.

If you think about it, telling a 3, 4, or 5 year old kid that you like their clothing (that they probably had nothing to do with acquiring or possibly even choosing for themselves to don in the morning) is very strange behavior. What message is that then telling the child? What are we placing value on in that moment?

I love giving compliments. I love making people feel good about themselves. Often, looks are the easiest thing to compliment because we are designed to take in visual information very quickly. I also love fabrics and textiles, and am drawn to visually artistic expressions and delicious tactile fabric sensations (soft velvet = bliss). So, commenting on clothing is something I tend to do A LOT. In grown women who have been conditioned to see our clothing as an extension of our personality and expression, I think this can be a fun thing, and I don't want to diminish having fun in that arena. But since having daughters, the way I do this, especially with children but even with my grown female friends, has changed dramatically.

How different would it be if, instead of someone telling us that we look beautiful, they said something like "you look so healthy and happy right now," or "you look radiant," or "it really looks like you have been taking such good care of yourself and it makes me so happy to see you looking so well." While still talking about looks, this changes the orientation from something that is an external factor to highlighting that true beauty is something that comes from health and an inner sense of happiness and ease. It encourages us to tend more to our inner world and experience than our outer expression. It's hard to do, but worth the effort, especially with our own children.

This is different from encouraging basic hygiene and self-care. Caring for our bodies, including good hygiene, can be an expression of deep love for ourselves. When we orient towards it that way, instead of as something we have to do in order to meet a certain social standard, it is reflected not only in our physical appearance but also in the kind of energy we radiate out into the world. Our beauty then becomes internally generated and we develop a certain magnetism that is with us even if we are having a season of sweatpants.

So when our daughter notices that she is starting to develop breasts, we honor this signaling of certain changes in her body. This is a marker of getting older, and there is a lot to celebrate about that. The presentation of breast buds can also be a great doorway into conversation about the other changes in her body that are inevitably coming.

One question that is going to come up at some point is training bras/bras in general. I am not the biggest fan of training bras, for a few reasons. The primary reason is that in young girls who only have tiny breast buds, they are completely structurally unnecessary. Also, putting undue pressure on the area under the armpits can restrict lymphatic flow, which is essential to healthy detoxification.

That said, there can also be something very appropriate about wearing a special garment around our developing breasts. It can be a way to honor this new change, and our breasts in general. Depending on the size of the breasts as they grow, this can also be a matter of comfort for a lot of women. I don't know about you, but I don't particularly enjoy jumping or running without one. There is also the matter of nipples starting to show through her shirts, which can feel exposing and embarrassing to a lot of young girls. Having an extra layer, whether it's a tank underlayer or a training bra, can help minimize the discomfort that comes from feeling like our bodies are on display.

If you are going to go the training bra route with your daughter, it's essential to get one that fits well. I have linked some of my favorites for young girls in the resources. Bras that are too tight or restricting around the rib cage or chest are a developmental no-no. If they leave a deep mark on the skin, they are too tight and need to be replaced. Also, you want to make sure that whatever training bra you give her is made of natural fibers. A polyester bra is essentially wrapping your daughter's chest in plastic.

There are 5 different stages of breast development, and these stages will evolve over the course of her puberty as her body grows the glands and tissue that is eventually necessary to sustain newborn life via the production of breast milk. The chances of her breasts being fully developed before or when she starts her first bleed is actually pretty small, as the mammary tissue continues to grow and develop throughout the teenage years.

Like vulvas, breasts come in all different sizes, shapes, and varieties and it is essential to normalize this from day 1. It is incredibly common for one breast to be slightly larger or higher or lower than another. In a culture that prizes symmetry as a primary feature of beauty, this can be very troubling when we discover one breast to be of a slightly (or dramatically) different size or position than the other. Nipple size, shape, and color is also quite varied, and is one of the most pronounced things that changes throughout the 5 stages of breast development.

I don't think it's possible to completely prevent our daughter from visually comparing herself to her peers. If body image stuff is going to come up, it's likely going to start with the development of breasts and the extra layers of fat around the hips and stomach that full maturation and puberty bring with it. Bringing joy, gentle celebration, and a feeling of specialness to this development can help foster a greater sense of security in her process. Normalize everything about her growing breasts. They might feel sore sometimes as they grow. Nipples might be slightly inverted at first. Or, one might be and the other one isn't. Stretch marks might develop. They will change throughout the course of the cycle. They'll tingle sometimes, burn sometimes, and/or feel soft or lumpy, depending on our hormones and where we are at in the cycle. It's all normal and it's all part of the changing landscape of the female body. Let her know that her breasts are another part to get to know, as a way of knowing herself and being intimate with the terrain of her body as it grows.

Normalize that our bodies change, because they will FOREVER! We are Changing Woman, and the breasts are yet another place where this change is evident. Having some kind of special breast oil to massage on the breasts as they grow can help to minimize the discomfort of stretching skin, as well as establish a healthy practice of self love and care. Violets are an excellent support for the lymphatic system, and I love to use the violet oil recipe from Susun Weed's *Healing Wise* for breast massage after showers. Not only am I loving and honoring my breasts when I do this, I am also encouraging their overall health. A simple coconut, olive, or almond oil can also be used. Avoid lotions and anything with scents (we go into a deep-dive on chemical-free living later). A simple, single oil, maybe plant-infused, is best.

Breast massage has been shown to increase circulation and blood flow, keep the breasts toned, help avoid and detect early signs of breast cancer, and release oxytocin, which can help reduce stress and anxiety. A healthy breast massage uses a firm but gentle pressure, lasts up to 15 minutes and includes the area around the pectoral muscle and into the armpits. Breast massage should feel good and should not be so aggressive or long lasting as to be painful. It is also not recommended to focus your massage on the nipple itself, but more on the tissue surrounding the nipple and the breast, moving your hand in a gentle, circular motion. Breast massage can be done any time of the day or night, and at any point in the cycle. Notice what changes your breasts go through during different points in your cycle. This will allow you to have deeper conversations with your daughter about how our breasts and bodies change over time.

Normalizing breast massage and teaching your daughter how to do it will be a gift you give her that will benefit her overall health for her entire lifetime.

Exercise: The Mirror Exercise

Note: You will need a hand mirror for this exercise

Find yourself a moment in a room where you can be completely undisturbed. Ideal would be a beautiful, quiet setting with decent lighting, but if all you can grab is 10 minutes locked in the bathroom, that can work too.

For this exercise, you will need to remove all clothing from your lower half. Find yourself a comfortable seat where you can have your legs comfortably open.

This is not a sexual exercise, but one to be done with open curiosity. If it gets sexual, that is totally fine! But really, this is about getting to visually know ourselves, which can absolutely include what we look like in a state of sexual arousal.

Take your hand mirror in your hands and open your legs. Angle the mirror so that you can see all of your vulva. Breathe and just take a moment to gaze at this intimate part of your anatomy.

This is a judgment-free zone! We are not looking to analyze or compare to other images we may have seen. We are looking to understand, to bear witness, and to get to know ourselves "down there" in a deeper way.

Look at your vulva as it appears on the outside. Then take your fingers and spread your labia apart to reveal the inner layer of your vulva. See if you can clearly identify where your clitoris is, your urethra, your vaginal opening, your perineum, and your anus.

What colors do you see? What layers do you see? How do the two sides of your labia differ from one another? What can you see or find that you can appreciate about your vulva? What stories does it tell?

Take as much time as you need or can with this exercise. It can bring up a lot - especially if we have never looked at ourselves this way before. This is one to return to again and again, with gentleness and total reverence.

Exercise: Soft Belly

This exercise is exactly what it sounds like it's going to be. In our culture, we are repeatedly told - through media messaging and imagery everywhere - that the best kind of body is one with a flat stomach and toned abs.

This leads to most women holding a tremendous amount of tension in their bellies and pelvic bowls in an attempt to "suck it in" and appear to have less of a stomach. Over time, tension in the belly and pelvis can lead to digestive disturbances, difficulty sleeping, hip pain, anxiety, prolapse - the list of seemingly unassociated problems it can create is actually quite extensive!

This exercise encourages you to let it all out! I find this exercise best to do in non-restrictive clothing, though it can be done anywhere and at any time. (You might feel encouraged to change your outfit afterwards, depending on what you discover.)

Step 1:
Bring your awareness to your breath. You don't need to change it or breathe differently, just notice your breathing and where it falls - in your chest, your belly, your throat?

Step 2:
Bring your awareness to your belly. It can be helpful to first intentionally push your belly out with your breath in an exaggerated extension in order to feel the contrast between a puffed-out belly and your normal holding pattern.

Step 3:
Consciously release *any* tension that you are currently holding here. This may take a while. It can help to close your eyes, and for some, placing a hand (or both) on your belly can really help.

Visualize the muscles in and around your belly and your pelvic bowl softening, like slowly melting butter. Breathe.

Soften.

Breathe.

Soften.

Breathe. Soften some more.

Step 4:
When you feel you have softened your belly as much as you can, see if you can soften it even just a little more. Can you extend the softening to your hips? Your pelvic bowl? Your perineum? Your jaw? (I know it sounds random, but our jaw and our hips/belly tightening are actually very closely connected. It can actually be almost impossible to fully relax our bellies and pelvic muscles if we are holding tension in our jaw). Rest in the softening for several breaths, or as long as you like.

You have now completed the soft belly exercise! Feel free to return to it often. See if you can bring this practice into moments in your daily life: walking the dog, sitting at your computer, washing the dishes.

CHAPTER 3

WHAT TO DO WHEN YOUR DAUGHTER IS AN ASSHOLE

Let's be honest, probably part of why you picked up this book is because you are having moments (perhaps even entire days) where you wonder where your sweet little child went and where this totally sassy, a-hole monster came from. She's rude, snappy, sarcastic, overly-literal, and entirely in love with pointing out everyone's shortcomings, especially all the ways you are wrong and failing as a parent and as a human being. Sound familiar?

Here's the thing: Yes, if this was an adult speaking to you and acting this way, you would have full license to write them off as a total jerk and turn the other way, never to include them in your life again. For better or for worse, though, we can't do that when it's our own kid (even though there are times when you probably want to). Developmentally, she's actually not trying to be an asshole - even though it might really seem like it. She just doesn't have the tools and the skills yet to understand what she's feeling and how to communicate effectively. She's also flooded with hormones that she's never dealt with before, and there are actually parts of her brain that have gone "offline" for updates. It can be a brutal combination.

When our daughters are treating us like dogshit, we've got a couple of options. We can drink wine (not very helpful, but I know it's become quite an insta-mom fad and a popular choice). We can take it personally and get super triggered (for me, this looks like getting annoyed, reactive, and pissed off, and is my default when I'm not present or I'm feeling under-resourced). Or, we can pause and ask ourselves some questions: *What might she be expressing or trying to express that I'm missing? What might be underneath this behavior?*

I love questions. I spent five and a half years asking questions when I had my podcasts, and it's the primary tool I have used with my coaching clients for over a decade. When we find the right questions, it's like a portal into another world opens up - especially when we are triggered. When we are triggered (or "brain-hijacked" as I like to call it), the main brain activity that is happening occurs in our reptilian complex. This is the part of the human brain that developed first and is also often referred to as our lizard or reptilian brain. You know, the part responsible for all the f's: fight, flight, freeze, fawn, or fuck.

When we ask a question, though, our brain automatically has to shift out of the reptilian brain into the prefrontal cortex to find an answer, because the reptilian brain doesn't do questions. The result in real time in our lives is that we can immediately shift out of the trigger and into inquiry, if it is the right question. Instead of feeling like we are the victim of the world and everything is out to get us, we start to unfold into a different way of looking at and approaching the world. It's kind of like magic. (Side-bar: this is also why asking a birthing woman a barrage of questions is the WORST thing to do, because she needs to be in her primitive, instinctual brain in order to birth effectively.)

When we ask "what's underneath this behavior," it allows us to start to really get curious about our daughter's internal world. Getting curious about her helps us approach her in an entirely different way. And here's the thing: if we want to develop a relationship with our kid where they feel comfortable coming to us and telling us *anything* and asking us questions about uncomfortable topics, it starts with us getting genuinely curious about what's going on inside them - instead of thinking we know.

4 Reasons Why She Might Be Behaving Like An Asshole

1 - Stress

We don't tend to think of kids getting stressed, but they absolutely do. There are a lot of things that can stress kids out nowadays, far more than when we were kids. The pace of life, of tech, of extracurricular activities and pressures at school, matched with a subtle knowing that the environment is a hot mess and they are being saddled with an immense responsibility/liability in the form of earth stewardship. Add in all the normal, awful tween and teenage social dynamics (compounded by social media) and you have enough to stress the hell out of any person. And these are kids! They have waaay fewer tools in their back pocket to deal with this stuff.

We don't want to shield our kids entirely from stress - we can't anyway. But we do want to help them become more resilient in the face of stress, which means including in their day an ebb and flow that helps them integrate their experiences. Sometimes this may mean restructuring some things in their life, and maybe even taking a thing or two off their plate. Studies have shown the important role of unstructured time and free, unsupervised play in the healthy brain development of children.[12] (There are even studies coming out now on the importance of having unstructured times as adults, but that's a different book.)

When we have every inch of our kids' lives scheduled and planned for them and it's go-go-go all the time, this requisite unstructured time becomes less and less, the amount of stress becomes greater, and the capacity to handle the stress diminishes. Also, stress is hard, but handling stress on an empty stomach is way harder. Hangry has become a popular term because it's a real thing. Make sure they are adequately nourished!

It can be easy to forget, when they seem able to do many of the things that adults can do, when they are growing to be almost-as-big-as or bigger than you, when they can now fit into your shoes and are stealing your clothes and makeup, and are verbally articulate, that they are actually still underdeveloped children. Their brains are not at the same level as an adult's by any means, and they are not yet developmentally capable of the same functions. They are still kids. They still need and want us to teach them things (no matter how much they pretend they don't). They are just bigger and have hormones now, which are often compounded and thrown horribly out of whack by stress. And the manner of things they need us to teach them, and the way to do so, has now changed.

2 - Hormones

Hormones are no joke. As we've already discussed, unbalanced hormones will knock us off our feet, turning us into a dribbling pile of mess at the drop of a hat, messing with our sleep and energy levels, and interrupting our mental clarity and function. We'll talk more about how to minimize

---

[12] The Coddling of the American Mind - Greg Lukianoff and Johnathan Haidt

hormonal disturbances in your environment in the next chapter, but let's just acknowledge right here and now that hormones play a *way* bigger role in our lives than most of us give them credit for.

So, when our daughters' hormones start to really come online, it can (and likely will) take everyone by storm. And these changes happen earlier than we expect them to. According to Jasmine Reese M.D. at Johns Hopkins Medicine, the normal age nowadays for girls to start developing is 8 years old. Yup, you heard that right! 8! And sometimes even as early as 7. For most young girls, the hormones kick in a couple of years before menstruation will happen, so as moms, we get blindsided with a hormonal barrage that we weren't thinking we were going to have to deal with until they were teens.

With the introduction of hormones, her needs are going to start changing. Where she was once totally content to be in imaginary play with her younger siblings for hours at a time, this is going to start becoming less satisfying to her. She's going to want to chat with her friends more often. Talk becomes more interesting than action. She'll need more down and alone time to integrate the changes her body is going through. If she's attacking her siblings (or you), it might be because she actually needs to be alone and she doesn't know how to ask for it because it's something she's never needed before. In fact, aloneness was probably something she expressly *didn't* want before. But now all of that has changed and it can be confusing and disorienting - for her and for us.

This is new territory, and together you get to discover what will nourish her in this new space. As her interests shift, we need to pivot along with her. We can still suggest things, but how our suggestions are given will need to shift too if we want them to be well-received. This is where the power of third party authority (other respected and beloved adults, books, media, and influencers) starts to become valuable to lean into, as our kids see the humanness of their parents emerge, and their view of us as infallible and all-knowing that they may have held as small children begins to erode.

3 - A Bid for Power

Adolescence is this weird time where they aren't little kids anymore, but they aren't grown ups either. They feel capable (remember how adult you felt when you were a young teen?), and in many ways, they are, but they still don't always clean up after themselves, or think things through all the way, or have a developed sense of timing. The part of their brain that is responsible for making good decisions is actually shut down for maintenance and upgrades during this time period. This is normal and actually part of the process of learning and growth, but can be incredibly infuriating to deal with as a parent. And it most often accompanies the adults still constantly telling them what to do.

They do need responsibility at this age. They crave it. It is good for kids of all ages to feel like they are contributing to something bigger than they are. They need agency. They need something that they can be in control of and that is theirs, even if they aren't perfect, or frankly even that good, at it. It's how they get good. They need to feel powerful in some area of their lives. Sometimes a bid for power looks like pushing against the things we ask them to do. This is normal. And it is also a sign that whatever the thing is they are pushing against isn't something they feel like they own.

We have talked at length with Sunna about power and power dynamics. These conversations started in our household when she was pretty young, when there were some kids at school who were treating her in ways that didn't feel kind or respectful and were verging on bullying. We spoke about how, most of the time, people who are trying to exert power over someone else do so because they don't feel powerful themselves (which doesn't make it okay, btw). They have forgotten (or have never known) that the only true power is in knowing themselves as divine in nature. We discussed how the true source of power is feeling connected to one's sense of self, and understanding of our perfect divinity as a precious child of the Creator. And these foundational conversations are ones that we regularly fall back on when Sunna is clearly in a bid for power (which happens most frequently with her little sister).

As girls who will be women someday, having an understanding of how power plays itself out, in healthy and unhealthy ways, is crucially important. The majority of troubling dynamics in our society can be traced back to imbalances in power. When your daughter pushes against you, as irritating as it is, it is her practicing standing up for herself. As parents, we are the safest people possible for her to do that with. Don't we want our girls to know how to stand up for themselves, speak their needs, and advocate for what they want?

Our kids need a sense of autonomy and agency over some aspect of their lives. Just because they are children doesn't mean that they shouldn't have a voice and a sense of dominion over themselves. Of course, one of the most important senses of dominion we can cultivate in our children is dominion over their own bodies. But having an external something to have dominion over becomes very important in adolescence. What this external something is and what agency looks like is going to be different for every family and every kid, but knowing that this is a need at this age is crucial. Because sometimes when your daughter is an asshole, it is because she is feeling powerless and she is looking for a way to feel more powerful.

So what are things, events, timeframes and/or spaces you can give her total agency over? Example: In my house, I no longer go in the kitchen when my daughter is baking, even though it's something I love to do, taught her to do, and in many ways, am still better at than her (and could give her pointers if she let me). Baking is a passion of hers and it has become clear that the best thing I can do to let her explore it is to give her the tools she needs and then get out of the way entirely. When she bakes, the kitchen belongs to her. It was SO hard for me to do this at first because the kitchen is historically my domain and I love to teach, but the shift in her since I have gotten out of the way has been palpable. She really feels proud of her bakes and knows they are something that she did entirely on her own. She owns them completely, and is now even playing with starting her own cookie and cake business.

In your house, it might look like letting your kid set their own bedtime, staying 100% completely out of their room unless they invite you in, cutting and dyeing their hair however they want, or having one area of the house or garden they are in charge of. Aligning it with their interest and passion is key, so again, this is going to look different for everyone.

An interesting question to ask your daughter is some version of "if there was one thing that I or someone else currently has control over that you could have control over instead, what would it be?" While it might not be possible to grant your daughter's request, her answer can give you an interesting insight into what is important to her, and could lead to you finding something in the same vein, or some piece of the thing that she *could* have total agency over.

4 - Emotions She Doesn't Know How to Process

Related to both stress and hormones, emotional processing (or lack thereof) can either help or hinder how stressed we feel and how our hormones respond. Or, conversely, how we respond to our hormones and stressful experiences. Children are not born with emotional language, but they are born with a ton more emotional intelligence and fluidity than most adults. Watch a three year old when they have a full blown emotional explosion and then move on and act as if nothing happened. As difficult as it may be to be around, it's actually pretty healthy to be able to feel free enough to fling your whole body onto the ground in a full-fledged temper tantrum. I kind of think more adults should try it, to be honest.

In our house, we sometimes have an intentional whine-fest. We started this when Sunna was about 7 or 8. If it's clear that at least one of us is feeling pretty grumpy, sometimes a big old whine-fest is just the thing to shift the energy. This involves everyone's participation. We sometimes even set a timer, with the agreement that when the timer goes off, all complaining has to stop. For the allotted time, everyone then flops around and loudly and openly shouts and complains about all the things we are feeling victimized about - the sky's the limit! Sometimes my husband and I do actually throw ourselves on the floor for dramatic effect. Usually the whine-fest ends in a lot of giggles and an entirely shifted family dynamic. I encourage you to try it out! It can be incredibly cathartic and fun.

If we don't give our children language for what they are feeling, they will never develop the ability to communicate effectively what they are feeling. The problem is, most adults nowadays weren't ever taught this kind of language, either. In fact, most of us had our emotional intelligence trained out of us. So how are we supposed to teach it to our kids?

With my kids, I started when they were little and just beginning to talk. I would mirror back to them in words what it seemed like they were feeling. "Looks like you are feeling frustrated by that," or "I can see that you are really angry right now," or "I love seeing how happy that makes you," or "it's okay to feel scared, and I am here with you, and you are safe," or "you seem sad, would you like a hug?"

As my oldest has gotten older, I still do this with her, it has just evolved a bit in complexity as she has matured. We have a lot of great and nuanced ways to describe how we are feeling in the English language, but underneath it all, we are still just variations of happy, scared, sad, angry, or turned on/creative. Emotions aren't actually as complicated as we like to make them.

With my clients, I often refer to emotions as weather that moves across the body. When we let it flow and let it through, it passes, just like weather. The same is true with our kids. The key is helping them to let it move through. This brings us back to inquiry.

Sometimes we won't get it right away when we guess what's up with our kiddos. And we want to be careful with asking *too* many questions, lest we drive them off entirely. And sometimes all they need, especially during these tween years, is really for us to just listen to them, as my friend Laura Froyen - a couple and family therapist specializing in parenting and child development - so graciously reminded me recently. Mirroring back to them verbatim what they just said to us is a simple and powerful way to help them feel heard and understood. Also, a few carefully placed observations (I'm seeing that you are feeling really upset right now), followed up with some simple questions and tools, like mirroring, can also be powerfully effective in both helping our girls move through their emotional weather and strengthening our bond with them during this challenging emotional time of adolescence.

Processing Your Own Stuff

First things first, when we talk to our kids we want to make sure we are coming from a place of genuine inquiry instead of a forced-curiosity-but-actually-still-triggered place. Sometimes this is better done after the heat of the moment has died down a little bit and you've both had some space from one another. Be vocal about that. "I'm feeling too triggered to talk about this right now, so I'm going to take some space until I have calmed down." It's okay (and healthy) to give *ourselves* timeouts sometimes, and for our children to know that we get upset too. Make sure you don't have some hidden agenda or motive in approaching her, because she'll feel it coming from a mile away. Approach her with an open heart, a curious mind, and a genuine desire for connection. If you did lose your cool with her, start with an apology and acknowledging that you weren't at your best and you don't feel good about how you responded.

Adolescence is hard, and as I mentioned in Chapter 1, can bring up our own unprocessed stuff from our personal tween/teen journey. This is real and deserves our attention. It can also be an amazing opening into a deeper conversation about real life stuff with our daughters. If it's deeply triggering or traumatic material for you, make sure you have a trusted person that you can work through the depth of it with before bringing it up with your child. (It probably goes without saying, but don't use your daughter as your therapist). But do bring it up with her!

It is only that which stays hidden and in the shadows that can grow and strengthen and perpetuate itself. Secrets and shame are common bedfellows. No matter what may have happened in your life, harboring shame and keeping quiet about it is not serving you, it is only strengthening its grip on your life. Households that produce addicts are often households with the best-kept family secrets. I speak from experience on this one, having lost my brother to a heroin overdose which most of our extended family and friends had no idea he was struggling with for over 15 years. Naming things can, over time, take away the power they yield on us and start us on the path to true healing.

Opening up about our past with our daughters as they grow older does a number of things. First, it helps them start to see us as complete and fallible people, which at this stage is actually a good thing. This is already happening (remember how I started this chapter off with a description of her pointing out all the ways you are failing as a person and a human?), but when we are the ones to initiate opening the doorway to the truth that mom is just a person with a past and hurts and faults and fumbles, it helps our child be more compassionate and less of a jerk with us. Because she can start to see that mom has had struggles just like she has, too. This levels the playing field, which lessens the need to cajole and point out your wrongs and shortcomings (which is almost always #3 - a bid for power).

Second, it can be sooooo educational. Humans learn best through stories. We are designed this way, so that we don't repeat the mistakes of our ancestors. The number one thing we have lost as a culture is the art of storytelling, and therefore we have also lost many of the stories of the ones who came before us. I will never forget when I had my abortion and my mom then told me her story about when she had one - after the fact. I can almost guarantee that if she had shared that story with me earlier in my life, when I was a young teen, I would have been less likely to treat abortion as an alternative to contraception. The outcome might have ended up the same, it might not have, but my process of approaching it would have been entirely different.

There is so much to learn from someone else's story. Even if it's a hard one to share, think about how you might share it with your daughter in a way that's mostly what you took away from the experience. What would you have done differently? What do you wish you had known beforehand? How do you understand what happened now that you are older, that you couldn't see back then?

Opening the Door to Conversation

One of my first coaches, Katherine Golub, used to always say "never waste a good trigger." I find this to be a particularly apt phrase when it comes to our relationship with our tween and teen daughters, as the likelihood that we will get triggered by our kids is pretty high.

If we decide we want to do things differently and we approach our daughters with inquisitiveness instead of reactivity in the face of their tantrums and upstarts, we actually have a tremendous opportunity in those moments to teach them about some of the topics covered in this book.

If you look at the 4 primary reasons listed above for why your daughter might be behaving like an asshole, it starts to become clear what kinds of questions you want to be asking yourself. The next time your daughter is being a jerk, pause and reflect for a minute. Which of the 4 reasons - hormones, emotions, stress, or bid for power - is most likely the culprit here? Or is it some sort of combination? Context is key. Did this come out of the blue? If yes, hormones or stress are most likely. What happened earlier in the day? How has her sleep and diet been? Is there something going on at school, or with her friends?

It's important to note here that we aren't doing this kind of inquiry to fix something in the moment, but more for our own understanding so that we can be less reactive and more compassionate and present for our child. There might be adjustments that need to be made, but often these are on a larger scale and aren't going to happen immediately in the moment the melt down or eruption is happening.

If we think we might have a sense of what is underneath, we can approach her something like this: "Hey, I'm noticing that you are having some big feelings. Would you like to talk about it? I have some ideas of what might be going on, but I'd love to hear from you what you think is happening." If hormones are a likely culprit and your daughter is open to conversing with you, this can be a great time to a) introduce the topic of hormones and body changes if you haven't yet, or b) circle back around to the puberty conversation and ask if she wants to try some hacks you have up your sleeve. Don't have any yet? You will by the time you are done with this book! That's why you're here, right?

If she isn't open to talking to you right then and there, then she might just need some space and cooling off time. Which, hey, that's usually what I need when I'm hormonally hijacked too. Try circling back around to it later when she's not in the middle of a fit. "Remember when you had that big meltdown? I was curious about what might have been happening for you. I had some thoughts but wanted to hear from you what you think."

"Our Biology Was Promised a Village"

I recently sat down with my friend Laura Froyen, whom I mentioned a moment ago, to get her take on what exactly is happening in this timeframe in the brains and emotional bodies of our children. Laura's PhD expertise is in attachment parenting, so I really appreciated her perspective and what she had to say. According to attachment theory and research, children do best when they have at least 4 significant attachment figures in their lives. This is a far cry from what most children experience in today's age of the nuclear family, where they are lucky to have 1 or 2. As Laura so beautifully put it when we sat down together, "Our biology was promised a village." The truth of this phrase hit deep for me. It still gives me full body chills just to write it. Our biology was promised a village. Which means that if we don't have something analogous to that in our lives, it is up to us to consciously create it, helping our children cultivate relationships with safe adults.

Laura also shared with me some of what is happening in the tween/teen brain during puberty. According to Dr. Becky Bailey, there are three levels of the brain - the reptilian brain (fight or flight), the limbic brain (emotional processing), and the prefrontal cortex. Each level of the brain has a question that is associated with it. For the reptilian brain, the question is "am I safe?" For the limbic brain, the question is "am I loved?" And for the prefrontal cortex the question is "what can I learn?"

As small children, that "am I loved" question involves us, the parents. Do we love them, even if they are wild and crazy and aggressive in their emotional expression? As they get older and go through puberty, around the age of 13 or so, that "am I loved?" question is no longer geared towards us as much as it is towards their peers and their community. This is where the work of having consciously cultivated healthy relationships with others around you that you can trust comes into play in a huge way. Hopefully, by this time, we have encouraged and fostered healthy attachments with others from many generations, and not just us.

Ideally, in the teen years is where they start to form a strong sense of self, of the upright "I." One of the things I adore about Waldorf education is that there is a conscious awareness of developing a healthy "uprightness" in children around grade 7 and 8. The curriculum is designed to support this healthy maturation and developed sense of self. What happens when they don't have a healthy sense of attachment leading up to these years is a desperate need for belonging and security from their peers. Some of this is normal and will happen even with healthy attachments. Leaving the comfort and safety of the bubble of home is a crucial phase of developing their personhood, but it can be scary for them. They want to be caught by something, and inevitably it will be their peer group that does the catching. While some of this is a healthy part of development and to be expected, needing peer recognition to feel like a valid human is not. This is why peer pressure is a thing. It's badly named because the pressure isn't coming from outside. It's internally motivated by a deep need to know who we are, and to find ourselves in others.

Laura used an analogy that I absolutely loved and clicked immediately for me. She talked about unhealthy couples being like an "A": two "I's" in search of someone to lean on. In this dynamic, if one person in the couple moves away, the other person falls over because their uprightness was dependent on the other person's stability. In healthy couples, the pair looks more like an "H" - if one moves away, the other is still standing upright. She said teenagers are just A's that have been leaning on us for so long, now they swing out and look for someone else to lean on. So the work of parenting in the teen years is to help them become that upright "I" all on their own.

Being Okay with Fumbling

You are going to make mistakes. It's one of the only guarantees of parenthood. It's okay! Just give it your best shot. You are working against literal millenia of programming in opening up these conversations with your daughter. So go easy on yourself if you don't get it perfect on the first try. In fact, I would be shocked if you did. Expect to fumble through it at first. I sure don't always get it right, and I've been studying this stuff for years! In my mind, if you have the conversation, it's a win, even if it goes sideways at some point. Just brush yourself off, learn from your mistakes, and try again. That's the most anyone can ask of you.

Acknowledging to your daughter that you are aware of your shortcomings and awkwardness when it comes to talking about certain things, but you're going to keep trying with her because this topic is important to you, can also be a great way to keep the conversations going. Like I mentioned before, she's already quickly becoming aware of your fallibility. Why not own it and be real with her? You will feel better because you're not trying to be perfect or something you're not, and she will feel better because she can see right through that shit anyway and it makes her trust you less when you pretend. It also models that you don't always have to have it together all the time to be a functional adult. What a relief!

Exercise: I Love You

This is a simple exercise with often very profound and far-reaching effects. I invite you to practice this whenever you are in front of a mirror, out loud in front of your children, and alone.

If the thought of telling yourself that you love yourself feels monumental and is new to you, maybe try it alone first.

Step 1 - Find a mirror.

Step 2 - Look into your own eyes in the mirror. Do not analyze your face or your features - just look into your own eyes the way you would look into a lover's eyes.

Step 3 - While maintaining eye contact with yourself, say the words "I love you" out loud. Words and sound have vibration and power. Don't just say this in your own head to yourself. Speak the words audibly.

Try to mean it. If you have a strong self-hating voice, this can feel like faking it till you make it at first. That's fine. Fake it till you make it. But also ask yourself - what would truly meaning it take? What would that feel like? Can you look yourself in the eyes with love - and mean it?

Step 4 - Breathe. Notice the impact of having these words said to you by you.

Step 5 - Repeat steps 3 and 4 until you have said "I love you" to yourself 10 times. Cry if you need to. Laugh if you need to. Feel your heart opening and the love for yourself permeating deeply.

When working with clients, I have often recommended this exercise be done daily for 10 days in a row. Once you are well practiced at this, do it every time you find yourself looking in the mirror.

The eye contact is an essential part of this exercise. As women, we have been so conditioned to put all of our focus on our external features that we can forget the depths that exist under the surface. This exercise can help to bring us into deeper connection with the essential part of ourselves that is eternal, expansive, and not limited to this changing physical form.

Exercise: Tapping or "EFT"

Tapping, also known as EFT or the Emotional Freedom Technique, is a fantastic tool to have in your back pocket. It can help in a variety of different situations where the amygdala, the body's alarm system, has been activated. This activation triggers a stress response, our "fight or flight" mechanism, and leads to elevated cortisol levels (and all the ways we habitually respond to elevated cortisol levels). It can be a chronic conditioned response, or due to an immediate traumatic event.

Tapping got its name from its simple technique - tapping your finger quickly but lightly on a series of acupressure points. A seemingly magical and mystical exercise in its simplicity, tapping's efficacy has been verified by a number of scientific studies that Nick Ortner writes about in his book *The Tapping Solution*. I've learned tapping from a variety of different sources, and everyone has their own spin on it. I'm going to give you a quick overview on the simple method and the points here, but for a visual of how to do this, you can go to www.thetappingsolution.com.

What I love about tapping is that you can do it anywhere, anytime - as long as you have one free hand. I've even done it while driving. Considering that you can get activated just about anywhere, this is a pretty awesome tool to have!

Technique and Pressure

Tapping pressure is pretty light, but can be firmer too. Imagine you are making a little "pitter patter" drumroll sound with your first two fingers on your desk. That is about how hard you want the pressure to be. You should be able to feel it, but it shouldn't hurt if you do it a few times in a row (which you will be doing). There isn't really a wrong way to do it, as long as you're not hurting yourself.

I usually use my middle finger to do the actual tapping on the individual points, but whatever finger feels most comfortable to you is the best one. Kind of like the "pitter patter" sound, the tapping happens kind of quickly - maybe 2-4 taps a second. I stay on each point for about 5 seconds or so, but you will find your own rhythm that feels right to you as you get more comfortable with the points and the process.

The Opener

Before any tapping session, there is an opener that we use to get started. Consider this a kind of "priming the pump," if you will. It starts with what is called the "karate chop" and saying an opening phrase. The "karate chop" point is on the side of the hand, and you will usually hold your hand up in front of you and tap it, like you're doing a karate chop. It doesn't matter which hand you use.

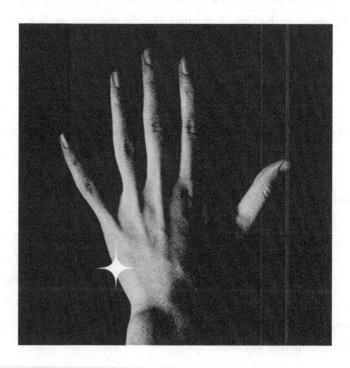

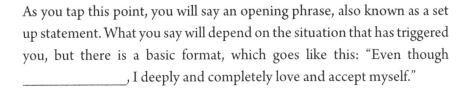

As you tap this point, you will say an opening phrase, also known as a set up statement. What you say will depend on the situation that has triggered you, but there is a basic format, which goes like this: "Even though _____, I deeply and completely love and accept myself."

So, it could be something like "Even though I'm mad at my husband for what he said, I deeply and completely love and accept myself." Or, "Even though I feel stressed out about this deadline, I deeply and completely love and accept myself." Or, "Even though my daughter is being a total asshole and I want to strangle her and drink wine, I deeply and completely love and accept myself." You get the picture. This acceptance sets the stage for you to be able to say whatever you want, completely uncensored, in the next step.

You'll cycle through this opening phrase about 3 times, tapping on the karate chop point the whole time. Then you will move onto the points.

The Points

Okay, the points. These are the points you will be cycling through as you do the tapping protocol. Once you've made it through the end of the circuit, go back and start over again. You will likely find yourself cycling through the circuit at least 3 times before you start to feel a real shift. You can do these points on either side of the face/body.

The first point is located directly at the top of the head, in the middle. The second point is on the inside of the eyebrow, directly to the side of the bridge of the nose. The third point is on the outside of the eye - kind of in the corner, where your eyebrow ends and you can feel the eye socket ridge. The fourth point is directly under the middle of the eye, right at the top of the cheek. The fifth point is under the nose, in that divet that Google says is called the philtrum. The sixth point is directly underneath that on your chin, right below the lips. The seventh point is right below your clavicle, closer to your midline.

There are actually eight main points. The picture I have here only has 7 listed. This is in part because of the limitations of the photo I chose to use, but also because the eighth point I tend to struggle with. I have talked with others who have also found it a kind of awkward and ineffective point, as it is directly under the armpit, on your side body. Maybe it's because I am more padded, but personally, I have found that tapping it hard enough to create any kind of effect is challenging and totally weird so, instead, I make the 8th point in my sternum, just between the top of where my breasts start, or I leave it at 7. But try it for yourself and see - you might like the under the armpit thing. According to the pros, it does complete a circuit.

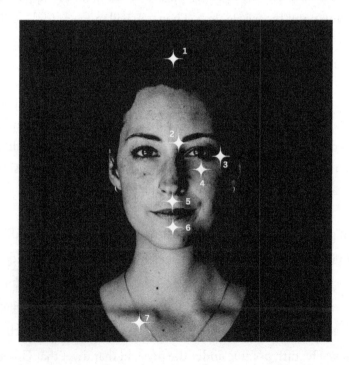

The Monologue

This part is, in my opinion, also optional, but there can be some real power in speaking what is happening out loud, and with as much specificity as possible. You will likely feel better just from tapping the points alone without speaking anything, but giving voice to what is happening can do a few things.

First, it can help you to clarify exactly what is happening for you. If you are a verbal processor, speaking out loud what's coming up for you can help to clear it more effectively, as you are basically rewiring your nervous system with the tapping.

Speaking what you're feeling and clearing aloud also helps to get more specificity, which can make the tapping more effective. So, instead of just "I'm angry," getting more specific like "I'm angry at my daughter" is more clear. From there, we can get even more explicit: "I'm angry at my daughter because what she did was so rude and it makes me feel like I'm a horrible parent and she will never succeed in the world and she is going to end up an awful human being and will probably do drugs and end up in prison." Now we are getting somewhere!

It's also totally okay if you can't come up with anything, and all you can say is "I'm angry" or "this anger that I feel." Just speak the emotion. The idea with this is that as you cycle through tapping on the 8 (or 7) points, you will speak your emotional state out loud. Be as crass and uncensored as you can, really letting the negative emotion and all the thoughts attached to it flow out of your mouth. If you can, this is the time to really let it rip.

You can tap on different emotions, limiting self-beliefs like what we covered in chapter 1, and self-destructive habits like addiction. The sky is the limit! Tapping is like an energetic detox, so whatever it is that is running in your system that you would like to rewire, you can try tapping on it. Deeper issues will likely require multiple tapping sessions, but I've heard some amazing one-and-done stories too!

The Pause

Once you have cycled through the points a few times, speaking your feelings out loud, pause for a moment and rest in silence. Take a few deep breaths. Let yourself tune in. Do you feel a shift from where you were at when you started?

If you are still feeling some pretty strong activation, keep tapping the negative feelings. There is likely something underneath you didn't quite get to! If you feel a significant shift, i.e. much better than when you started, you are ready to move onto the next phase if you want - the reframe.

The Reframe

This one is also optional, but I like to include it sometimes too. Now that you have allowed all of the negative voice to come through, this is where we get to rewrite the story line. This time, instead of saying all of the negative things that are bothering you, you can say what has shifted, also while tapping on the points.

So, instead of "I'm so angry at my daughter for being a totally rude ass," you can start to say "I love my child. I am a good mother. Everyone has hard moments. Maybe she's going through something I don't know about. I am making more space for her feelings. We can do this." - or whatever feels accessible and alive for you.

One thing I like to be really attentive to when I'm speaking the reframe out loud is what happens to my vibrational state. How does it land when I speak a specific phrase out loud? Is it resonant? Does it make me feel better or worse - even subtly? The reframe should feel good and accessible. It should feel true. Overblowing it - "my daughter is the best daughter in the world and I will never get mad at her again" - is not helpful.

That's it! That's tapping. It takes some practice to get the points, but once you've got it down, you now have a very valuable tool that is available to you at any time and in any place.

If you want to make tapping even more powerful and effective, there is also the Aroma Freedom Technique, or AFT, created by Benjamin Perkus, which combines blends and singles from Young Living* essential oils with the methodology of tapping. Because of the proximity of the ending of the olfactory nerve to the amygdala, adding unadulterated plant scent consciously into this process has been shown to dramatically increase its efficacy. You can read more about the specific process using oils in his book, which I've listed in the recommended reading.

*A note about oils: Not all essential oils are created equal! The essential oil industry is unregulated in the US, and brands can bottle just about anything, and as long as it contains even just 10% essential oil, then they can call it 100% pure and for some reason that's allowed. Of all the companies I have encountered, the integrity of this one is beyond compare with anything else out there. This includes the purity of their oils, the vast library of knowledge they have about harvest timing, if the plant needs to rest before it is distilled, and if so, for how long, and the temperature and timing of distillation for *each plant* to yield the most therapeutic oil possible.

If you don't have oils, you can use fresh or dried aromatic plants crushed in your palm. Just inhale the scent as you go through the process. Especially for something with a therapeutic purpose like AFT (but really also all the time), if you aren't going to use these oils, just use the aromatic plants directly. Whatever you do, do NOT use brands like NOW, or buy oils off Amazon!!! Just don't. Please.

CHAPTER 4

THE UNSEEN FACTORS THAT WREAK HAVOC ON HORMONES - AND WHAT TO DO ABOUT THEM

I was 15 years old the day I came home from school in excruciating abdominal pain. I spent the afternoon on the couch, cuddled up in a blanket in too much agony to move.

It must have been winter because I remember talking on the phone with the doctor and it was dark outside. He asked me to walk around the room while I was on the phone with him, despite my adamant response that it was far too painful. I took three steps, felt the most searing pain of my life spread across my abdomen from my right side, and collapsed to the floor in tears. I heard him say to my mother, "I think she had an ovarian cyst that just popped. She probably has PCOS. There is nothing to do tonight - just give her some Tylenol and the pain will subside, now that the worst is over. I will see you in my office tomorrow."

PCOS is a problem that affects millions of women around the globe. The symptoms of PCOS include painful menstruation, irregular periods, hirsutism (excessive hair growth caused by high testosterone levels), acne, infertility, depression, anxiety, cysts on the ovaries, and obesity. The most commonly prescribed "treatment" for PCOS is some form of hormonal birth control.

147

When I went to the doctor's the next day, lo and behold, he prescribed me "the pill." I was 15 and not yet sexually active or in a romantic relationship of any kind. But the thought of being on birth control was somehow exciting to my 15-year-old self. It felt like a status symbol, a way of being part of the "cool kids" club, even though I hadn't had sex yet. Losing one's virginity was a huge milestone back then, and one that I had yet to attain. But with the pill, now I had a doorway in, albeit a side one. I took it into my life with gusto.

I was no stranger to taking pills every day. I had been on antidepressants for 3 years already when I was prescribed the pill. When I look back on my life now, I feel so sad for the young girl who so naively walked into and embraced the world of pharmaceuticals. If there is one thing I could go back and change when I look at the historical arc of my life, it is the consumption of these chemical drugs. The lifelong effects of these so-called medications have bred devastating results in my life, including being unable to successfully breast-feed either of my children.

It is so clear to me now, in retrospect, what the underlying causes of my depression and PCOS were (an overabundance of sugar consumption, which totally disrupted my gut microbiome and my overall energy levels, combined with lack of exercise, which were both tied to an energetic/ emotional response to family and social dynamics that were playing them-selves out in my life at the time. Also, environmental chemicals, which we will talk about shortly). But instead of addressing the root cause, we live in a culture and society that is trained merely to treat the symptoms. More often than not, this leads to more symptoms, more need for different drugs, and no real healing taking place. It's a self-perpetuating spiral of ill-ness, with a whole lot of profit for the pharmaceutical industry.

I happily and willingly took the pill for the next three and a half years. It was the summer before my second year of college when I went home to see my original doctor, the same one who had been my primary care doc since birth and who originally prescribed me the pill, along with a cocktail of continuously changing antidepressants. This visit was when he suggested I change the birth control I was taking, from the pill that had the 7 days of placebo so I would bleed every month, to a pill that would ensure that I wouldn't bleed at all. I was only 18, but I remember distinctly thinking that this couldn't be a good idea. He assured me that it was perfectly safe, that because we have fewer children nowadays we have more menstrual cycles than we "need," and that I would be completely fine.

I had been well-conditioned at that point in my life to trust an external voice of authority over my own intuition (especially a male authority), so even though something deep inside me knew that this was not a wise move, I went ahead and, as I had done for so many years leading up to this point, took the new medication.

I was on it for four months before I started uncontrollably hemorrhaging. My body, in her infinite wisdom, revolted from the attempt to stop up her sacred blood and opened the floodgates. It was as if all of the blood I didn't bleed over those four months decided to come out at once. The pain was immense - worse than anything I had ever experienced up to that point. I remember practically crawling on my hands and knees out of the lecture hall to the payphone (remember those?) to call my only friend with a car to come and get me from class because I physically could not walk from the pain and had already soaked blood through my jeans.

I spent the next 9 days on the couch, missing class, smoking pot, and making little clay figurines because the focus required to do the detailed work was the only thing that would make me momentarily forget about the pain. It was so painful to walk, I had to have my roommates help me to the bathroom. I was covered in blood for 9 straight days, needing to change my pad every 2 hours so as not to soak the couch. It was horrific.

After this episode, it was very clear to me that my body was rebelling against having my period stopped up, and I made the decision to stop taking the pill. I was starting to question my doctor's choices and didn't trust him anymore. I was also very far away from home and in another country (I went to college in Canada) so I decided to seek out another doctor who could perhaps shed some light on my uterine situation, why I had started bleeding so uncontrollably like that, and why my periods had become so aggressive and painful.

I went to doctor after doctor (all male) and had a variety of different tests and ultrasounds done. There was even one in which the unknown-to-me male doctor had me insert the ultrasound wand into my vagina myself in front of him, my spread-open legs facing the direction of the door to the room, which had been left slightly cracked open. To my 19-year-old self, this was an utterly horrifying scenario, and I felt totally violated afterwards. At another visit, the doctor told me to "just stop eating carbs and lose some weight," with no understanding of my medical history, which included a long-standing eating disorder. Also, what college student doesn't eat carbs? He didn't give me any suggestions of what or how to eat. I went virtually without food for weeks afterwards, kicked into an anorexic episode and starving myself because I didn't know what was and wasn't okay to eat.

All of these visits and tests yielded zero results, other than trauma. Zero. Results. After every visit, I was told that there was "nothing wrong with me" and that what I had experienced was completely within the realm of normal.

Let me assure you right now that there is NOTHING normal about what I was experiencing. Menstruation is *not supposed to be painful*, nor should it be plentiful to the point of completely soaking through a pad every 2 hrs. That's right, I said it's not supposed to be painful!! If this is happening to you or your child, there absolutely is something that is off in your physical or energetic body. The main reason that western medicine doesn't recognize menstrual pain as an imbalance is because the solution lies entirely outside of the western medical paradigm. They have no fix for this one.

At this point in my life, my diet consisted mainly of bagels and cream cheese, Kraft macaroni and cheese, cheeseburgers (there's a theme here), ramen noodles, Redbull and vodka, marijuana, and Little Debbie snack cakes. Vegetables were a non-entity, and I had never given a thought to reading the ingredients of anything I put on or in my body.

I was fortunate enough at the time to have a lover who was also a farmer and very into organic food and alternative living. This was the early 00's and organic food, yoga, and natural body care products were still pretty fringe. There was a small cafe with odd hours in a far-off corner of campus that was the go-to place for smoothies, lentils and rice, and people who practiced yoga and knew how to turn food scraps-into compost-into food again.

There was a vibrancy to the people who worked at that cafe. The light in their eyes and their vitality was noticeable and pronounced. They knew and understood something I wanted to know, too. Lucky for me, they were more than happy to share their enthusiasm for living in ways that were closer to the natural rhythms of the earth.

My first major initiation into the world of alternative living was the elimination of two ingredients from my diet: high fructose corn syrup and hydrogenated oils. Taking out these two ingredients alone turned my whole world upside down in an amazing way. Now that I was reading labels, I realized that virtually *everything* I regularly consumed had one or both of these non-food, food-like substances in it.

Over the course of just a few months of removing foodstuffs with these ingredients from my diet and replacing them with real food, I lost 20 pounds. I felt lighter and more self-confident. I was still having painful periods, but my overall health and vitality began to improve dramatically. It wasn't until I learned about EDCs and switched out my body care products and detergents that my cycles completely normalized.

Why Chemical-Free Living Matters When it Comes to Hormones

We are the only species to combine ingredients from nature in such a way that they have become completely toxic and harmful to our health and wellbeing. I'm not going to pretend I know the origin of all the weird ingredients that are in practically EVERYTHING nowadays, because I don't. But what I *do* know is that there are a whole host of chemicals, known as Endocrine Disrupting Chemicals or EDCs, that can wreak havoc on our hormones, and therefore our overall health. And they are EVERYWHERE.

As we saw in our little science class chapter, hormones are responsible for way more than just reproduction. From metabolism to heart health, hormones impact almost every other system in the human body. So when we surround ourselves with EDCs, usually unintentionally and unawares, the natural result is that our hormones can go totally out of whack. And as women, we are particularly at risk with these chemicals.

But don't just take my word for it. Here are two excerpts from papers in the National Library of Medicine:

"Endocrine Disrupting Chemicals (EDCs) are a global problem for environmental and human health. They are defined as "an exogenous chemical, or mixture of chemicals, that can interfere with any aspect of hormone action". It is estimated that there are about 1000 chemicals with endocrine-acting properties. EDCs comprise pesticides, fungicides, industrial chemicals, plasticizers, nonylphenols, metals, pharmaceutical agents and phytoestrogens. Human exposure to EDCs mainly occurs by ingestion and to some extent by inhalation and dermal uptake. Most EDCs are lipophilic and bioaccumulate in the adipose tissue, thus they have a very long half-life in the body….Developing fetuses and neonates are the most vulnerable to endocrine disruption. EDCs may interfere with synthesis, action and metabolism of sex steroid hormones that in turn cause developmental and fertility problems, infertility, and hormone-sensitive cancers in women and men. Some EDCs exert obesogenic effects that result in disturbance in energy homeostasis. Interference with hypothalamo-pituitary-thyroid and adrenal axes has also been reported." [13]

"A key question arises as to whether EDCs contribute to the development of female reproductive disorders, particularly those occurring during a critical window of susceptibility: *in utero*, neonatally, in childhood, during puberty, and during adulthood. There are increasing data from wildlife studies and laboratory studies with rodents, ungulates, and nonhuman primates that support a role of EDCs in the pathogenesis of several female reproductive disorders, including polycystic ovarian syndrome, aneuploidy, POF, reproductive tract anomalies, uterine fibroids, endometriosis, and ectopic gestation."[14]

---

[13] https://pubmed.ncbi.nlm.nih.gov/31792807/

[14] https://www.ncbi.nlm.nih.gov/pmc/articles/PMC2726844/#:~:text=The%20 group%20of%20molecules%20identified,%2C%20plasticizers%20(phthalates)%2C%2 0pesticides

As I mentioned earlier, I first learned about EDCs when I was on my journey of healing my PCOS in the early 00s. After the change in diet, the next phase for me was to switch out my laundry detergent, body lotions and soaps, shampoo and conditioner, dish soap and cleaning products - including anything with the mysterious "fragrance" ingredient. I remember being totally shocked to learn that something I didn't even ingest or put directly on my skin, like my laundry detergent, was a likely culprit in my hormonal issues. It seemed so unrelated to me at the time. But the difference after switching it out was undeniable.

Eliminating toxic and endocrine disrupting products from your home and environment can feel like a daunting and overwhelming task. But it doesn't have to be, and it doesn't mean that you can't take care of yourself in the ways that you are used to. Like I mentioned, there are so many companies nowadays that are aware of EDCs and are committed to making their products without them. Nearly every product you are used to using in your daily life has a toxin-free alternative. I've included some of my favorites in the resources section, as well as a checklist to use to help clear out your home of EDCs.

Ewg.org is also a great resource that has a massive database of a wide variety of personal care products that it has analyzed and scored according to their presence of disruptive and harmful ingredients, or lack thereof. You can type in almost any personal care product that you currently use: soaps, shampoos, lotions, makeup, perfumes, etc, and see its score and if it has any ingredients that are concerning, as well as find products that have been certified by the EWG as completely safe to use. (I would still look at the score of the individual ingredients in a product and not just its general score, as their database isn't always perfect, and I have definitely noticed some anomalies and mistakes in certain product ratings). But overall, it's a pretty good resource. They have a consumer guide for many different kinds of products, the "clean 15 and dirty dozen" when it comes to organic produce, as well as food additives, and a guide to what is in your tap water - and the best countertop water filters to use to get the crud out.

Fortunately, greater understanding around the toxic implications of EDCs is making its way into the mainstream, which means there are more and more products available to us that don't contain them. I don't think we need to live our lives in fear of encountering these chemicals outside of our homes. If we go out in public spaces, we will occasionally encounter them. I don't think it serves a positive outcome in our bodies to walk around in constant fear and vigilance. But I do think that, when we have a choice about what we put in and on our bodies and use to clean our clothes and our homes, we can use this information to make smarter choices. Believe it or not, it's actually most people's homes that are the most toxic environments. Information is power, and a cornerstone of true sovereignty.

So, with that as a sounding call, here is a list pulled directly from the National Institute of Environmental Health Sciences website of the most common EDCs and their sources:

Chemicals That May Disrupt Your Endocrine System
According to the Endocrine Society, there are nearly 85,000 human-made chemicals in the world, and 1,000 or more of those could be endocrine disruptors, based on their unique properties. The following are among the most common and well-studied.

- **Atrazine** is one of the most commonly applied herbicides in the world, often used to control weeds in corn, sorghum, and sugarcane crops.

- **Bisphenol A (BPA)** is used to make polycarbonate plastics and epoxy resins. It is used in manufacturing, food packaging, toys, and other applications. BPA resins may be found in the lining of some canned foods and beverages.

- **Dioxins** are a byproduct of certain manufacturing processes, such as herbicide production and paper bleaching. They can be released into the air from waste burning and wildfires.

- **Perchlorate** is a colorless salt manufactured and used as an industrial chemical to make rockets, explosives, and fireworks, which can be found in some groundwater.

- **Per- and polyfluoroalkyl substances (PFAS)** are a large group of chemicals used widely in industrial applications, such as firefighting foam, nonstick pans, paper, and textile coatings.

- **Phthalates** are a large group of compounds used as liquid plasticizers. They are found in hundreds of products, including some food packaging, cosmetics, fragrances, children's toys, and medical device tubing. Cosmetics that may contain phthalates include nail polish, hair spray, aftershave lotion, cleanser, and shampoo.

- **Phytoestrogens** are naturally occurring substances with hormone-like activity found in some plants; they may have a similar effect to estrogen produced by the body. Soy foods, for example, contain phytoestrogens.

- **Polybrominated diphenyl ethers (PBDE)** are used to make flame retardants for products such as furniture foam and carpet.

- **Polychlorinated biphenyls (PCBs)** were used to make electrical equipment, such as transformers, and are in hydraulic fluids, heat transfer fluids, lubricants, and plasticizers. PCBs were mass-produced globally until they were banned in 1979.

- **Triclosan** is an ingredient that was previously added to some antimicrobial and personal care products, like liquid body wash and soaps.[15]

I love it when scientific studies validate what I know in my bones to be true and the feedback my body gives me. While I don't revel in the fact that we have created so many harmful chemicals and spread them all over the place, I do appreciate knowing that it's not just the hippies anymore who want to do something about it. If there was ever a stronger argument than the above list to go as natural as possible, I have yet to find one.

Once you open your eyes to the prevalence of EDCs, you cannot close them again. You also start to see the relationship between the higher prevalence of reproductive disorders in poor women and women of color and the amount of environmental EDCs that tend to be concentrated in areas with higher impoverished and/or minority populations. This is known as environmental racism and is a huge problem, not only in the US but in the world at large.

The main categories where EDCs tend to present in our homes are hair and body products, makeup, skincare, fragrances, and cleaning products. The worst offenders and most common ingredients you will likely find in personal care products are:

- Diethyl phthalate (DEP)
- Dibutyl phthalate (DBP)
- Butylbenzyl phthalate (BBzP)
- Diethylhexyl phthalate (DEHP)

---

[15] https://www.niehs.nih.gov/health/topics/agents/endocrine

- Dimethyl phthalate (DMP)
- Anything ending in "paraben"
- Anything containing the ingredient "fragrance"

In addition to being chock-full of endocrine disrupting chemicals, makeup can also come with a whole host of problems that are tied to societal standards of beauty and female sexual objectification. We've already touched on this a bit, but I think it bears repeating. Like clothing, makeup can be a fun way to play and express ourselves outwardly to the world and so I don't want to dismiss it entirely. But it can also become a chore, a mask, a way to berate ourselves, an expectation, and an attempt to prove something to ourselves or the world. Again, it's all in how we orient toward it. This deserves a fair bit of conversation and inquiry with your child. If you are going to let your daughter play with and explore the world of makeup, please make sure that you are providing her with mineral-based makeup free from EDCs, as excessive use of makeup products in her teen and tween years can have a detrimental impact on her hormones.

When it comes to cleaning products, the list of ingredients to watch out for is far more extensive. The majority of cleaning products on the market today contain extreme toxins. A few years ago, I visited a friend who, in anticipation of my arrival, deep-cleaned her bathroom with a product called Ka-Boom. Sunna came with me on the trip. She was 7 at the time and I was pretty pregnant with her sister. In the middle of our first night there, Sunna started having several bouts of violent vomiting and diarrhea, seemingly out of nowhere. While I felt quite nauseated, I did not end up throwing up, but also had some diarrhea. Assuming we had a stomach flu, we shortened our trip and left the following day, hoping we hadn't also infected our friends.

Two weeks later, I got a sincerely apologetic call from my friend. She and her family had been having a mysterious stomach bug that seemed to be happening every two weeks. It wasn't until our visit and then her family coming down with it again two weeks later that it dawned on her that this "stomach bug" was directly associated with the timing of cleaning her bathrooms. Upon deeper investigation into this "cleaning" product she'd been using, she discovered that stomach pain, diarrhea, and vomiting were potential side-effects from coming into contact with some of its ingredients. Why on earth this product is allowed on the market at all is beyond me, though I'm sure we have capitalism and greed to thank. So there you have it. Your stomach issues might have nothing to do with your diet or what you put in your body at all. It might be your household cleaning products. Again, for a deeper dive into all of this, go to EWG.org.

Replacing your current EDC containing products with healthier ones that don't contain EDCs can be so beneficial for your and your family's overall health, and while it may seem daunting at first, it actually is not that hard. Switching to natural products across the board would be my first step to alleviating any mystery symptoms that you, your family members, and your pets might be having. In the case of places like salons and medical offices, never underestimate the power of consumer advocacy to make a change in what products are used and carried. As for your home, I can almost guarantee you that you can find or make a healthier alternative, oftentimes for even less money than what you currently pay for said products or items. And it can be fun! I've included a few of my favorite at-home recipes at the end of this chapter.

Below is a checklist for areas where EDC's are likely hiding in your home or places you frequent (like the salon or medical office). With products in your home, I have created a downloadable PDF checklist that you can use to go through and detox your house, which you can find in the resources. This is by no means an exhaustive list, but is a good place to start. In most cases, these products can easily be switched out for alternatives. Use this list to go through your home, make the switch, or toss them out! Your and your family's health will thank you for it.

EDC Checklist:

- Lotion - body, hand, face and foot
- Facial cleansers and toners
- Hair spray, hair mousse, hair gel
- Hair dye and treatments
- Shampoo and conditioner
- Body wash
- Soap - bar soap and liquid hand soap
- Hand Sanitizer
- Vaginal douches, 'intimate feminine' washes - *You don't need to replace these, just throw them out. The vulva needs only mild soap and water to be clean, and then only on the outside, as the vagina cleans itself regularly. These products are the main cause of recurrent yeast and other vaginal infections and are harmful and unnecessary.*
- Toothpaste
- Nail polish and remover
- Deodorant/Antiperspirant - *Antiperspirants should also be tossed, as we need to sweat for healthy detoxification. Stopping our body's natural sweat response over time leads to a build-up of toxins in the lymphatic system.*
- All makeup products
- Laundry detergent, fabric softener and dryer sheets
- Dish soap and dishwasher detergent
- Perfumes, air fresheners, scented candles
- Scented trash bags
- Any and all cleaning products

The prevalence of EDCs also extends to farming, manufacturing, cookware, furniture, carpeting, fragrances, and sometimes even clothing as well. These are all areas where, if we can make a choice with them, we should. Non-stick cookware can be so nice to cook with, for example. But is the trade-off of potential hormonal disruption and carcinogenic action on you and everyone you cook for really worth the "convenience?" Same goes for the plastic cooking utensils that so often accompany said cookware that, when heated, leach EDCs into the food.

Cast iron, enamel, glass, ceramic, silicone, and stainless steel are the only kinds of cookware that I have in my kitchen. Stainless steel and wood, bamboo, or silicone cooking utensils are the only cooking utensils I have in my kitchen. My kitchen is a healing kitchen. Our food choices, including what that food is cooked in, is one of the biggest health insurance investments I can give my family.

While it certainly can be, it does not have to be costly to replace your kitchen items. Cast iron pans are easy to find and rehabilitate. They last forever and you can usually find a neglected one in the back of someone's garage for free. With a little elbow grease, you can clean it up, use it your whole life, and pass it on to your grandkids later. Garage sales, estate sales, and second-hand stores, while a hit-or-miss treasure hunt, can sometimes yield some great finds. (Just watch out for pans made of aluminum if you're going retro, as aluminum cookware has been linked to Alzheimer's.) Replacing your pots and pans doesn't have to happen all at once, either.

I highly recommend doing a deep clean-out of your entire home and getting rid of anything containing EDCs, especially if you or anyone else in your household is regularly getting sick or experiencing hormonal issues. As you can see, EDCs are everywhere. To reiterate, I don't think we need to walk around in a state of constant fear or vigilance. Start where you live. Making a sweep of your home to eliminate the EDC-containing products, and then keeping them out of your home, is a huge step forward.

Diet, Health and Wellness

As I briefly mentioned in the introduction, I have struggled with a compulsive eating disorder since I was 8, so I am not interested in offering anyone restrictive eating protocols and diet recommendations. I do have some pretty strong thoughts and opinions that I will share with you regarding health and wellbeing, though, that have been formed in big part because of that struggle. What I'm about to share is a result of *years* of gathering information and testing it in the laboratory of my own life, as well as with clients. As with anything in this book, take it or leave it.

I have spent my entire adult life in various alternative health and wellness circles. I will begin this section by saying that I think there is so much garbage out there about diet and exercise, and a lot of it is either utter bullshit or tested and designed for the male body. This is including, and sometimes especially, in wellness circles. The majority of popularized wellness advice is either rooted in pathologizing our brilliantly wise female forms, or is designed to make us feel horrible about ourselves so that we will buy things and stay stuck in a loop of needing to constantly improve our already divinely perfect selves. What better way to keep a woman from her full creative potential than to make her constantly think that she has to be focused on looking a certain unattainable way? I refuse to comply.

Dietary Advice, Fat Phobia and Eating Disorders

Outside of the consistent screams of "portion control" from my mom at almost every meal when I was growing up, and the continual diets she would put me on as a growing kid, I have tried a full gamut of diets in my adult life. Keto, paleo, raw, GAPS, gluten-free, vegan, vegetarian, macrobiotic, Whole 30, metabolic eating, intermittent fasting, ancestral eating, eating more beans. It's honestly been EXHAUSTING!

After traveling through many different countries and continents, I kinda think at this point that the majority of Americans have some kind of eating disorder - even (sometimes especially) in alternative health and wellness circles. Take intermittent fasting, for example. Quite often, when applied to women, this whole intermittent fasting thing becomes one giant eating disorder sold to us as health. It is a classic case of something that has been studied on men and postmenopausal women being sold to everyone, especially women in their childbearing years. The thing is, when applied to women who are not post-menopause, this kind of eating (or not eating) consistently can have detrimental hormonal effects.

I do think our digestion needs times of rest, and I love engaging in an annual spring or fall (or both) cleanse. But daily getting all your calories in within 1-5 hours of the day? Or skipping days entirely? For months - or years?! That's for rare times of famine when we don't have access to enough food. Without the catchy label that has become such a fad, if you were to prescribe that kind of eating to an anorexic person, you would have folks up in arms. But hear that an overweight person is doing it and everyone cheers.
Why?

When I went through my bout of anorexia in college, I lost a bunch of weight pretty quickly. I was quite literally starving myself and dying on the inside. My life was a complete mess and I was falling apart, but everyone I saw would tell me how great I looked because I was losing weight. What a head trip!

Fat is not the problem. It never was. It isn't what makes you unhealthy. Women especially actually need some fat on our bodies. It is protective. The BMI is one of the most unscientific measurements that has been readily accepted by the mainstream, without question. There is zero science behind it. It's completely made up.[16] *Unhealthy excess weight is almost always a symptom of another imbalance.* In women it is most often hormonal or energetic, usually both. Correct the imbalance and the weight changes automatically, like magic. Telling someone with a hormonal imbalance, or a toxic living or employment situation to just "lose some weight" is one of the absolutely least helpful things you can recommend. If you are chronically stressed, your body will go into a holding pattern. (Or you won't be able to gain anything, and will be stick-thin, which is problematic in a different way, but more socially acceptable.) The fat is not the problem.

I have been termed "overweight" almost my whole life, but with a few minor exceptions, over the past 20 years, whenever I have labs done, I am healthy as a horse. I have no problems with sleep and never have (save when I have had a baby nursing or a toddler kicking me in the kidneys). I know plenty of skinny people who struggle a LOT with sleep, and getting adequate sleep is essential for good health. In case you hadn't heard, *skinny does not equal healthy!*

It's rarely ever just about the diet (unless you eat mainly non-food "food-like" substances, which we will get to). An often overlooked reason for people putting on weight is energetic protection. I cannot stress the reality of this enough. Putting on weight is a safety mechanism. It is our energy body's response to help shield us from perceived energetic threats and toxins. It creates an energetic safeguard. I know it doesn't feel protective

---

[16] https://www.medicalnewstoday.com/articles/265215#:~:text=BMI%20(body %20mass%20index)%2C,of%20Medicine%2C%20University%20of%20Pennsylvania.

in a world where being fat isn't allowed and we are shamed, either by ourselves or others or both, for carrying excess weight. But to the energetic body that's what it is. So a diet change is unlikely to have any impact if that is the case.

There are SO many bullshit rules about what you "should" and "shouldn't" eat, when to eat or not eat, and which supplements to take - it can be pretty maddening. This is especially true for women. Do you have any idea how much money, time, and energy we waste on how we look, what we eat, and how we work out?! Billions of dollars are spent every year on female body modification, and this commodification of "health" has seeped into the alternative health and wellness sector as well.

Everywhere you turn, there is another diet recommendation that conflicts with the last one you just heard. And the people offering these diets are SO CONVINCED that they are right! I find it fascinating that different people can be so strongly certain about their version of reality being the correct one, and the realities are as different from one another as night and day. So who wins? Who is right and who is wrong? How do we figure it out?

What this all boils down to for me is this: you've got to test things out in your own experience. All bodies are not the same. The same bodies aren't even the same all the time! As women, we are cyclical beings. We do not operate on the male 24hr clock. Ours is approximately a 25-32 day rhythm, depending on the length of our cycle. We change - constantly. We are Changing Woman. So, it's pretty likely that if we make it the same each and every day, whatever new diet or exercise protocol we adopt will fail for us.

I have studied countless healing modalities and made A LOT of lifestyle and dietary changes over the course of my lifetime. I've spent years being unhealthy, years feeling fabulous, and years in toxic situations that spent my wellbeing to the point that I've had to start the healing journey over again. Of the things that have had the most sustainable impact, I list them for you here now. I have put these in the order of general importance as far as their beneficial impact on your life, but it's not static. You might find that the order of importance for you is different than it has been for me. Test it out!

Sunshine

A highly overlooked source of energy and wellbeing, your daily dose of sunlight (*without* sunglasses or sunscreen on), is likely going to have a greater impact on your health than any change in diet and exercise combined, especially first thing in the morning at sunrise. As we've already discussed in the chapter on hormones, early morning sunlight (not through a window, but actually outside under it) triggers the major brain hormones leptin, cortisol, and melatonin, which then signal all the other metabolic functions in the body. When it comes to your hormones, there is no diet change that can compete with adequate sunshine intake. It's just not popularized because it's free. No one can make a living off of selling sunshine (though California has done a pretty good job with the sunshine tax). But the science is there.

So get outside! Do some inventory for regular activities in your day that could just as easily happen outside. Can you take that call outside? What about setting up a little outdoor office? Take light breaks - even just a few minutes at a time can make a huge difference. We were made for outdoor living, and we are too often indoors, too much of the time. I guarantee you that wherever you live on the planet, whatever your economic status is, the sun rises where you live. It's up to you to make it a priority to access it.

Happy lights aren't really a substitute for the actual, real, live sun, even though they can help some in the dead of winter. What helps more, though, is getting outside first thing in the morning. Even on days when the sun isn't shining, there is still beneficial UV light that we can absorb from being outside. Even just 10-15 mins first thing in the morning when the sun is rising will make a huge difference. Even just 3-5 minutes. You will not get skin cancer from the sunrise. Change this one thing and you will change your life. And did I mention it's free? (I live in Wisconsin, FYI, if you are complaining that you can't 'cause of the weather. There is no bad weather, only bad clothing for the weather. I know it's hard sometimes to get motivated to get outside. Believe me, I know! But it is SOOO worth it. Wool is awesome. Get bundled. Get outside).

When your kids are little, they are natural early risers. This is because children are born with innate wisdom that hasn't been trained out of them yet. Rise with them early enough to catch the sun. Take your kids outside with you. I wish I had started this earlier. This is one of the best things you can do - for yourself and also for your daughter. Get into the rhythm before she is an angsty teen, if you can. It will help her hormonal development tremendously.

One of my elders and fire teachers once shared with me that the sun is the literal physical portal for Source/God to enter our planet. For years, I could grok this on a spiritual level, the sun being the original fire. But the more I learn about the tremendously beneficial impacts of imbibing early morning sunlight on the physical body, I am more and more wholly convinced of this as true.

Looking directly at the sun *briefly* in the first 5 mins of its rising over the horizon and 5 mins before setting over the horizon helps to activate the pineal gland, sending essential signals to all of the major hormones in the brain and initiating essential functions in the body. These early and late rays will not blind you the way looking directly into the sun at midday can. It's okay to look at the sun in these tiny time windows. It actually feels really, really good.

Light, Screen Time and The Outdoors

As we discussed in chapter 2, a general rule of thumb is that when the lights go down in the sky, the lights in our homes should be going down, too. This can be *so hard* if you live in a place with winter! We have adopted a lovely routine in our home of turning down the lights and having mainly candles or no-flicker, low-watt, yellow light bulbs on once the sun goes down. We've also adjusted the screens on our phones to be red, as this is less disruptive to the circadian rhythm. While it took some adjusting at first, everyone has agreed that our new nightly routine creates a really cozy and peaceful atmosphere in the evenings. And we're all sleeping better too!

The light from screens, fluorescent lights and LEDs can wreak havoc on our metabolism, impacting our hormones, sleep, and overall mental and physical health. There are a whole host of blue blocking glasses, screen protectors, lightbulbs, apps, and software you can get to help minimize the negative light effects of too much screen time and artificial lighting. (Check the resource section.)

This is especially important to think about for your daughter, as the amount of time young people spend on screens is increasing dramatically. Unfortunately, in the majority of schools in the US, our children are now spending more and more time on computers. Just the other day, my daughter came home from her karate class and shared with us that the local public schools were closed that day **because the internet went down.** To say my husband and I were flabbergasted that this would be a cause to cancel school would be an understatement.

This is a big part of why, in our family, we send our girls to the local Waldorf school, as Waldorf pedagogy is especially dedicated to educating children in the classroom without the use of screens and over-reliance on technology. I recognize that not everyone has this option, but if you do have a Waldorf community near you, I highly recommend checking it out. There are other schools and pedagogies, like Montessori and a variety of outdoor schools popping up nowadays, that are also far less technologically dependent. And while not everyone can, homeschooling is also a very viable option.

Not only does excessive exposure to blue light have a damaging effect on their hormones and circadian rhythms, but when our daughters are also on social media, there is a whole other social and emotional component of negative side effects that will trickle into your family's life. In our house, we have just opted out.

The rise of cyber bullying is real. The rise of depression in teens is real. The research linking cyber bullying, the use of social media, and the rise of depression, anxiety, and suicide or suicidal ideation in teens is real - and is higher in girls. Online grooming resulting in rape and/or sex-trafficking is, unfortunately, very real. (We will go more in-depth with all of this later). There are around 10,000 cults active in the US alone today, the majority of them connected online.
I don't share all of this to scare you, but simply to ask: Is it really worth it?

Look, I know it can be hard. The world has become increasingly more reliant on everyone having a mini supercomputer in their pocket everywhere they go. If you are self-employed like both my husband and I, chances are your kids are seeing you on screens all the time. It can take a Herculean effort and resolve to opt out and change behaviors. It helps to have like-minded parents and community on board who are making the same or similar choices.

If your child absolutely has to have a cell phone, there are more and more options that don't include web browsers or social media apps, which I will also include in the resources section. Just know that if she's got access to texting, she's also open for cyber-bullying - albeit less likely. Just like conversations about sex, talking to her about what is and isn't okay in online communications is paramount.

More time on screens can also mean less time moving their bodies and less time connecting in real life with their peers. We need real, in-the-flesh connections for healthy cognitive, social, and emotional development!!!! Online relationships are not a substitute. And our bodies need to move!

If any one of us were to trace our ancestral roots back far enough, we would find that we are descended from people who lived in harmony with nature. Ancient humans had to in order to survive. The evolution of our species and our bodies involved continual, regular, daily contact with the natural world. We were not designed for the pace and speed of industry, and definitely not for the pace of technology as we know it today. The timeframe between the industrial revolution and now is a pretty small blip in the evolutionary timeline of the human form. We have not adapted.
I'm not anti-tech by any stretch. I'm writing and disseminating this on a computer, have social media accounts, and own a smartphone. But being born in the generation just before the advent of the internet, I have definitely seen the detrimental effects of overuse and over-dependence on technology - both in my own life, but also on society as a whole.

I'm not going to go into a whole philosophical diatribe about the detriments of technology, but my point is, in order to be fully healthy and developed human beings, not just stunted and emaciated versions of what a human is designed to be, we need to get outside and in nature. And we need to do this as often as we can, with our children.

There are forces in nature that we cannot see and are only just beginning to be able to measure somewhat that have an immense impact on us. (For all of our "technological ability", we really are still pretty lacking in being able to quantify and measure the unseen). Original people knew and understood this, and in some places still understand this. We are not separate from nature. We are part of nature. And so when we separate ourselves from the natural world, we suffer immensely.

We need fresh air and clean water and plants and trees and bodies of water and mountains and desert. We need them more than we need anything else. And we don't just need them sometimes. We need them as much as we can get them. It is well known that immersion in nature helps to heal many illnesses. Nature is our original mother, and just as human mothers are designed to do, she helps us to regulate our nervous systems. Without contact with her, we don't know how to do that very effectively. Stress, as we will discuss, is the most common underlying factor in most diseases. Which is another way of saying that not knowing how to regulate our nervous systems (i.e., not being in regular and consistent contact with the natural world) will lead to early death for most humans.

I have traveled across many continents and in many countries on this planet, since a very young age. Every place I have been on this planet that has been left mostly untouched by human hands, regardless of climate or landscape, has inspired awe, reverence, and a sense of union with the divine in me. If there is one thing that you take away from this whole damn book, let it be this: get out into the natural world, get out into the natural world, get out into the natural world!!! And bring your kids.

Movement

It doesn't really matter what kind of movement you prefer, but your body is designed to move. Our bodies are between 75-90% water (there seems to be no general consensus on the exact percentage). Regardless of consensus, it is clear: more than we are anything else, we are water. Water that stagnates and sits for too long becomes anaerobic and a breeding ground for bacteria, parasites, sickness, and disease. Water that moves, while it can still become polluted from external inputs, is far more likely to be clean and healthy water.

Again, we are mostly water. We are designed for movement. So do something to move your body for at least a cumulative couple of hours a day. I like to combine this with the above-listed sunshine and outdoors as often as I can.

That said, water that moves too fast and too much can be destructive. There are countless stories of female athletes who have overdone it, with detrimental effects on their bodies. One example is Meredith Kessler, who was an Ironman champion and professional triathlete who started her athletic career young. All of her intense training messed with her hormones so much, she still hadn't started her period by the time she was 19, and she developed borderline osteoporosis.

So, yeah, movement is important, but again, so is checking in with your body. How do you feel after the movement you engage in? Does it change during different times in your cycle? Your body is *so* wise. Don't push her just because we live in a man's world where "pushing past your limits" is the mantra of success. Sometimes that's how you fall off a cliff.

Water

Drinking water that is free from chemical additives can be unreasonably difficult to do nowadays. But coming back to the whole "we are mainly water" premise, the water you drink will have a huge impact on your wellbeing. We want to filter out fluoride because it calcifies the pineal gland, which impacts hormonal function as well as our ability to feel spiritually connected to a larger source. We want to filter out chlorine and nitrates from farming. We want to filter out PFAS as much as we can. Heavy metals too. Again, EWG.org has some good water filtration info and resources. Filtering our water can be crucial. But we want minerals!

Water stripped of all its natural minerals (such as that which is processed through reverse osmosis) has the effect of stripping the body of minerals. Water molecules will naturally bond with essential minerals, which is why spring water in its original, unpolluted form is the best water for you. It has pulled all the essential minerals out of the rock and soil for you in the most bioavailable form. (It's all designed so perfectly when we don't mess it up.)

So, that means if our water is devoid of minerals, the water molecules we drink are looking for minerals to bond with when they enter our body. So instead of putting minerals in, when we drink reverse osmosis water, it's taking minerals that we really need *out* of our bodies. Minerals are so, so important to basically every function in the body. So make sure your water has some good minerals in it, and your filter is the real deal. Again, I've got you covered in the resources section.

Stress

A fact well-documented by plenty of research is that chronic stress is one of the largest underlying factors in almost all diseases. It depresses our immune systems, making us more susceptible to getting sick. It triggers gene expression, turning on genes for certain diseases that wouldn't have been activated without it. It wears on us slowly over time, putting undue pressure on every major system in the body. It is a silent killer.

Some stress is normal and natural, and humans are amazingly resilient, but the way most of us live our lives these days is stressful beyond anything our nervous systems are designed to take. And different people respond differently to various stressful stimuli. What is stressful for me might be exhilarating for you, and vice versa.

Examining your life for sources of stress is important to do. Just like caffeine, sugar, drugs, and alcohol, we can get addicted to stress hormones. So, for this inquiry, it is really important to slow down and be honest with ourselves. Sometimes, the things that we do in an effort to be "healthy" are actually stressing us out tremendously.

Learning techniques to mitigate stress, such as meditation, tapping, and breathwork, is also crucial in today's day and age. Meditation is no longer just for yogis. It is an ancient technology that we would all do well to learn and have in our toolbox for moments of extreme stress and overwhelm.

The breath is our gateway back into wholeness. It is always with us, it never leaves (until we die), it is free, and it is ours to learn how to be with in a way that improves our overall well-being. Breath is the original antioxidant. For years, I would get off a coaching call with a client and think to myself, *is it true that I really just got paid to remind someone how to breathe?* It was true. It still blew my mind every time. Sometimes when someone asked me what I did for a living and I was feeling sassy, I would say, "I remind people how to breathe." Sure, there was more I did, but the breath was always what we came back to, every time.

I bet you're focusing on your breath more right now just because I brought your attention to it. That's how easy it is. You just shift your attention. Doesn't it feel good? If you want to play with conscious breath manipulation, a really easy exercise to start with is what is sometimes referred to as the "box breath." This is a simple 4-count breath: inhale through your nose for a count of 4, hold for 4, exhale through the nose for

4, hold for 4. You can increase it to a 5, 6, or 7 count as it feels comfortable, just keep them all equal length. Sometimes you have to give it a few rounds before your body understands how much air it needs to take in and release to make it work. Try it right now!

How did it feel?

Another one I like is to inhale through the nose for 4, hold for 4, and exhale through the mouth for 8. Again, you can lengthen each one as is comfortable; just try to keep it proportionate. Try that one too!

Did you like it more or less than the box breathing? Why?

These are just 2 in a long line of possible ways to consciously focus your breathing. Play with them and see how each one feels in your body. Alternate nostril breathing is another one I love for downshifting an overworked nervous system. You can find videos online for how to do that one - it's easier to show than to explain in writing.

Based on these two exercises, would you say you are more comfortable with fullness or emptiness? That in and of itself is an interesting contemplation and study, if you think about it in the context of the rest of your life. What did sitting in the space of no-breath feel like for you? With all breathwork, only take it as far as feels comfortable for you. The minute you start to feel the slightest bit dizzy or off, just resume your normal breathing. Notice the difference in how you feel afterwards. Calmer? Probably.

Trauma

And then we have trauma. Trauma is a catch-word that has essentially come to mean how we respond to different stressors in our lives. Post

Traumatic Stress Disorder, or PTSD, is another beast entirely and deserves its own special category in the realm of trauma and stress, because living with PTSD or complex PTSD is *hard* and not the same as simply having a conditioned stress response. Overcoming PTSD (or learning how to live a mostly functional life with it) is not impossible, but it is its own separate universe. We all have little traumas from stressors in our lives, but we do not all have PTSD. I think the language of trauma and knowing our default trauma responses can be incredibly useful as we go about our daily lives and work to further understand how to manage our stress better. Though I do think calling them conditioned stress responses instead of trauma responses is more helpful, less stigmatizing, and more respectful to those who actually suffer from PTSD.

There are 5 major responses to triggering or stressful stimuli: fight, flight, freeze, fawn, and the lesser known, but still true - fuck. You have likely heard of the fight or flight, as those are the most commonly known responses. Either we put up a fight, kick, scream, yell, throw things - or we go running in the opposite direction. We avoid, we leave, we run away, both literally and figuratively. I tend to be more of a fleer than a fighter. What about you?

"Freeze" is when we either literally freeze our bodies or just shut down/dissociate. "Fawn" is when we act overly nice and agreeable as a form of appeasement to avoid a potential violent outburst from the person we are interacting with. These responses are also just as common as fight or flight, and I believe are variations of the two. More complicated and, therefore, less discussed is what I like to call the "fuck" response, which is when we are in a hijacked or triggered state and we seek out sex as a way of changing our state, or repeating dominance patterns to feel in control. (I have usually seen this in people who were victims of sexual abuse, but that is not a rule.)

We all have one or two of these responses as our go-to default when we feel under stress or pressure. I think that's important to recognize. There is not a single person in the western world who doesn't have some kind of conditioned stress response built into their nervous system. (And yes, I did say western world. There are 100% cultures out there that are designed for a healthy ability to metabolize stressful stimuli, that in our culture turn into chronic conditioned stress responses.) So none of these stress responses is better or worse than the other, or somehow makes us a bad person for having it. They are a result of living in the world in which we do. It's just important to know which one is your default - because it is totally liberating to know ourselves. It also takes the shame out of it. There's nothing wrong with you - that's just your default. Good information to have! It doesn't excuse inappropriate behavior, but it can help us to understand why we do it.

For me, for example, my default stress response is freeze. I shut down or dissociate in the face of stressful or overwhelming circumstances and events (this can make parenting super hard on the days when the kids just being loud is a trigger for me). I have been known to even get triggered just by having someone ask me to schedule an appointment (neurodivergence is amazing). Knowing this about myself is super helpful, however, because when I recognize that I am shut down, if I can just *keep moving*, I can get through it without it consuming me entirely. I just do the next thing in front of me, even if I want to cry. Or, I go for a walk and move my body, dance, shake, get angry, roar, or growl. This is the opposite of sitting and meditating. That is actually not the most helpful thing for me to do when I'm activated in my freeze response (though it would totally be my preference).

If fighting is your default response, however, then taking a moment to pause, slow down, close your eyes, feel your feet, get still, and take a breath are likely going to be more helpful for you when you feel that activation or trigger. Meditation would be great for you! And you probably hate doing it! It's usually going to be the thing you are resisting the most in the moment that would be most helpful for you in working through the trigger. That's why it's called a trigger!

On the other side of fight or flight, we have rest and digest. When we don't live in a chronic state of activation, we have access to states of regeneration and healing. Digestion is essential for the healthy assimilation of nutrients in the body. If you are chronically stressed or triggered, it will affect your digestion. Changing your diet is unlikely to majorly shift things for you if this is the case. Also, our body needs periods of rest to be able to heal, rejuvenate and repair itself. Again, if we are chronically stressed, we shut down our access to this innate power.

Learn how to manage your stress. It all comes down to knowing yourself. Know what sets you off, what makes it worse, what helps, or what you are just using as a crutch that might actually be making it worse underneath. Sometimes it means making major life changes. This can be scary as hell, especially if making a change means introducing uncertainty into your financial or living situation. But if you are in a life that majorly stresses you out, ultimately making the change your heart is telling you to make is worth it. Stress kills. Don't be one of its victims.

If you want more resources and tools for managing your stress, go to the resources and recommended reading sections of this book.

A Sense of Purpose

Knowing what thrills you in life is one of the most important pieces of knowledge you can have. If we aren't happy and fulfilled in our lives, it will take a toll on our health. Laughter, pleasure, joy, and a sense of purpose are all essential parts of being human. A feeling that we are somehow contributing to something larger than our small selves is crucial for living a purposeful life.

We are creators by design, and when we aren't clear on how or what we are creating, we begin to feel stagnant. It doesn't matter how large or small the creation. It could just be a scarf you're knitting or a meal you're making for your family. Or, it could be a whole business venture or charity project - or something in between. Whatever it is, it should be something that lights you up.

When I was in my toxic business and work relationship that lasted way longer than it should have, in the last two or three years of it, I would get horrific migraines that became more frequent and stronger in intensity over time. It was also during that time period that I gained a significant amount of weight that I was completely unable to shed. (Energetic protection much?). At first I thought my migraines were hormonal, as they often linked up with either ovulation or menstruation. But then I started to notice that they would interestingly coincide with conversations or events that had to do with my business and work.

When I left that business relationship, my migraines all but entirely disappeared. There was nothing else in my diet or exercise that I changed. Coincidence? I think not. Our bodies are wise beyond measure. We would do well to listen to the feedback they give us.

Focus and Gratitude

We have been gifted with the choice in where we put our focus. Every day, and in every moment, we can focus on what is wrong with ourselves, with our environment, with the world - or we can focus on what is working. There is always something we can find appreciation for and something to be grateful for, no matter what the circumstance.

Entire tomes have been written about the beneficial impacts of gratitude and focus on health and wellbeing that I'm not going to go into too much here, outside of saying: it's not trite. It actually does work, and it actually does have a huge impact on our wellbeing.

I understand that shifting focus is not easy for everyone. Like building a new physical muscle, shifting focus can be something we have to train in ourselves. But it is a muscle worth building. There are things we can change in life and things we can't. Most things we can't. We can't change the weather, when someone we love dies, someone else's thoughts about us, someone else's behavior or beliefs. But we can change what we focus on. And we can always find something to be grateful for if we really are committed to finding it.

This is another one I like to combine with the first morning sunshine. It is the way I have been taught by my elders as well. Greet the sunrise with an offering of gratitude that we are alive another day. We have been given another day here on planet earth, and that in and of itself is something to be grateful for. We have water. We have shelter. We have relatives in the birds and the trees, the plants and the animals, the swimming ones and the creepy crawlies. All of these relatives help us to live, and for that, for them giving their lives so that we may have ours, we can give thanks each and every day.

Food

And finally, there is food. I don't know if you noticed, but it's at the end of the list. I do have two general guidelines I like to follow with food. Here they are: #1) Eat a wide variety of foods #2) Don't eat non-food.

I classify food as something that, if properly prepared, could reasonably be consumed by itself. A fruit or veg, a spice, a grain, a nut, meat, dairy, eggs, legumes, honey, etc. - all of these, if individually offered outside of the context of being mixed with anything else, could be consumed alone.

Hydrogenated oils, biologically unavailable vitamins and minerals, mono-sodium glutamate, and red dye 40, on the other hand, would not be something you would take a solo sampling of if you found them sitting on your kitchen counter. These and other chemically altered and lab-created food additives are what I call non-food "food-like" substances. Unfortunately, they are often mixed in with real foods.

So, this does mean reading ingredients on things. (I'm sorry to break it to you, but McDonald's hamburgers are not just made of wheat and beef). Know what's in your food. The front of labels are designed to make you think that what is in something is only two or three things, so you have to also read the back of the label to know what's *really* in your food. Make sure it's actually food. That's just generally a smart thing to do.

Eat primarily food made of ingredients that are easy to recognize growing or living before it gets to your plate. Even better if it hasn't been sprayed with or fed a bunch of chemicals beforehand. Best if it came from nearby where you live, or your own backyard. Wild food is supreme in its nutrient density. The benefits of eating locally are plentiful: your body adapts to the place where you live; produce that is in-season and local has the highest nutrient density and, therefore, the highest health benefit for you. And eating locally means you support your local farmers, without which we'd all be pretty fucked.

That's pretty much it. It's pretty simple. You don't need to be counting carbs and weighing every macro of everything you eat. Just eat fewer things in packages and more things you can easily pronounce (though I know a lot of people who struggle with pronouncing "quinoa").

Our cells need minerals, carbohydrates, protein, and fat in order to function, and our digestion needs fiber. So eat those things. Eat plants. Eat animals. Eat things that make you feel good - including chocolate cake. Don't eat things that don't make you feel good (sometimes including chocolate cake). Eat things that give you solid energy, not fake energy you crash from later. What that is for you might be different for someone else, or at different times in the season, or your menstrual cycle. Experiment. Be honest with yourself. *Only you will know.*

What food gives you more energy for longer? Does it change at different points in your cycle or times of day? Your body is not like anyone else's body, and there is no formula to follow that will work for all bodies. Sorry to break it to you. Eat when you are hungry. Don't eat when you are not hungry. Simplify.

I personally love the concept and practice of cyclical eating. As someone with an eating disorder history, this kind of eating works so well for me because it is not restrictive, it's cyclical. Everything is allowed, just at different times of your cycle, to accommodate the different nutrient needs your body has at different hormonal phases. (We covered this in the section on hormones). I've also personally found that eating 20-25 grams of animal protein first thing in the morning helps me have sustained energy throughout the day, as does prioritizing high protein intake with most meals. But everything anyone suggests, letters after their name or not, you have to test through the laboratory of your own life experience.

We are omnivorous by design, so I do believe in including animal foods in the diet in some way. There are people out there who have really strong feelings about this, on both sides of the fence. I just stick with what feels right for my body. I've been vegan and vegetarian, and I feel better when I eat meat, but not when I eat too much meat. This is ultimately personal preference and needs to come from direct feedback from your body, not someone else's idea of what is right.

Our bodies need fats to function properly, and good sources of dietary fat are very important. However, a lot of the fats that are in many of the things we eat (especially if they are processed) have been chemically altered so that they will be shelf stable. Naturally shelf stable fats are fats that are solid at room temp. Plus they are delicious. This includes things like lard, butter, coconut oil, and tallow. Olive oil has amazing health benefits, but that industry is also mafia controlled, and much of what is sold as olive oil isn't actually pure olive oil. Knowing the source is crucial.

Fats that are extracted from nuts and seeds tend to go rancid pretty quickly. (That's why you'll often see it labeled on whole nuts and seeds to store them in the fridge for a longer shelf life.) Eating rancid things isn't very healthy for you, in general, so I tend to stay away from things like canola, sunflower, safflower and corn oils in my cooking, unless they are fresh-pressed recently from a local farm or something. I'm also shying away from them more and more when it comes to putting them on my skin. But again, you do you. How does eating these oils, or not eating them, make you feel?

I think our approach to diet is way overcomplicated in most circles. It can be simple. Eat real food and pay attention to the feedback from your body. That's really it. I honestly believe that the stress of watching everything we put into our mouths can be more harmful than it would be to just eat the fat and carbs. Can we please stop demonizing macronutrients that our bodies need for survival? Enjoying yourself is not evil!

Diets and Your Daughter

Please do not put your daughter on a diet, unless it is somehow medically necessary (even then, I would encourage you to do some deep digging and investigation around potential other root causes). Give her whole, recognizable-as-food foods at home on a regular basis. Train her palate towards fruits and veggies as much as you can because they have great minerals, vitamins, and fiber in them that our bodies need. Make sure she's getting adequate carbs, protein, and fats. Switch it up from time to time (our microbiome, and our world, thrives on diversity). But for the love of everything, please do not put her on a diet, ever!

Try not to categorize foods as "good" or "bad." There is food, and there is non-food, and unfortunately, a lot of what Americans eat nowadays in the form of processed junk is not actually food, which is a contributing factor to why so many are so sick. But in terms of actual foods, there are not inherently good or bad foods. Just preferences. Likes and dislikes. Things that work for our bodies and things that don't. Harmony and balance - or lack thereof. Teach her that she can have preferences. Because she will.

If she's an athlete and is taking dietary advice from a coach, make sure that advice is inclusive of the female hormonal cycle, like what the US women's soccer team follows. Alisa Vitti has some great advice on this in her book *In the Flo* if the coach or team leader needs some resources on how to recommend appropriate training diets for young women.

Your relationship to food is what is going to be modeled to your child, and is what she is most likely going to follow, especially later in life. This has been one of *the hardest* pills to swallow in my parenting journey, because I still struggle sometimes with my relationship to food (though far less since I have adopted the above philosophy and stopped listening to diet/food gurus). I talk to her about my struggles. I let her know my challenges and what I've been through

I can see how some of the toxic beliefs and patterns regarding food that I absorbed in my childhood have trickled down to my oldest already, and it has pained me so much that it's forced me to do things differently with my youngest - or try at least. But I'm not going to pretend this part of the journey has been easy for me. Sometimes it takes all my will to stay silent about what is going into her mouth. I don't always succeed. It can be so hard.

One thing I can say that I feel pretty passionate about is this: If you have a specific diet or way of eating that you follow in your house - paleo or vegan, for example - I highly encourage you not to make your daughter follow that diet when she is not in the house (unless it's because of an actual allergy). This kind of restrictive eating, the kind that is due to philosophy instead of actual physical requirement, sets our daughters up for a lifetime of confusion around food and diet. It might also mean that she stops herself from reaching for something her body actually needs from a nutritional perspective, thereby rendering her nutritionally deficient. Or that she is drawn to something but feels she needs to sneak it behind your back. My mom's "portion control" mantra and forced diets led to me stealing every kind of awful packaged cake and candy, stashing it under my bed, and binge eating it in private when no one was looking. Needless to say, her mantras didn't work.

Share with your daughter why you eat the way you do, why it feels important to you - absolutely. Let her know that it's different in different households and different families. That doesn't make your family better or fundamentally right. Just different. If she tries eating something different outside of the house that you don't normally eat at home, ask her how she feels after eating it. Ask her how it was. Don't shame her for it; just introduce inquiry.

For example, we generally don't eat fast food in our family. When my daughter's class went to Culver's on a school trip, I didn't throw a tantrum (well, maybe I actually did just a tad. I was not expecting the food culture that has come along with this particular Waldorf school, and sometimes I have my moments). But not to her. With her, I just asked her how it was and how she felt after eating it, and she said "not that great" to both, and that was that. Her classmates were shocked that she had never eaten a fast food burger before, but it didn't phase her. She even recently shared with me that one of her life's ambitions is to make it through to the end without ever having eaten at McD's. Good for her.

As she grows, she is going to make her own decisions about how to eat that feel right to her. Her body and her preferences might not be the same as yours, and that is okay. Let it be fluid. Tastes change. Preferences change. Don't be too rigid about it, because I can almost guarantee you that if you are, it will blow up in your face at some point.

Around the world, in other cultures, food is a way of sharing our love, respect, and care for other people. It's a form of wealth. Food is how people around the world come together. When we are militant in our food choices and it's not due to actual allergies, we can inadvertently limit the kinds of places we can go, and the experiences and degree of connection we can have with the people we meet. The healthiest food in the world is the food created and given in love. Please don't rob yourself, or your daughter, of that.

Recipe: Homemade All-Purpose Cleaner

This is an easy and inexpensive way to make a lot of non-toxic, all-purpose cleaner that also smells good.

Ingredients:
- White Vinegar
- Citrus peels
- (You can also use a variety of pine clippings or cuttings from your Christmas tree or wreath before you throw it out)

Materials:
- Half-gallon glass mason jar

Directions:
Spend a week eating lots of citrus and using it in all the recipes, and save the peels. Fill the mason jar as full as you can with citrus peels, pine clippings, or both! Cover with the vinegar and allow it to soak, away from direct sunlight, for a minimum of two weeks, or up to a month. You may want to put a piece of parchment between the jar and the lid, as the vinegar can eat away at the metal. Agitate the jar occasionally. Strain the vinegar and store it in a spray bottle. Use as you would any all-purpose cleaner!

Recipe: Fabulous Face Scrub

This is my go-to recipe instead of any kind of commercial facial exfoliant. It's luxurious, smells amazing - and if you even wanted to, you could eat it! (Though I think it's much nicer when used on the face.) Play around with different herbs and flowers and see what you like best! I make a double or triple batch of this and split it with my daughter. It also makes a nice gift.

Ingredients:
- 2-3 Tbsp Oats
- 3-5 Raw Almonds (omit if there is an allergy. You can replace the almonds with sunflower seeds, pumpkin seeds, apricot kernels, etc. - just make sure they are raw and unsalted)
- 3-5 Tbsp Dried Herbs of your choice.
    - Some of my favorites are: lavender, rose, chamomile, calendula, frankincense, and butterfly pea flower. You could also experiment with herbs like lemon balm and peppermint for a more uplifting and invigorating experience!
- Raw Honey - enough to make a thick paste

Materials:
- Bowl
- Herb Grinder
- Fine mesh strainer
- Clean container to store scrub in

Directions:
Place all dry ingredients into the herb grinder. (I have a designated coffee grinder that I use specifically for herbs so as to not contaminate them with the coffee oils.) Grind until you have a fine powder.

Place the strainer over the bowl and dump the ground oats, nuts/seeds, and herbs into the strainer. Press the powder through the strainer by stirring it around and around using your finger, a spoon, or a stick. Any larger clumps will be left in the strainer and can be re-ground until you can't get it any finer. Discard compost any coarser materials left over.

Mix in the raw honey until all the dry ingredients have been incorporated and you have a thick paste. Place your finished product into the clean container(s).

Usage:

Use this scrub every 3 days, or once a week. You don't want to over-exfoliate, so use it a couple of times a week at most. I don't usually follow with a cleanser on days I use this scrub, but you can find what works best for you in your face care regimen. Finish with your favorite moisturizer. Enjoy the softness and clarity of your beautiful skin!

Recipe: Rosemary Hair Oil

People often comment on my hair, as I have quite an abundance of it. It is long, it is naturally flowy, it is FULL (I do NOT need volumizing shampoo), and it's definitely got a mind of its own. I sometimes joke that my hair has a plan for world domination, because you can find lonnng strands of it in many random places. It also likes to collect twigs and leaves in it when I go for walks in the woods, and I am often pulling random detritus from nature out of my hair.

The "secret" to my hair, other than a healthy, mineral-rich diet, is actually that I very minimally care for it. I finger comb it more often than I brush it. I wash it about once a week. And when I do wash it, I *never* blow dry my hair. I wrap it in a towel when I first get out of the shower for about a minute so it's not dripping all over the place. Then I just let it dry naturally.

I do, however, apply hair oil to it when it's still wet. I find this keeps it from getting frizzy, adds shine, and also helps define its innate desire to curl.

Plain coconut oil can work just fine - you just have to warm it up in your hands first to get it liquid (unless it's the heat of summer or you live in the tropics). But when I'm wanting something a little more luxurious, this is one of my go-to oils. It is simple, easy to make (I'll give you two recipe versions), and smells amazing.

Recipe Version #1 - Plant-infused Rosemary Hair Oil

Ingredients:
- Jojoba or olive oil (or a combination of the two)
- Dried or fresh Rosemary
- (optional) Vodka, Everclear, or some other 100 proof, clear spirit

Materials:

- Pint-sized mason jar
- Mesh strainer
- Cheesecloth
- (optional) 8-12 oz. bottle with a pump top

Directions:

Gather enough rosemary to pack whatever glass container you will be using to make this oil. (I like to just use a pint-sized mason jar so I can use it up before it goes bad.) Chop or crush the herb finely. This increases the surface area of the plant material, giving you a more powerful oil.

If using, place between a teaspoon and a tablespoon of vodka into the jar with the herb and toss it around, coating the herb in the alcohol. You want enough to coat it, but not so much that it is pooling at the bottom of the jar. The alcohol helps to maximize extraction. It makes a more potent oil and can help give the oil a longer shelf-life, but it is not necessary to get a good oil. Cover the herb completely with the oil, making sure all plant parts are below the surface of the oil. Seal the jar.

Now you have a few options: you can place the jar in a sunny windowsill for a week and let the heat and light of the sun infuse the oil with the plant's medicine. OR, you can place the jar in a cool, dark cabinet for a month, coming back to shake it regularly. Some herbalists say that the oil will have a longer shelf life if you infuse it in the dark, which I do actually believe is true, as the oil is never exposed to heat. Others prefer having the energy and heat of the sun infusing the oil, as the sun has its own medicinal properties. You choose what feels most alive for you.

You can also do the fast version, which involves placing the glass jar in a pan of gently simmering (not boiling) water on the stove for 30-60 minutes. This will quickly transfer the properties of the herb into the oil. You have to be mindful that you don't heat it too much, as excessive heat will destroy the beneficial oils in the herb, giving you a crispy herb menstruum and a burnt oil. Heating the oil will also give it a shorter shelf life, but it works fine.

When you are ready to decant your oil (whether after 30 minutes, a week, or a month, depending on the method you choose), you will need a strainer and a cheesecloth, or a fine cloth that you can strain the oil through.

Set the strainer over whatever container or bowl you will be straining the oil into and line it with the cloth. Pour the oil and herbs into the strainer and let it sit and drain into the bowl. Avoid the temptation to squeeze! Squeezing will release any water that is still in the plant material into the oil, significantly decreasing its shelf life. Let it drain completely. Discard the plant material and cloth.

Voila! Bottle up this beautiful oil and use it on your wet hair after washing. I usually use it after showers, but you can also use it as a deep-conditioning hair treatment beforehand. Just coat your hair in it, put it up in a shower cap for 15 minutes, and wash your hair as you normally would.

And guess what? Now you know how to make any plant-infused oil! The process for making any fresh or dried herb into an oil is the same.

Recipe Version #2 - The Cheater's Way - EO infused Rosemary Hair Oil

Ingredients:
- Olive or Jojoba oil (or a combination of both)
- Therapeutic-grade Rosemary essential oil
  (https://www.myyl.com/tatiana-berindei?share=rosemary-oil#hwm/rosemary-oil)

Materials:

- 8-12 oz bottle with pump top

Directions:

Put the essential oil into the base oil. I put about a teaspoon or more of EO in a cup (8 oz) of olive or jojoba oil. You want to be able to smell it.

Cap. Shake. Voila!

Told you it was the cheater's way!

FYI - I do prefer the first oil over this one, both for the finished product and the witchy process of making it. But in a pinch, this works great.

Recipe: Making Herbal Infusions

Herbal infusions are, in my opinion, one of the best things you can add to your overall well-being regimen. Made from a strong decoction of plant material, they are chock full of minerals and nourishing compounds that, as women especially, we tend to be deficient in. I highly recommend making herbal infusions a part of your daily practice.

Making herbal infusions is pretty simple. All it takes is 1 oz. of dried plant material to 1 quart of boiling water. (1 oz. might not sound like a lot, but when you're talking dried herbs 1 oz. can equate to a cup or more of dried plant material. A kitchen scale comes in handy here.) Pour the boiled water over the herb, cover, and let steep for a minimum of 4 hours (best overnight). Strain and drink throughout the day.

Here are some of my all-time favorite herbs for infusing every day:

Oatstraw (Avena Sativa) - a fantastic balm for the hair, teeth, skin, nails, and nervous system! Oatstraw calms and cools, while supporting us in strengthening our foundational structures. Oatstraw is also a tonic for the endocrine system. One of my all-time favorites!

Nettles aka Stinging Nettle (Urtica Dioica) - Nettles are the highest source of magnesium found in the plant world. That fact alone makes this one of my go-to herbs for infusions, though its benefits extend far beyond magnesium. Nettle infusions can help to reduce overall inflammation in the body, strengthen the kidneys and urinary tract (and adrenals), stop hemorrhage bleeding, strengthen nails and hair, and fortify our immune systems. So drink your nettles!

Red Clover (Trifolium Pratense) - Red clover is an amazing and nourishing tonic herb for our reproductive system. It is full of isoflavones which can help lower inflammation, benefit cardiovascular health, reduce the severity and frequency of hot flashes, and help strengthen our bones.

Red Raspberry Leaf (Rubus idaeus, Rubus occidentalis) - A uterine tonic and relaxant, red raspberry leaf is also beneficial to digestion. Not just for pregnancy, raspberry leaf infusions are a fabulous tonic to be taken regularly, especially right before and during menstruation as it can relieve cramps and help with water retention. Full of antioxidants, red raspberry also has anti-inflammatory properties.

As with most natural and herbal remedies, the magic of infusions really kicks in with regular and consistent use. While we can absolutely see some short-term benefits from drinking them one time, our overall health improves and vitality kicks in when we drink infusions on the regular.

My preference is to harvest the plants I use for medicine. When I can't harvest them myself, I buy my herbs in big, bulk, one-pound bags. When it comes to medicinal herbs, you want to source your herbs from ethical harvesters or growers, as over-harvesting has led to some plant species becoming endangered. I suggest searching for a local farm in your area or in a neighboring state or province that grows the herbs you are looking for if you don't want to, or can't, grow them or wildcraft them yourself. Farmers and herbalists, in my experience, tend to be pretty rad people. So, not only might you meet some cool folks, you will also be supporting their efforts in growing these magical plants!

Recipe: Cramp Bark (Viburnum Opulus) Glycerite Tincture

This tincture is a great alternative to over-the-counter meds for cramps. It doesn't come with the crazy long list of potential side-effects that otc meds do - and it works! Cramp Bark is effective in relaxing smooth muscle tissue - specifically uterine tissue.

Cramp Bark (also known as Highbush Cranberry) grows in the Eastern United States, as well as many parts of Europe. The part harvested for medicinal use is primarily the bark (hence the name) but sometimes the berries are gathered as well. If you plan to wildcraft this plant, make sure you have 100% positively identified the plant before harvesting to make into medicine. The best time to gather this bark medicine is in the spring, before it has leafed out.

Well-respected herbalist, Dina Falconi, has an excellent video on harvesting cramp bark. (Guess where I put it for you?)

As with all herbal medicines, harvesting your own will provide you with a far superior product, as well as a relationship with the plant. I always leave an offering when I harvest, either some tobacco or some of my hair, as a thank you to the plant nation for providing their medicine. I also make it a general rule that someone with an untrained eye should not be able to tell I was there harvesting, and I never take more than I need.

If harvesting feels out of reach, there is no shame in buying the dried herb! Just make sure it comes from a reputable source. (You can also just buy a premade tincture - resources! But that's not as fun or satisfying as making your own.)

This recipe uses vegetable glycerine as the main base, as this is intended for your child - though adults can 100% take glycerite tinctures, too! They are yummy! But you can absolutely make this as just an alcohol tincture. The amounts will vary depending on how much tincture you want to make. The nice thing about alcohol tinctures is that they last a very long time, whereas glycerites have a shorter shelf life. I have tinctures I made 10-15 years ago that are still good.

Glycerites don't last as long, so you might want to make less at a time unless you plan to give some away. A pint-sized jar would be the perfect size for a starter batch of glycerite tincture. Once made, this tincture will last about one year.

Ingredients:
- Dried cramp bark herb
- Vegetable glycerine
- Alcohol - such as brandy, rum or vodka

Materials:
- Glass jar with a tight-fitting lid
- Cheese cloth
- Metal strainer

Directions: Gently fill the jar with the dried herb. Don't pack it down; just fill it loosely to the top. The more surface area on the herb, the more medicine that can be extracted, so crushing or chopping it first will make a more potent medicine.

Once the jar is loosely filled, cover the dried herb completely in a solution of 70 percent glycerine and 30 percent alcohol. The alcohol helps with extraction of certain medicinal properties, as well as with the stability of the tincture.

Once the herb is completely covered (make sure there are no loose bits sticking up out of the glycerine), cover the jar and let it sit in a cool, dark place for 4-6 weeks. About once a week or so, you can shake the jar to make sure the medicine is being well-released.

After 4-6 weeks, strain out the herb (you can compost it after this) and put the liquid into tincture bottles. Voila! You have your cramp bark tincture!

Dosage: 30-40 drops of tincture in a little water 3-4 times a day/as needed for cramps during menstruation

CHAPTER 5

"LET'S TALK ABOUT SEX. BABY.."

Of all the chapters in this book, this one is the most likely to trigger the highest number of people. In this chapter, we will cover some of the hottest topics with the strongest opinions and sometimes even political movements behind them. You might want to re-read the "How to Use this Book" introduction again before you dive in. And remember to take deep breaths and breaks if you need to.

Also, each of these topics could be their own book. I did my best to touch enough on each one to give you something to work with, but I also did my best to keep it within bounds. Alright, all, here we go! "Let's talk about sex, baby…" (I'm a child of the 80s, remember?)

"The Talk" is Not a One-Time Thing

If there is one phrase I could do away with in our current-day vernacular surrounding this topic, it would be "the talk." This phrase erroneously leads us to believe that a conversation about sex with our children happens one time and that's it. That might have been true for us with our parents when we were growing up, but if your parents just had the one "talk" with you, let me ask you this: how did that work out for you?

It is no wonder we have such a sexually dysfunctional society. What of depth and value have you ever learned from one conversation, one time?

Repetition is key to retaining information. How many times do you have to ask your child to clear the dishes from the table or brush their teeth before it becomes an automatic habit? Maybe 105 - if we are lucky?! How have we been led to believe that a single conversation about sex and the body is going to adequately prepare our children for the minefield of human sexual relating?

When It Starts

In our society, our media and cultural references are rife with images of that super uncomfortable moment when our kids ask us "where do babies come from?" and we, the parents, awkwardly fumble for an answer. We poke fun at the discomfort, and we've gotten really good at giving creative answers. A stork? Really? (No, but actually, I was in Romania once with my dad and we saw storks nesting on someone's house and my dad said it was a common belief that storks were a fertility symbol, and that if they nested on your house, you were more likely to get pregnant, so I guess the myth has some origin in something...)

But it starts even earlier than that. How we interact with our children during a diaper change or potty training, how we answer their questions about their body parts, and the names we give their body parts, all have a bearing on how our children will grow up to feel about their bodies. While naming body parts in childhood might not seem relevant to intercourse as adults, it can have a big impact on our sexual life.

A penis is a penis, not a wee wee. A vulva is a vulva, not a peanut or a cookie (also - who the fuck came up with edible names for a young girl's genitals!?). We have used the Sanskrit term yoni in our house, as I like planting the seed early that this is a sacred part of the body, but my daughters still know that the proper term in English is vulva.

Correctly naming body parts helps to reduce sexual shame later in life and boost confidence in how children feel about their bodies. If we have to give something a secret name and the adults can't even call it what it is, then children internalize that there must be something dirty or wrong with that part of the body. Accurate naming of genitalia can also help reduce rates of childhood sexual abuse, as predators can often be disarmed and turned off by a child saying something like "why are you showing me your penis?" or "I don't like it when you touch my vulva."

How to Talk to Your Kids About Sex

"But I'm not ready!"

Actually, usually this feeling in parents tends to masquerade as "*they* are not ready" - meaning your kids. If we are honest with ourselves, though, it is we who are not ready to start having conversations about sex with our children. This is very common, and comes up for a lot of parents; I'd venture to say *most*. We have so much conditioned cultural shame and confusion around our bodies and sexuality, it is only natural that we would have conflicted feelings about how to talk about this with our kids, if at all. So I want to make sure that you don't feel any shame if you are reading this and you have not really initiated a conversation with your daughter about sex yet. It's incredibly common.

If this is coming up for you, though, ask yourself this question: what is it *exactly* that you don't feel you are ready for? I invite you to really sit with this one. Write down your answers, if that helps. What is the fear? Or is it just that you have no idea where to start? (Surprise! An exercise in the middle of a chapter!)

One of the most common concerns I have heard parents express is that if we start to talk to our kids about sex, then they will go out and have sex.

But this is rarely, if ever, the case. More common, actually, is that if we *don't* talk to our kids about sex (outside of just telling them not to have it), then they go out and have sex. Or "learn" from porn. Or both. Because they're curious! They want to know! And what better way to find out than to try it themselves?

Maybe a better way would be if a trusted adult in their life were to talk to them about it *before* they get to the experimentation phase…

Get my drift?

There is no force in nature more powerful than sex. That is why it is capitalized on everywhere you go. Nothing sells better than sex. Nothing manipulates better than sex. Nothing else in nature has the power to create new life. Nothing else has the power to destroy reputations, relationships, and even entire empires. Sex is the ultimate force of creation, and on the flip side, it can also be immensely destructive. This is most true if we are not aware of its power and how we wield it, or if we intentionally misuse that power. No wonder we want to shield our children from it for as long as possible.

It's also foundational, fun, and a totally normal part of life as a teenage and adult human. There is nothing wrong with sex. Sex is normal, natural, and a healthy expression of vitality and well-being. Sex is healthy. Sex is good for us. Sex can also be a portal into divine connection.

What to Talk About

With my own children, I have functioned under the principle of "if they are old enough to ask the question, they are old enough to receive an answer." An answer doesn't mean a full-length powerpoint for a three year old asking where babies come from. Sometimes the simplest answers, rooted in biological fact, have the most impact. If your short answer is unsatisfactory for a young child, rest assured, they will follow up with more questions. But as a general guideline, simple is better - especially when they are little.

This is where most parents get stuck. Their kids are asking them questions that they think they need to give adult answers to, when kids are not asking for adult answers. But they are asking, and they deserve to be given information that will not only satisfy their curiosity, but adequately prepare them for the truth of living in a human body. These conversations need to start way earlier than we think. If you are waiting to broach the topic of puberty and sex with your daughter until she has started puberty, then you are missing the boat. In our house, we have conversations about bodies, if not daily, at least a couple of times a week. Some last a minute, some for much longer. Most of these conversations are initiated by questions from my daughter, but I also initiate them sometimes too.

There is no way that you are going to fit all of these topics we are about to dive into in one conversation with your children. And that is a good thing! Because, as I have mentioned previously, "the talk" is not a one-time thing, but an ongoing and evolving conversation that grows in nuance and complexity as your children grow and mature. Which means if you try one time and totally flub it, you get to try again. And again, and again, until your daughter knows that you are the best and safest resource for conversations about bodies and sex, even if you might not always know the answer right away.

I recognize that every family is different and will approach this topic in different ways. We all come from different religious, cultural, and social backgrounds, and have our diverse ways of thinking about and addressing the topic of sex with our children. I make no pretense for this book being a prescription of what you have to do in talking to your child about sex (though, obviously, I have my own opinions and biases). The main point I want to get across is that we need to start talking to them about it in healthier ways than just "Don't have it." Period. And we would do well by them to make those conversations not only safe but commonplace in our households.

Does Talking Really Help?

Mangala Holland is a Woman's Sexual Confidence and Pleasure Coach based in the UK who focuses her support on women in their 40s and up. She is also the author of the bestselling book *Orgasms Made Easy: The No-Nonsense Guide to Self-Pleasure, Sexual Confidence and Female Orgasms*. I first met Mangala when she was a guest on my podcast *Sex, Love and Superpowers*. I asked her recently what her take was on what is the biggest mistake parents make when it comes to talking about sex with their kiddos. She went above and beyond, offering not just her professional opinion, but also polling some of her clients, some of whom also asked their adult children to give an answer. After gathering all that information, here was her response:

"(*The biggest mistake parents make is...*) Not talking about it at an early enough age, and not doing their own inner work about sex and pleasure. If a parent is feeling awkward and uptight, kids will pick up on that. So many of my clients who struggle to communicate about sex, or feel shame, are able to identify that this came from their parents' attitudes and communication.

Some parents assume their kids aren't "doing that yet" or have had no exposure, but in the current digital age, the average age that kids are being exposed to porn is 12. As more youngsters get their education (and misinformation) from social media, it's important to highlight that things like choking, rough sex, non-consensual, etc., aren't considered "normal" or welcome.

I think it's also important for parents to talk about wider concepts of sex, which might include kissing, oral sex, foreplay, consent, pleasure, and self-exploration, and not to assume your youngster is heterosexual. Using correct medical terminology, such as vulva rather than "down there", can make a huge difference to how people relate to their bodies.

Find out what is age-appropriate to share with your kid, be prepared to go at their pace, and let them know that they can ask anything if they're not sure."

So, does talking really help? Looks like the answer is yes.

Why You Can't Separate the Puberty and the Sex Conversation, As Much As You Might Want To

I have read and heard countless accounts of women who want to teach their daughters about how their bodies work but don't want to have the sex conversation with them "yet." Here's the problem with this line of thinking: The way our bodies work, especially in regards to the changes that happen in puberty, are SO THAT we can and want to have sex and make babies.

The definition of puberty, according to the Oxford Dictionary, is "the period during which adolescents reach sexual maturity and become capable of reproduction." Whether we actually ever end up making babies or not is irrelevant. That is the biological function and purpose of puberty.

205

To try to separate these two is not only kind of impossible, it's a bit naive and potentially harmful to your child. Puberty exists solely so that we can procreate. Which, last time I checked, involves having sex. Unless we're wanting to make all of our babies in petri dishes in labs. But my guess is, if you picked up this book and have gotten this far, that's not your desire for humanity.

Your daughter is going to grow up in a highly sexualized culture, whether you like it or not. Regardless of your personal or religious beliefs or feelings about it, the fact is that we live in a world and culture that is dramatically impacted by the ubiquitous presence of pornography. This pornographic influence is heightened by the Puritanical beliefs foundational to this country that deem the body and sex sinful and shameful. The distortion that this concept of "original sin" created still runs as a silent undercurrent in our society. Whenever you suppress something and push it into the shadows, its pull and its power grows. We can see this phenomenon play out more clearly in the world of sex than almost anywhere else.

As her body changes and she starts to grow breasts and emit pheromones, the likelihood that your daughter will attract male attention is high. She, in turn, will likely also find herself sexually attracted - either to the same or opposite sex (or both). To not educate her about this fact and ignore it in the hopes that it will be different for your child is to do her a grave disservice. It sets her up to be ill-equipped to handle inevitable advances and interactions with the opposite sex, and could even lead her to naively walk into undesirable situations. She needs to know that if something ever happens to her that feels off, she can tell you about it. She needs to know that she will not be shamed for it, and that she will be believed.

Our Bodies are Sacred

I want girls and women everywhere to get excited about the magic of their bodies and their periods, to be honored and proud to be womb bearers. One of my early teachers, Natem Anank Nunkai of the Shuar tribe in Ecuador (who has since crossed the threshold), confirmed this for me after a very powerful ceremony we had together. In the ceremony, I was shown many things about the mysteries of the womb. I was instructed that the womb is a spirit house that we, as women, were entrusted to carry inside of us. So we need to take care of it. When we do, we therefore also have the good fortune to be able to tap into that "house of spirit within" to harness its beyond-the-veil wisdom any time we want to.

Whether we ever choose to go on to bear children or not is irrelevant, as the womb is a sacred storehouse of power and wisdom that extends far beyond birthing. I also believe, however, that a generation of women raised proud to be womb-bearers will have a far easier time getting pregnant, maintaining their pregnancies, and going on to birth in power and sovereignty.

I know that part of that might freak you out. "Pregnancy - ack! Hell no, I don't want it to be easier for my daughter to get pregnant!" But that fear and that freak-out are coming from a place of not trusting your child, not trusting your ability to have hard conversations, and not trusting the process of spiritual maturation that we are embarking upon in this journey together throughout this book together. I submit that girls who hold themselves with sacredness and reverence are far less likely to be victims of unwanted experiences, including pregnancy.

Teaching our daughters how to claim and own their sacred bodies can be a revolutionary act. So often in the case of sexual abuse, women have the experience of feeling like their body was never fully theirs before it was claimed by someone else. When we teach our girls that their bodies are sacred vessels for spirit, we at least give them a strong and healthy baseline. Regardless of what may occur in their lives, they will always have this set point to fall back upon. In my years of working as a coach, I can say that a healthy baseline when it comes to a sense of ourselves, and who we are in relation to the larger world, is invaluable. The clients that I have coached who had some sense of their Higher Self at some point in their life prior to working with me had a much easier time returning to that knowing than the clients I had to introduce to themselves for the first time.

The last thing any mother wants to envision is her daughter being the victim of sexual abuse. And if you're reading this, you know that sometimes it happens anyway. Not thinking about it and not talking about it is not the way to avoid it from happening. Our daughters need to know that there are wolves in the world. Not just so that they can travel in a pack and protect themselves from them, but so they can become a wolf when they need to be. Wolves are wild creatures. Outside of actually putting our daughters into the wilderness for a time, connecting our daughters with their innate biological process is one of the best ways that I know of to return them to their wild nature. (There are also some fabulous, guided rites of passage ceremonies that include some kind of solo wilderness component, which we will talk about later.)

Wild things can be inconvenient and hard to tame. They push at boundaries and borders that we sometimes wish they wouldn't. They aren't obedient all the time - or ever. But this is where we have to ask ourselves as mothers what qualities we want to foster in our daughters. Do we want them to always be submissive? Do we want them to do everything they're told? Or do we want to ignite the spark of the wild within them? These are questions that only you as a mother can answer. But I entreat you to ask them.

I want to take us back to the drama triangle here for a minute. What if we were raised not believing that we are victims - of our culture or our bodies? While totally socially unacceptable to say, I can't help but wonder how much our unconscious beliefs and unconscious identification as victims, of our menses, our pregnancies, our births, and the patriarchal culture at large, play a part, however subtle, in the continuation of sexual violence.

Men do not get off the hook, and they 1000% need to be taught differently and held responsible for their actions. Rape should not be so hard to prove in court, and we need to believe survivors. Rape is never okay, and our boys and men need to know that drugging a woman and/or taking her by force is *never* an acceptable option, no matter what your friends say. At the same time, the kind of preparation for our girls that Simpson Rowe was undertaking is clearly effective against sexual coercion, and, I would hazard to say, therefore, essential.

I'm in no way suggesting that changing this narrative is an easy task. Almost everywhere you turn, there are very real reminders of this identification as either victim or sexual object. There are systemic abuses that happen every day to remind us that our lives and bodies are still property - of the medical establishment, of the courts, of our partners and spouses.

But what if our core operating belief about ourselves and our bodies was that we are sacred and deserve to be treated as such? What if we actually treated our bodies as such? What if we learned the language of our bodies deeply enough so that we could hold ourselves that way? What kind of impact might that have on the way we carry ourselves, the places we hang out, the people we spend time with, and the kinds of activities we engage in? What would a legion of women and girls embodying sovereignty do to the sexual violence statistics? There is no way to know, of course, and ultimately, it is not women's responsibility to stop men from raping. But wouldn't it be an interesting experiment? Can it hurt to try?

It is my hope and goal that by the time we are through here together, you feel equipped so that you can start to be the woman who carries herself as sacred - and that you can teach your daughter to do the same. For as we've mentioned, we can talk at our kids until we are blue in the face, but it is what we embody that they will learn the most from. Yes, there are suggestions and ideas of what to discuss with your child as she matures, and practical things to do - because we all love *doing*. But love it or not, how you hold yourself will speak volumes, and louder. When you carry and own yourself as a sacred woman, when you follow your intuitive impulses and act on instinct, you are teaching your daughter and the other young women in your life in the clearest way possible. This is our life work as women.

Will we always get it right? No. Will we fumble along the way of discovering a new way of inhabiting ourselves? Most certainly. Is there any guarantee that by doing this work our daughters will not go through some of the same struggles we did? No. Will it be our fault if we give it all we've got and something unfavorable happens to our child? No. Is it worth doing anyway? Unequivocally, yes.

Sex and Power

As a young woman, I was fascinated by the authority I could wield over men who were sexually entranced by me. I had some distorted idea that the more men I could get to sleep with me, the more powerful that meant I was. I have spoken to many women over the years who also had a similar storyline in their youth: sex meant control, and the more sex with more men they could have, the more accomplished they would be. There was also, of course, the delicate balance between having enough lovers to be accomplished, and being labeled a "slut," but as someone who had been the fat kid in school, for me getting men to sleep with me seemed the more potent avenue at the time.

Seduction did indeed feel very powerful at first. The ruse was that, at the end of the night, it was I who had willingly given my power away in this desire to exercise might over these men. I knew sex was compelling, and I knew it would bring me places if I used it. So I did. It didn't always bring me places - not that I actually wanted to be anyway. And in the process, I cheapened and chipped away at the integrity of my own being. I was left with a deep inner hollowness that I couldn't shake. It wasn't until I was in Hawaii, reclaiming my body, befriending my blood, and doing Ho'oponopono rituals to honor my womb that I finally started to restore some of that integrity.

I often wonder what my journey would have been like if my mother had had conversations with me about sex, power, and influence as I was growing up. I wonder how different my experience might have been if I had had solid female role models, other than just my mother, that I could confide in and talk to. Would I have felt the need to go through all of that?

Outside of my older brother telling me one night when I was 16 when we were smoking a joint together "don't let men use you as a toilet," (true story - thanks, Lazlo), and my grandmother's dying words to me of "don't give yourself away to men who don't care about you," (which, at the age of 12, just made me super uncomfortable to hear from my grandma), no one ever mentioned sex, power, or agency to me at all when I was growing up. And definitely no one ever told me what TO do - just what not to do. I knew that my dad would make creepy little "mmmhmmm" sounds at attractive women on TV and in public, and my mom would be visibly and audibly irritated by that. But there was no conversation about those exchanges and what they meant or didn't mean. I was left to interpret that on my own. How was I supposed to explore my budding sexuality in a healthy way if *no one*, outside of my peers who were in the same boat, would talk to me about it?

There is some level of needing to figure things out for oneself that is a healthy and essential part of adolescence and maturation. No matter how much we talk to our girls, we are not going to completely prevent them from experimenting and trying things out at some point that we may rather not think about, thank you very much. But having "I wish I had done things differently" or "I'm so grateful I learned _____" kinds of conversations with our girls as they grow older can go a long way. We are designed to learn from stories, and if we don't share the stories of our lives with our girls, then they can never learn from them.

The sexual objectification of women is one of the most ingenious ways the patriarchy has used our most powerful natural resource to keep us ensnared. And the truly brilliant part about it is that we have unconsciously been willing participants in our own captivity. We are trained from a very early age that if we are deemed sexually desirable by men, then we are more influential - which, unfortunately, is often true. We equate sex with power. In some cases, without sexual desirability, there is no entry - to the job, to the club, to the social circle. And there are *billions* of dollars invested in an industry deeply devoted to perpetuating this narrative.

The sad part of this is, when we fall in line with this fallacy, we end up giving all of that magnificent power away. It gets us places - oh, boy, does it get us places! But at what cost?

How do you want your daughter to be able to hold herself sexually? We like to pretend that our children will never grow up and have sex. They are so young and cute and innocent and we don't want to think of them that way. So let's just ignore the subject, push it back and back and back until it's so in our face, we just can't ignore it anymore. Hopefully, it has sunk in by now that, by that point, it is too late.

While we don't want to fall into the trap of sexual objectification, going too far in the other direction is not helpful, either. Let's not pretend sex isn't power, because it IS. It is the pure, raw, wild power of nature. But it doesn't have to be the power-over dynamic of domination and subjugation.

One of my favorite plays growing up was the Greek play *Lysistrata*. This play tells the tale of how Lysistrata stopped the Peloponnesian war by organizing with all the women of the warring cities of Athens and Sparta - wives and prostitutes alike - to refuse the men any sex until the war ended. It took approximately five days to end a war that had been going on for 30 years. So, yeah, sex is powerful.

Sex is the number one driving force of any species. Nature's drive is for growth, for creation. We are designed to reproduce, and the forces that drive reproduction in all species are some of the strongest forces on the planet. Sex has the power to create new life, to drive major life decisions, to blind us from important factual information, to build and create, to sell just about anything, to destroy families, and to topple empires.

When channeled positively, sex is vibrantly creative, regenerative, health-giving, and useful. When driven by shadow, perversion, and distortion, sex is exceedingly destructive - to our bodies, psyches, and spirits.

We don't want to hide the power of sex from our children. They can feel it. The more we try to hide and disguise it, the more intriguing it becomes for them. And the more we hide it or refuse to talk about it, the more driven into the shadow it becomes, where it is prone to perversion and distortion.

Sexual Violence and Predation

While I would never imply that being the victim of rape or violence is a woman's fault, EVER, I do believe that if we educate our girls differently, we will likely have dramatically different results in the statistics of sexual violence. In Peggy Orenstein's thoroughly researched book *Girls & Sex*, she refers to a pilot study that was being run by Lorelei Simpson Rowe, a clinical psychologist at Southern Methodist University. It's an accepted fact that around 80% of acts of sexual coercion and violence happen with someone the person knows. Based on this understanding, Simpson Rowe's pilot program ran simulations to train high school and college girls to successfully ward off the kinds of unwanted advances and pressure that tend to be responsible for the majority of occurrences of sexual coercion and violence.

Although the girls went into the study self-identifying as confident and capable young women, in trial runs of the simulation program, they froze when faced with this kind of coercion. So, while they felt confident in many other areas of their life, the skills to not freeze when faced with a potential predatory situation were simply not there for them. Once successfully completing the pilot, initial follow-up data showed that after a three-month period, participants in the program were *half as likely* to experience sexual victimization as the control group. In my view, those are some pretty compelling statistics.

In her book *Call of the Wild*, Kimberly Ann Johnson describes how each of us have inclinations either towards predator or prey within the makeup of our nervous systems. She does a wonderful job in her book of destigmatizing the predator response, which women can also be inclined towards. She also has fabulous exercises on how to engage your predator and know when you are in prey mode and when you are in predator mode from a nervous system response. I highly recommend this book as a resource to further your studies.

Over half of all women have experienced sexual coercion, abuse, or violence. That is a heavy statistic. You may be one of those women. And if you aren't, you definitely know a few - whether you are aware or not. I am one of them. So how do we protect our daughters without cloistering them from the world or inducing a tremendous amount of fear? How can we teach them in a way that doesn't lead us directly into the trap of the drama triangle?

I don't believe there is one simple answer to this question. As a mother of two daughters, this is something I think about a LOT. But I do believe that consistent conversation and education about bodies, pleasure, and sex is crucial to developing a deeper understanding in our children than we were likely raised with. I believe it is possible to raise our girls with a strong sense of themselves (and some hardy self-defense skills) without going into depth and detail about the intricacies of sexual violence with a 9 year old. Scaring our children in the hopes of protecting them is a surefire way to bring about a host of other problems. But so is keeping them entirely in the dark.

Naivety is a Turn-On For the Wrong Kinds of People

I will never forget a story shared with me years ago by a friend who had spent a period of time in an institution for mentally unstable individuals. Diagnosed with borderline personality disorder, this was a woman you didn't want to be on the wrong side of. (While we were quite close for some time, I did eventually end up on her bad side, and needless to say, we are no longer friends - but that is not the point of this story.) I remember her sharing with me once how at one point, when she had been institutionalized, she found herself alone in a room with a young man who was in this same institution because he was a serial rapist. She told me how, after his attempts at intimidating and coercing her to have sex with him failed, he bluntly and openly expressed to her why she would never be one of his targets. He told her how he could literally smell the fear on women, and that is what he was drawn to. It turned him on. The women who were fearful and unsure of themselves in response to his advances were his targets. He told her she was far too confident and expressive for him to therefore be attracted to her.

Sick, I know. Stories like this can bring up a lot for us - especially if we are survivors. How are you doing in this moment, Mama? Where's your breathing right now? How about your feet? Knowing that there are people like this out in the world can pop a bubble many of us like to walk around in, believing that everyone is good and kind.

Tribal law in many traditional cultures took care of individuals like this differently. Without jails or institutions like this one, having individuals like this around was simply not an option for cultures that relied on the health and safety of their communities for survival. A story Natem once shared with me was about the shrunken heads in his tribe, and how and why they were used. In the Shuar tribe, if someone was acting out of line - say, beating their wife, for example - a shrunken head would mysteriously arrive hanging at their door. This was considered a warning to the person - clean up your act, or you will be the next shrunken head. This was how they kept tribal law in a jungle full of things that could kill you at every turn. There was no space for additional threat from within the tribe. When I first encountered this kind of tribal law, it flipped my sense of reality on its head. While it may seem like a barbaric way to run a culture, (and please don't think that I'm insinuating we should be offing some of our kids) the resulting societies were overall peaceful and kind. In fact, Natem was one of the most genuine, sweet and sincere human beings I have ever met in my entire life. I have heard of other similar ways of keeping tribal law, that, while harsh upfront (especially for our modern sensibilities), produced some of the most peaceful overall societies.

These forms of tribal law were wiped out with the missionaries. They are part of what the colonizing people used as support for calling Indigenous people "savages." But if you consider that in Medieval Europe it was not uncommon to find yourself on a street lined with impaled body parts on sticks, it kind of makes you wonder which cultures, in fact, were the more savage ones? Tribal law merely places the emphasis of wellbeing on the community, rather than the individual. And the result was healthy societies.

Why Fear-Based Abstinence Education Doesn't Work

Back to sex. If it's not already clear, I do not promote an abstinence-based form of sexual education. Not because I have something against the concept of abstinence in-and-of-itself. I understand the draw and the concepts behind it, and I myself have had some really beautiful years of intentional abstinence that taught me a tremendous amount about myself. The problem with abstinence-based sex education with youth, however, is that there is no proof that this approach to sexual education is in any way effective. In fact, the proof is that the opposite is true. When we are told not to do something, we want to do that thing even more. This is especially true of teenagers.

According to Peggy Orenstein's research in her book *Girls & Sex*, of all the religious groups of teenagers in the US, evangelical Christian teens (who receive primarily abstinence based sex-ed) are the most sexually active of all.[17] On average, they lose their virginity younger and are less likely to protect themselves from sexually transmitted diseases or pregnancy. Of those who pledge not to have sex until marriage, males are 4 times more likely to engage in anal sex, and both males and females are 6 times more likely to have oral sex as teenagers. Orenstein writes, "The only lesson that sticks is that they remain less likely to use contraception and drastically less likely to protect against disease." Those who do successfully save themselves for marriage have reported serious shame and confusion around sex that lasts well into their married years, and has negative impacts on their relationships.

In 2018, I interviewed Nathan Novero, a former Bible Belt youth pastor, for my podcast *Sex, Love and Superpowers*.[18] As a youth pastor in his Southern Baptist evangelical church, he was a leader in the "True Love Waits" purity movement in the 90's. Teens in his church would make

---

[17] Girls & Sex: Navigating the Complicated New Landscape by Peggy Orenstein

[18] https://open.spotify.com/episode/1wRKmg6NnfZoOlnuOyhUCA?si=i3Girnn OQ/KcyTE1dXFXGA

abstinence pledges, promising - on paper - that they would not have sex until they got married. He shared about the giant rock concerts that were a foundational part of creating the culture that included the shame and guilt-based abstinence education for the youth.

He met the woman who would become his wife through the church, and they married young. (It has been shown that teens raised in the evangelical Christian, abstinence-based communities tend to marry much younger than their peers, which makes perfect sense. Teens want to have sex, and if marriage is the only way, then so be it. These communities also tend to have statistically higher divorce rates, which also comes as no surprise, if sexual desire is an unconscious and primary motivating factor in getting married in the first place.)

Navaro shared with me how both he and his wife thought that, once they were married, they would have a passionate and robust sex life, having saved and prepared themselves for exactly that. But nothing could have been further from the truth. They both had been so conditioned to believe that there was something sinful or shameful in enjoying their bodies that, even as a married couple, they were virtually unable to have sex. Their sexless marriage lasted 13 years, after which he moved to Los Angeles and became a film director and producer, and also began producing short, erotic art films he calls "Holy Erotica." This has been his way to find healing and reconciliation with the deeply negative sexual programming he received from his upbringing, and in his words, has been his true path to God. Navaro, who still identifies as a Christian via Christian mysticism, now believes that it is through the beauty and depth of feminine sexuality that Christianity will find a healthy bridge into embracing the world of sex as the holy and divine portal that he has now seen it can be.

Pleasure

One thing that has been consistently left out of the majority of education around sex is real-talk conversations about pleasure - specifically, female pleasure. There are entire generations of people globally who were educated about bodies out of textbooks that completely eliminated the clitoris from anatomical drawings. Ooops! Forgot that part! Which is ironic, considering that women are the only ones with an *entire organ* that serves no other function than our own enjoyment and pleasure. The result is that women have become seriously divorced from our pleasure. Male pleasure is a given, and female pleasure is an afterthought. This is a belief that both men and women carry.

In my research for this book, I found a fascinating study from Finland called "Determinants of female sexual orgasms" that stated that, on average, men orgasm more than 90% of the time in sexual encounters, contrasted with 50% of the time for women. The full results of this study? Well, you can read them for yourself:

"Contrary to expectations, women did not have orgasms that are more frequent by increasing their experience and practice of masturbation, or by experimenting with different partners in their lifetime. The keys to their more frequent orgasms lay in mental and relationship factors. These factors and capacities included orgasm importance, sexual desire, sexual self-esteem, and openness of sexual communication with partners. *Women valued their partner's orgasm more than their own.* (Italics mine.) In addition, positive determinants were the ability to concentrate, mutual sexual initiations, and partner's good sexual techniques. A relationship that felt good and worked well emotionally, and where sex was approached openly and appreciatively, promoted orgasms.[19]"

---

[19] https://www.ncbi.nlm.nih.gov/pmc/articles/PMC5087699/#:~:text=More%20than%2090%25%20of%20men,2001%3B%20Kontula%2C%202009),

Whew! There is A LOT to unpack in that one little paragraph. Orenstein mentioned this phenomenon I highlighted as well - that teen girls overall tend to be far more focused on their partner's pleasure than their own (even, and often particularly, in casual sexual encounters). When we break it down, what this means is that one of the main determining factors in women's general inability to climax comes from their and their sexual partners' lack of belief that they deserve to. Ouch.

What would it be like if we taught our daughters that pleasure - that *their* pleasure - was important? Looking at the results of this study, it seems like one of the most revolutionary things we can impart to our daughters. But where do we start?

I asked my friend Juliana Rose Goldstone, who is a Somatic Sex Educator based in Brattleboro, Vermont, to share her thoughts on teaching our daughters about pleasure. Here's what she had to say:

"The blueprint for our childrens' relationship to sex and pleasure begins to form at a very young age. As a mother, you hold prayers deep in your heart for your daughter to have beautiful and positive sexual experiences as she grows up. You pray for her relationship with pleasure to be one of joy and empowerment. But how do you offer that to her when you yourself are still healing from generations of sexual shame, violence, and oppression? How do we model a more holistic understanding of sex to our kids? One that values pleasure, consent, respect, and sovereignty when it was not necessarily modeled to us?

It begins by creating a pleasure-positive environment in our homes from the very beginning. And I don't just mean in how we respond to our children as they explore and touch their own bodies or genitals - though that is important also. Our children's sexuality is not something that just pops up out of nowhere overnight. It is a part of them from the very beginning, and it is expressed in different ways as they grow.

As young ones, our children express their sexuality through curiosity about new sensations, preferences around food or activities, and experimenting with how their big or rambunctious energy may or may not be received by the people around them. We could say that the three pillars of healthy sexuality at any age are curiosity, access to choice and voice (preference), and the ability to be seen in our authentic expression of who we are. My many years as a Somatic Sex Educator working with adults has validated this theory over and over again.

The notorious toddler years can be some of the most challenging for parents because this is when our childrens' instincts towards sovereignty really start to kick in. How you respond to your child's curiosity, choice and voice, and expression of their feelings, no matter how big or small, is crucial to how these parts of them will evolve into a healthily expressed sexuality later on.

So, notice what your child is curious about. Instead of snapping at them to take something out of their mouth, if it is a safe and clean object for them to explore, can you honor their curiosity and desire to feel new sensations in their body? Can you stay curious and ask them what they like so much about that food that they are demanding instead of the broccoli that you served them? Can you celebrate their tastes and love of that food even if they can't or shouldn't have it right now? Can you give them a choice of clothing to wear and truly honor the choice that they make? Can you gift them the experience to safely feel cold or hot or scared or sad or wild or silly in their bodies and see what the world echoes back to them without telling them to bundle up or sit down or be quiet?

Obviously, your child's safety is your number one priority. But I invite you to notice, is it really about "keeping them safe", or are they just wanting to have an experience that you were told was not okay to want somewhere along the way? Or, might it actually be about how it could reflect on you as a mom if you let them explore that? Take a deep breath with that one. This is vulnerable work that asks you to really look at yourself in the mirror.

Teaching our children about sex is so much more than one awkward "talk" on the way to school. Creating a home environment that honors our childrens' curiosity, innate sensuality, big wild energy, and choice and voice is how we begin to lay the scaffolding for a life of healthy sexuality from the very beginning."

Contrary to the distortions our society tries to sell us, it is not sex that holds the most power for us as women, but our willingness to claim our pleasure. A woman who is sexually attractive on the outside but completely divorced from her pleasure is not in her power. She is a shell of herself, operating on external cues and directives. A woman who knows her pleasure is magnetic, for she is the one who can access joy and playfulness, and open portals to other realms of existence through embodied pleasure.

Consent

Consent has made a big entrance into the sexuality conversation - for good reason. Non-consensual sexual encounters are what classify as sexual abuse and violence. I am glad that this conversation is becoming more common. It makes me happy to see the memes going around social media about not forcing your kids to hug people - even family (even you!) if they are not feeling like they want to. And, there is so, so much more nuance to

223

this conversation than what I am currently seeing out there in the mainstream.

Nikki Ananda is an Integrative Embodiment Coach and Feminine Mysteries Guide who supports women in reclaiming their personal power and, as she puts it, "embodying opulent radiance." (Yes, please!) She is a powerhouse in her field, and a fun and amazing woman, colleague and friend.

Having worked with women for many years, she's seen the nuance of how consent can play out in the female experience. Here's what she had to offer on the topic:

"We talk about consent with other people, but what is often overlooked is our relationship to consent with our own bodies. This simple practice is one of the most powerful practices that I have seen transform my clients' relationships with their own bodies and life itself. Before inserting a cup or a tampon, before moving into internal pleasure with our fingers or a toy, simply slow down to ask the body, "May I enter you?" and listen for the response. This is such a profound step towards healing the deep wounds that we all carry around premature penetration. Women are often surprised at first at how often the body will say "no" or "not yet" to their own request! And what we do with that "no" becomes an art form in itself.

This is the true art of learning consent. To be present in the moment, to learn to listen to what the body is open to or not open to, and to respect the response we are given. As we do this, we are creating more safety and trust in our body. We soften. From this place of grounded awareness, we become more empowered to advocate for what our body desires and where the boundaries are with other people. Our authentic and healthy boundaries are not fixed. They change moment to moment, always in motion. The only way we can ever truly cultivate safety in consent and boundaries without creating armor or hardening is to listen in the moment. It is from that place that we get to tap in deeply to the Feminine Mysteries and all the magic that dwells within for us."

I love what Nikki has to say here, and I agree with her wholeheartedly. Tuning into these messages in our own bodies is its own art form. It takes practice, especially if this is new for us. Sometimes our "no" or our "yes" can be a whisper. If we haven't been listening to ourselves for a long time, those signals get really quiet, as they don't have the experience of being honored anyway, so why bother? It takes listening to the whisper, honoring it, and following through without rationalizing why we can't right now, and doing that over and over again before those signals will get louder, clearer, and easier to read. And this extends far beyond just our experience with vaginal insertion. This is a worthy exploration to apply to every aspect of our life. It is a practice, and one of the most worthwhile practices there is.

As we learn how to honor consent in our own bodies, truly honoring it with our children becomes second-nature. And that is how they learn. They learn by us stopping when they say stop. By us modeling what it is to have a strong boundary about something. By asking them questions, tuning into their subtle cues that might be underneath their words or in their silence, and helping them to interpret those cues.

My years as a nanny and early childhood educator taught me that children do thrive when they have clear boundaries. But that is very different from having a controlling adult, hell-bent on being an authority figure. If you are like me and grew up in a household where authoritative parenting was the norm, and pleasure was considered unsafe, you might have a default "no" response when your kids ask to do just about anything. I found that "no" was, more often than not, my immediate response for most things, until I started to ask myself why? There is a difference between holding a clear and strong boundary out of respect and wisdom, and getting into a battle of wills with your child. I think my automatic "no" came from some unconscious idea that, as a parent, I was supposed to be "in charge", and that people in charge say no. When we can step out of an authoritative framework and are willing to slow down, tune into what our child is really asking for, converse with them, and be willing and able to switch course when provided with new information, we set the stage for a greater feeling of inner safety and help foster a sense of agency in our children, which is essential for successfully communicating our needs to others.

Porn

Yup. We've got to talk about this, too. If your child has access to a device that is hooked up to the internet (either their own or a friend's, sibling's or friend's sibling), their chances of seeing porn well before they are sexually active is pretty high. Even with parental controls on devices, it is possible for our children to stumble upon images that imprint a certain sexual throughline into their psyches. On social media, even on regular media, the explicit sexual displays that have become commonplace can border on pornographic. Western culture is a culture heavily influenced by the presence of pornography.

With few small exceptions, most commercial porn is objectifying of women at best, incredibly violent towards women at worst. In general, it perpetuates placing value and emphasis on male pleasure over female pleasure, and normalizes degradation and overt aggression towards women during sex. "Girl-on-girl" is one of the most watched categories of pornography,[20] which also seriously jeopardizes the legitimacy of true intimate lesbian relationships, as well as safety for lesbians, as it reduces them to a simple sexual fantasy for men's pleasure.

---

[20] The End of Gender: Debunking the myths about sex and identity in our society by Dr. Debra Soh

It's important that we talk to our kids about porn - what it is and what it *isn't*. According to a 2023 study done by Common Sense Media, "73% of teen respondents age 13 to 17 have watched pornography online—and more than half (54%) reported first seeing pornography by the time they reached the age of 13."[21] And almost half of those teens said that they felt porn gave them "helpful information" about sex.

There was some hopeful news that came from this study, too. The same study said that "Even as teens acknowledged learning about sex and sexuality from pornography, they were **far more likely to say they had learned a lot about sex from a parent, caregiver, or trusted adult (47%) than from pornography (27%)**. And while less than half (43%) of the teens in the research reported they've had conversations about pornography with a trusted adult, most who had these conversations said it encouraged them to find other ways to explore their sexuality besides pornography." Again, as with abstinence, we can see that talking to them about porn doesn't encourage them to watch more of it, but instead promotes the opposite.

So what *do* we tell them about it? Years ago, one of my friends gave my favorite response yet when she found out her teen son was watching pornography. She told him in no uncertain terms that porn was theater and had no bearing whatsoever to what sex in real life is, or what it should be. I love equating porn with theatrics, not only because it is the real truth, but because it also starts to detract from the pull to learn about "real" sex from watching it. These are paid actors, doing what they are doing because they are getting paid to do it. If they were following their own pleasure and a mutual respect for their partner(s), the sex would look very, very different.

---

[21] https://www.commonsensemedia.org/press-releases/new-report-reveals-truths-about-how-teens-engage-with-pornography#:~:text=The%20report%27s%20key%20findings%20highlight,first%20viewing%20pornography%20is%2012.

A Woman's Anatomy of Arousal by Sheri Winston is one of my favorite resources for information about the female body, and specifically female pleasure. I believe that everyone who has a female body or enjoys pleasuring a female body would benefit from reading this book. It is also chock full of beautifully random erotic pictures from historical archives. Having books like this, *The Kama Sutra*, the *Shunga* erotic scrolls of Japan, and *Sexual Secrets: Anatomy of Ecstasy* by Nik Douglas and Penny Slinger in your home gives your daughter a place to go to find information about sex and assure that it will be delivered in a sacred and pleasure-affirming way.

It was this last book, *Sexual Secrets*, which I discovered in my father's library as a young teen, that I credit for part of why I ended up on the path I have. Once I got over the initial horror that came with discovering such an explicit book in my dad's collection, I would page through it when no one was looking with rapt fascination. While I also watched some porn as a teen, I believe that having access to these very different images of sexuality than what we can generally find in porn planted a seed in my young mind as to what is possible when it comes to sex - and I wanted that. When my husband and I first started dating, we connected around a desire to explore and expand our horizons in the world of sacred sex and energy. For me, I can undoubtedly say that attracting a partner who was as committed to my own pleasure as I was came, in part, from the influence of this book on me as a teen.

Birth Control, Pregnancy and STDs

One of the biggest fears a lot of parents have is that if their daughters start having sex, they will get pregnant as teenagers and therefore "ruin their lives." While I won't start to get into the problematic societal issues that make teenage pregnancy completely taboo and stigmatized, I also would not want my teenage daughter to have a baby if that was not her express soul desire in life at that time.

So what do we do?

I am clearly a huge proponent of knowing the inner workings of our bodies intimately. I'm also deeply opposed to the use of hormonal birth control for a multitude of health reasons, some of which I have already shared. Outside of all the ways hormonal birth control wreaks havoc on our health and hormones, I'm also not a fan of birth control in teens especially, because it sends the false suggestion that they then don't need to use barrier methods of contraception once they become sexually active. Barrier methods of protection are the only known ways, other than total abstinence, to prevent sexually transmitted diseases.

The birth control pill was considered a revolution as far as women's liberation. Finally, instead of being damned to a life as a barefoot and pregnant homemaker, women could now take their fertility into their own hands, by chemically preventing it. I don't wish to diminish what it enabled us to do. As far as the feminist movement was concerned, the pill was what allowed us access into the workplace, side effects be damned. But side-effects there are. Headaches, breast tenderness, mood changes, nausea, acne, breakthrough bleeding mid-cycle, depression, fatigue, fluid retention, and low libido are just some in a laundry list of potential side effects of hormonal birth control. At the worst end of the spectrum, birth control side-effects can include blood clots that can lead to life-long debilitating conditions and, in some cases, death.[22]

---

[22] Everything Below the Waist: Why Healthcare Needs a Feminist Revolution by Jennifer Block

There's also the issue of infertility. While it has not been shown that the use of hormonal birth control alone causes infertility, it is often prescribed as a "treatment" for other problems like endometriosis and PCOS, masking symptoms which, when left untreated, can lead to infertility. It also makes us feel like we are doing something to address those issues, instead of getting at the root cause and actually healing ourselves. It can take up to a year, sometimes as long as 18 months or more, for fertility to return after long-term use of hormonal birth control. Women are also having their first babies later in life, which biologically introduces some more challenges to innate fertility, as we are designed to be most fertile in the late teenage years into the end of our 20s and early 30s. (This is by no means insinuating that women can't easily get pregnant in their later 30's or into their 40's, just highlighting that nature's design for the optimal fertility window is earlier than we are culturally lined-up with. That said, I find the term "geriatric pregnancy" being used to refer to women who are over 35 and pregnant to be highly offensive, and completely unnecessary.)

In desperation, women often turn to the drug Clomid during this 12-18 month waiting period after getting off birth control. Clomid, while encouraging the release of eggs from the ovary, also dries up the cervical mucus that is required to allow for sperm to travel to said eggs.[23] This is yet another case of medically-induced ridiculousness and the medical paradigm not understanding how all this stuff actually works (or understanding and not giving complete information to their patients because it's "all about that cash money").

Fertility is a marker of overall health and vitality for women in a certain age range. So, while we may not want our teenage daughters getting pregnant, we do want to be supporting their fertility as a health measure. The irony

---

[23] https://naturalwomanhood.org/pill-cause-infertility-yes-no/

of all of it is that we are not the ones who are fertile 365 days a year, men are. Women are fertile, on average, around 5-10 days out of our cycle at most. That's it. And there are very specific signs that our body gives us to alert us to that fertile window, if we know what to look for and how to pay attention.

While the Fertility Awareness Method (FAM) was largely dismissed by the liberal feminist movement as ineffective and merely a conservative Christian approach to birth control, it is actually the best way to know when you are fertile. Not to be confused with the Rhythm Method, which was based on the erroneous information that all women have a 28 day cycle and ovulate on day 14, FAM is highly effective. Using this information to prevent unwanted pregnancy has been shown to be as effective as hormonal birth control.[24] In my mind, there is nothing "conservative," or even political, about knowing what is going on in your body. It's just smart practice, and something I wish I had known about when I was younger.

Without the "egg white" cervical fluid we discussed in the 4 phases of the menstrual cycle section, a woman is not able to get pregnant naturally, as the sperm cannot survive in the vagina or travel into the uterus without it. Consistent tracking of your daily basal temperature first thing in the morning, along with analysis of the quality of your cervical fluid and cervical feel and positioning, can give you the information you need to be able to assess whether or not you are ovulating. While we covered some of the changes you can track and watch for in the 4 Phases of the Menstrual Cycle, a complete FAM education is outside of the scope of this book. My favorite books that go in-depth into how to use FAM successfully are in the recommended reading section.

---

[24] Taking Charge of Your Fertility by Toni Weschler, MPH

One of them is Toni Weschler's *Taking Charge of Your Fertility,* which has essentially become the bible on FAM. Lucky for us, she's also written a version for teens called *Cycle Savvy: The Smart Teen's Guide to the Mysteries of Her Body.* This is a great book to give your daughter once she has gone through a few menstrual cycles, and one you can use to help her read the signals her body is giving her. I believe that we can trust our daughters, and that when we give them our trust and respect as sovereign beings, they rise to meet that. Arming them with information about how to read their bodies is part of cultivating that trust.

All that said, FAM does nothing to help your daughter prevent contracting sexually transmitted diseases (STDs) once she becomes sexually active. Even in committed partnerships, STDs can occur. Knowing what they are, how to recognize them, and how to prevent them is, just like FAM, smart practice. Again, there is a serious stigma around STDs that leads us to avoid talking about them. This does nothing to help prevent the spread of infections, it just amplifies the shame associated with them. Being willing to talk about STDs with our children sends the message that this is a subject that is also okay and necessary to talk about with any sexual partners they might have in the future.

I haven't had explicit conversations with my 12 year old about STDs yet because I haven't felt it is necessary quite yet. She is nowhere near the stage of being sexually intimate with someone, and doesn't currently have easy avenues for that - she's not going to dances or parties, nor has she expressed any interest in a relationship outside of confiding to me that she has a crush, and those feelings are still uncomfortable for her. This is not true of all 12 year olds. If our circumstances were different - if she was different - I may have initiated this conversation with her already. I anticipate that over the next year or so, and definitely when she gets to high school, this will be the next evolution of the sex conversation for us. As with all the topics in this book, you will tailor the timing of this conversation to your specific child.

I think it's safe to say that most parents would probably prefer that their children wait to have sex until they are in a committed partnership. More conversation about sex and relationships throughout their youth can encourage a greater likelihood of that, as we work to reduce the shame and stigma around sex and desire. It's also important at a certain point in adolescence for us to trust that we've given our kids a solid foundation, and to start to let go of what they do when we aren't around. We have to start trusting them to have the experiences that are required for their soul's learning.

When it comes to STDs, let her know that if she brings up the idea of getting tested together with a potential partner and they have resistance to that, that partner is not someone she should be exchanging bodily fluids with. I strongly encourage normalizing STD testing once your daughter becomes sexually active, as many STDs don't present symptoms at first - sometimes not for quite a long time, until after irreversible damage has already been done.

I believe that if you follow the processes in this book and open a pathway for clear and open communication with your daughter, it will make you a safe zone for these conversations. The likelihood of her then telling you when she becomes sexually active is much higher. To help facilitate the STD conversation for you, I've gathered information about the most prevalent STDs in the US below.

When it comes to using conventional treatments for certain illnesses and disease, I tend to approach with caution, as many conventional treatments have side effects that natural remedies do not. For most things, like a fever or flu, trusting that this is a healthy signal from the body and that the fever is doing something necessary is the path I take. I give the body the support it needs to do the healing itself, usually through somatic inquiry, rest, nutrition, homeopathy, herbs and/or supplements.

For other more serious things, I will sometimes add a conventional approach to that list of natural treatments. For the three most prevalent STDs in the US listed below, the conventional treatment is antibiotics. The risk of these infections going untreated is so severe that this is a case where, if I were to contract any of them (or know my daughter had done so), I would absolutely go with antibiotics and focus on healing the gut afterwards.

Okay, here we go. Deep breaths! Take breaks if you need to, and try not to freak out too hard. Remember that conversation and prevention are key here. These are the 3 most prevalent STDs in the US today:

Chlamydia - Chlamydia is the #1 most prevalent STD in the US, and if left untreated, can cause permanent damage to a woman's reproductive tract.[25] Oftentimes, it doesn't present with any symptoms at all, which is part of why it is so widespread. Symptoms of chlamydia include burning during urination and abnormal yellow or greenish vaginal discharge, cramping, and occasional bleeding after intercourse.[26] Chlamydia can be contracted with any genital contact, including through oral or anal sex. Testing for chlamydia can be done easily nowadays at home, without the need for scheduling with a doctor or clinic.

---

[25] https://www.cdc.gov/nchhstp/newsroom/docs/factsheets/std-trends-508.pdf

[26] Sex, Love and Health: A Self-Help Sex Guide to Love & Health by Brigitte Mars

The risks of untreated chlamydia are permanent damage to the reproductive organs and pelvic inflammatory disease. If I found out that I or my daughter had it, and if trying a week or two-long intensive treatment with goldenseal root didn't, after a repeat test, show that the infection was completely cleared from the body, I would opt for a round of antibiotics. Everyone will have to make their own choice, but for me, that is a risk I wouldn't want to take, especially if I still had my childbearing years ahead of me.

Gonorrhea - The second most prevalent STD in the US, gonorrhea can also present with no symptoms. If the symptoms do manifest, they usually do so in women about two weeks after contracting the disease. Symptoms include painful urination and a greenish yellow discharge, bleeding between periods, and inflammation of the cervix. Gonorrhea is spread through sexual contact with the penis, vagina, mouth, or anus of an infected person. Untreated gonorrhea can lead to chronic pain, tubal pregnancy, and pelvic inflammatory disease. It is rare, but gonorrhea can also spread to the heart, brain, and joints. This is another one where antibiotics are the course of treatment and might even require multiple rounds, as gonorrhea has been known to have a high rate of recurrence.[27]

Syphilis - Yup! It's still around and is actually the third most prevalent STD in the US, though it is rarely fatal anymore because of treatment options. Typically progressing through 4 stages, the first stage includes the development of a painless, small, hard lesion, known as a chancre, between 10 days and 12 weeks after exposure. This lesion usually presents on the penis, vagina, or rectum but can also appear on the face or hands. Direct contact with this lesion, usually through oral, vaginal, or anal sex, is how the disease is spread. Close contact of any kind with the chancres can spread the disease.

---

[27] Sex, Love and Health: A Self-Help Sex Guide to Love & Health by Brigitte Mars

Several weeks after the first chancre appears, the second stage sets in. Sometimes there are no symptoms in this stage, but if they do appear, they are flu-like in nature and can include fever, fatigue, joint pain, swollen glands, headache, and a rash on the feet and hands. Concurrently, multiple lesions may form in the mouth, throat, rectum, and vagina. This is the most contagious stage of the disease, as the lesions are what secrete the bacteria.[28]

In the third stage, the disease can seem to disappear, and for many, it will not progress further than this. For others, it can resurface years later and fatally cause irreversible damage to all the major organs in the body. Again, the treatment for syphilis is early detection and antibiotics.

HIV/AIDS - Like many STDs, the symptoms of HIV might not appear for a long time - in some cases as long as 10 years - at which point it has usually become full-blown AIDS.[29] In people with early symptoms, they generally appear 2-4 weeks after infection and present with flu-like symptoms - fever, chills, sweating, fatigue, swollen glands, and body aches. According to the Planned Parenthood website, symptoms of AIDS can include: thrush, sore throat, recurrent bad yeast infections and infections in general, feeling tired, dizzy and lightheaded, headaches, rapid weight loss, chronic pelvic inflammatory disease, swollen glands in the throat, armpit or groin, shortness of breath, purple growths on the skin or inside of the mouth, deep dry coughing spells, skin rashes, long bouts of diarrhea, night sweats, numbness in the extremities, and loss of muscular and reflex control.

---

[28] Sex, Love and Health: A Self-Help Sex Guide to Love & Health by Brigitte Mars

[29] https://www.plannedparenthood.org/learn/stds-hiv-safer-sex/hiv-aids/what-are-symptoms-hivaids#:~:text=You%20may%20not%20have%20any,that%27s%20when%20HIV%20becomes%20AIDs.

When I was growing up, the AIDS epidemic was in full swing. The gay community was dying in droves from this horrible disease, and there were huge campaigns to combat the spread. Because of this, AIDS has been associated as a disease that attacks mainly gay people and drug users, but this is not the case - anyone can contract the disease if they come into contact with infected blood, semen, or vaginal fluids. While it is still a problem and deserves conversation and proper protection, the death rate for full-blown AIDS has significantly decreased since I was younger. While it is not considered curable, new ways to manage the disease have since been found that lead to greater success and quality of life, as well as a smaller chance of transmitting it to others if it is caught and treated early.[30] Focusing on supporting the immune system can allow a person with the HIV virus to live a relatively long life, as this is a virus that attacks the immune system and its ability to fight infection.

Other common STDs are: genital warts (caused by the HPV virus), pubic lice (commonly referred to as "crabs"), hepatitis, herpes, and trichomonias, all of which can be successfully treated with natural remedies. In her book *Sex, Love and Health: A Self-Help Health Guide to Love & Sex*, Brigitte Mars has some comprehensive nutritional, herbal, and supplement suggestions, as well as mindset suggestions for treating various STDs if this is something you are interested in learning more about.

Again, the only sure-fire way to prevent STDs outside of abstinence is by using barrier methods of contraception, namely condoms and dental dams. Easy access to condoms can make the difference in whether or not

---

[30] https://www.plannedparenthood.org/learn/stds-hiv-safer-sex/hiv-aids/what-are-symptoms-hivaids#:~:text=You%20may%20not%20have%20any,that%27s%20when%20HIV%20becomes%20AIDs.

your daughter contracts any of these diseases, so for me, making them available without question is a no-brainer. You may want to know in advance if your daughter is allergic to latex, however, as irritation and itchy rashes can occur with contact with latex. (There are a few brands out there that offer non-latex condoms.)

When I was younger and having a lot of casual sex, I used to carry around an Altoid tin with me in my purse wherever I went. In the tin, instead of mints, were a couple of condoms and a single-use, water-based lube packet. Being in a hard case ensured that my condoms didn't accidentally get punctured by random pens and things in my bag, and having them with me all the time meant that I never found myself unexpectedly in the heat of the moment and unprepared. I can gratefully say that I never contracted an STD, even with my 20+ sexual partners from that time period. With STDs, preparedness is key to prevention.

Social Media and Online Grooming

We don't do a lot of screen time with our kids in our house in general - maybe a couple of hours a week, if that. When I worked as an early childhood educator, it was quickly evident to me which kids had a lot of screen time and which didn't based on their play. The children who didn't consume a lot of media were far more creative in their play, and willing to try new things and create new characters, whereas those who clearly watched a lot of TV would be more static and repetitive in their play, doing the same thing and playing the same character over and over.

Sunna does not have a cell phone. She will not have a cell phone for quite some time, and if she does get one, it will not have apps connected to it. She has an ipad which we carefully monitor, and she does have Messenger Kids so that she can stay connected with her friends from back East, which has been a very sweet and positive thing for her. My husband and I felt comfortable with this compromise because of the intensive controls that Messenger Kids offer us as parents, as it allows us to see and manage who she is communicating with. (We have it set so that we have to approve every friend she is connected with on the app.) We also found that, due to these controls, the benefits of being able to connect with her friends who she can't see regularly far outweighed any risks we could identify. We are clear that she is not connecting with friends from school on that app, only ones who are far away and whom she can't otherwise easily connect with. I am, like with all the other topics in here, very clear and open with my daughter about why I feel the way I do, and why we have made the choices that we have when it comes to tech.

For me, low tech with kids is a hard and fast boundary. It may seem extreme to some, but there are few things in life that I feel clearer and stronger about than this. I have seen no research that suggests any positive benefits to the increased presence of technology in our children's lives that can't also be achieved, with more lasting success and positive impact, from contact with a loving and supportive community of in-person people, and/or more unstructured time in nature. Kids that are deeply woven into the web of tech spend less time outside and are far less able to have successful and meaningful social interactions with other humans in real time, neither of which are good things.

When it comes to social media platforms, I see no positive reason for a young girl to be on them. Not one that holds any weight against the myriad of negative ones, anyway. The research is unabashedly clear. Rates of depression and suicide, cyber bullying, body dysmorphia, low self-image and eating disorders is exceedingly higher in teens who actively engage in social media platforms, including gaming sites. This is particularly true of teen girls. Keeping a clear and strong boundary in this arena means knowing who is in your community and surrounding yourself with like-minded parents who are all willing to adhere to a similar ethic. Peer pressure in the area of technology can lead to some serious backlash for you from your child, if you are attempting a low-tech experience outside of a supportive community. I am immensely grateful to our Waldorf community for providing a container that, while still imperfect, at least has a greater measure of understanding around all of this.

In addition to the above-listed issues, teenage girls who have social media profiles are also more likely to become targets for what is known as online grooming. This is where an older person, generally male, will slide into her DMs. Often they will pretend to be of a similar age, "befriend" her, and then either send her unwanted graphic sexual images, coerce her into sending him nude pictures of herself, and/or lead her into meeting in real life, where she then becomes a victim of sexual abuse and/or trafficking. The psychological manipulation skills of some of these online groomers is not to be underestimated.

According to the Child Crime Prevention and Safety Center (CCPSC), children between the ages of 12 and 15 are the most susceptible to online grooming and predation.[31] The CCPSC also states that 89% of online predatory behavior happens either in internet or gaming chat rooms, or through instant messaging. Snapchat and Meta platforms (Facebook, Whatsapp and Instagram) are where 73% of online grooming crimes were committed in 2023, according to the NSPCC in the UK, and the overall rate of these crimes has gone up 82% in the last 5 years.[32] It is our job as parents to educate our children about this and stop giving predators such

---

[31] https://childsafety.losangelescriminallawyer.pro/children-and-grooming-online-predators.html

[32] https://www.nspcc.org.uk/about-us/news-opinion/2023/2023-08-14-82-rise-in-online-grooming-crimes-against-children-in-the-last-5-years/

easy access to our kids. Using these statistics and gathering together a group of parents to agree that you won't allow your kids to roam free on the internet or on social media until at least the age of 16 seems like a wise choice in the face of this kind of information. There is absolutely no need for children younger than that to be on social media of any kind.

The majority of parents have no clue what their kids are up to online (the stats I found were that between 7 and 15% of parents know the details of their children's online behavior, including if they have been groomed or not).[33] The natural world and physical reality are the best possible teachers we can give our young children. They can learn the tech later, when their brains are more developed and ready to incorporate it, and they can handle concepts like digital citizenship and moral ethics. Young kids just can't. And they shouldn't have to. None of the big tech giants let their children use their platforms. So why should we?

Sexual Orientation and Gender Identity

Some people are same-sex attracted. It has always been that way and is a normal variation of nature. Normalizing that some people are attracted to the same sex is healthy, and I would seriously hope that it's something you do in your home. If our children are attracted to the same sex or are questioning their sexuality but don't feel like it's okay to talk to us about it, let alone have those feelings, it drives them to find solace and community in other places. Often that looks like engaging in the above-mentioned online forums. Don't just assume your child is heterosexual. Depression and suicide rates are so much higher in LGBTQ teens, in big part because

---

[33] https://legaljobs.io/blog/online-predators-statistics#:~:text=66.7%25%20of%20 online%20predators%27%20victims%20are%20female.,-(Screen%20and%20Reveal &text=Similarly%2C%2077%25%20of%20offenders%20target,based%20sexual%20ab use%20(60%25)

of the lack of love and support they receive from their families and communities.[34]

Bullying and violence against this or any community is heartbreaking, and we would do well to teach our children that, above all, we treat people with kindness and respect no matter how different from us they might be.

Often in the LGBTQ community, there are also other concurrent mental health issues that, unfortunately, don't always get addressed nowadays due to the increasing focus in our society on transition as the sole solution to the pain of gender dysphoria and confusion in children and adolescents. "Emotional reasoning" is a term used to describe a cognitive distortion, whereby an individual concludes that their emotional response to something proves it to be true, despite empirical evidence to the contrary. The prevalence of emotional reasoning now being accepted as motivation for sweeping political policy change has contributed to this unfortunate phenomenon in the LGBTQ community and elsewhere, as Jonathan Haidt and Gregory Lukianoff discuss in their brilliant book *The Coddling of the American Mind*.

I grew up during the gay liberation movement in the 90s. As a tween and teen, I was marching in the streets for gay marriage rights, going to the BAGLY (Boston Area Gay and Lesbian Youth) prom and drag shows, and some of my best friends were gay men, lesbians, and bisexuals. I was an active member of our school's GSA (back then, we just had the Gay Straight Alliance) and was openly "out" as bisexual by 8th grade. I wore black lipstick and studded dog collars, and had a wide variety of colors of Manic Panic hair dye. The only time I ever woke up before sunrise in high

---

[34] https://www.thetrevorproject.org/resources/article/facts-about-lgbtq-youth-suicide/

school was to stand outside in the freezing cold in order to get $25 front row tickets to see the live musical "RENT." I took a girl to my high school prom. The gay artist community was my community, and I wouldn't be who I am today without those formative years.

I still have several friends from that community, and Sunna has grown up knowing that sometimes women love other women and men love other men. It's not a big deal - it's a known fact and just a normal part of the world in her eyes. It's led to some interesting conversations about virginity recently. (If a lesbian is never penetrated by a penis but has been sexually intimate with another woman, is she a virgin? I would say no, and likely so would she). This, in my mind, is *very* different than opening up a whole conversation around gender identity and gender as a construct, though Sunna does know that sometimes there are people born as women who feel male and vice-versa. Outside of that fact, I have found the gender conversation to be particularly vague and confusing for children (also, to be honest, for most adults). It is also scientifically inaccurate, as Dr. Debra Soh so rationally explains in her book *The End of Gender: Debunking the Myths About Sex and Identity in Our Society.*

When we first moved to our current home, in the middle of the pandemic, Sunna went to a different school than her current Waldorf school. This school prided itself on being a bastion of "progressive education." But we found that Sunna was having major anxiety and panic attacks almost daily after starting out there. Over the course of a few months, several children in her class started to change their pronouns, based on invitation and en-couragement from the class teachers and school culture. Sunna would come home from school warily questioning whether or not she was actu-ally a girl, wondering if she should still use the same pronouns, and becom-ing deeply concerned and anxious about potentially "misgendering" someone at school. She was in 4th grade at the time.

While the pronoun conversation was not the only factor in our decision to change schools, we did finally decide after the first semester to switch to the Waldorf school instead. While respectful, accepting, and welcoming of people of all walks of life, her current school does not place the same emphasis on pronouns that this first school did, even though there are a few people in that small community who are non-binary or gender non-conforming. Sunna's anxiety disappeared almost overnight once we transferred her to this new school, even though it was a new school for her and she didn't yet know anyone.

In addition to being vague and confusing, most conversations I have seen about trans ideology, including ones in well-meaning books geared towards children, instead of breaking down gender stereotypes, tend to reinforce them instead. How can we say that you can be a girl and be drawn to any activity on one hand, but on the other hand, if you are a boy and like wearing dresses and nail polish - and have ever since you were young - then you must be a girl? Why can't you just be a boy who is also gay?

Why is a woman who loves other women and is more masculine in her presentation now encouraged to go by "they," even if that pronoun usage is not true for her? One of my dearest friends is very masculine in her presentation, and for the majority of her life has been confused for a man. She often describes herself as having both male and female inside of her. She loves women. She is a she, though, and she's clear about that, though now many will misgender her as "they" by default assumption.

In the quest to "dismantle the gender binary", all I have seen this conversation do is strengthen a very different binary: either you agree wholeheartedly with everything the trans movement has to say, or you are contributing to the deaths of trans people - specifically children. The blanket label of TERF (which stands for Trans Exclusionary Reactionary

Feminist) allows people to completely throw out any kind of conversation with someone presenting an alternative viewpoint. Where is the room for nuance or critical thinking in that kind of rhetoric?

Also, where is the data to support the party line that if they aren't allowed to transition, children will kill themselves? Suicide is a complex issue, often with multiple mental health challenges accompanying it. Gender dysphoria tends to present with several other mental health comorbidities. Is focusing on transitioning as the primary treatment actually changing suicide rates amongst trans youth? The hard data seems to suggest it is not. Countries like Sweden have reasoned that, based on recent research, the health risks of giving children puberty blockers far outweighs the potential benefits.[35] While they have not banned the use of cross-sex hormones and puberty blockers in extreme cases of childhood gender dysphoria in Sweden, they are now prioritizing therapy as a more valid and effective approach.

This is a complex topic with A LOT of layers, and if we are not willing to hold nuance, to question, to investigate deeply our own biases and programming, including from the counterculture, and listen to the voices, concerns, and opinions of people on all sides of the issue, then I don't believe we should be discussing it.

Nowhere have I seen the suppression of dissenting voices be more pronounced in regards to this issue than in all-women spaces. Women's sports, for example, were created as their own category because of the fact that individuals who have undergone male puberty have physical changes that give them significant physical advantages. But women who have a

---

[35] https://segm.org/segm-summary-sweden-prioritizes-therapy-curbs-hormones-for-gender-dysphoric-youth

problem with male-to-female trans people entering into their sports and dominating the field are deemed TERFs, silenced as bigots, and receive threats that their athletic career will be ruined if they speak out.

Women have found solace and strength from gathering with other women since the beginning of time. It has actually been shown that a woman's physical health suffers when she doesn't get regular social time with other women. As anyone who has sat in a women's circle knows, they are profound places of healing and transformation. Powerful work gets done when women come together for their own healing. What we are seeing now in women's spaces is a growing trend that views women gathering together, without being willing to include men who identify as women in the space, as bigoted and insensitive. In some places, the vitriol has been so intense that I personally know women who stopped doing their work - work that positively changed the lives of hundreds of women - because of it. In other places, women continue to hold their ground but risk being "canceled," bullied, and in some cases, receive death threats.

While on the whole, I am a fierce advocate for all-women's spaces being just that, I have actually led a moonlodge once where a trans woman was welcomed in. In this particular case, it felt very good and right to all present to allow her in, and we discussed it as a community ahead of time without her present, making it clear that if even one woman objected or felt uncomfortable that we would not do it. I believe that this is something to be assessed on an individual, case-by-case, community-by-community basis. But that involves open dialogue and being willing to hold nuanced and difficult conversations as adult women, without resorting immediately to name-calling, screaming matches, and death threats.

If someone holds a boundary and you have feelings in response to that, it is not the person's job to change their boundary to accommodate your feelings. It is your job to learn how to deal with your uncomfortable feelings, which admittedly sucks sometimes. But if I need someone else to change in order to feel okay, unless that person is actually bullying or physically harming me, then I am the one contributing to an emotionally manipulative and potentially abusive dynamic. It seems to me that this is what we are now witnessing on a grand scale.

In some circles, it is no longer acceptable to refer accurately to female body parts and biological processes. Breastfeeding is now chest feeding, birthing women is being replaced with the term birthing person in many places, and the word woman is being co-opted, and in some places, erased entirely. In some circles, "inclusivity" means no longer using the word woman because it might hurt someone's feelings and make them feel like they don't belong. This is not saving anyone's life. It is a collective delusion which borders on insanity and is unabashedly misogynistic in origin, as this standard is rarely, if ever, applied to using the word man.

I was at a ceremonial gathering recently where I was on the team helping to lead and facilitate. Before meals, in line with teachings I have received, elders, children, pregnant, nursing, and mooning women are encouraged to stand at the front of the line to get their food so they can eat first. Elders can even sit and have a plate delivered to them by a younger person if they wish. This beautiful practice acknowledges that there are not only often very real physical differences in these populations that make giving them food first a kind and respectful thing to do, but also honors their very important place in ceremonial society. When making the announcement about "mooning women" at this gathering, I was asked to change it to "mooning people" in order to be more inclusive. When I said that I would not take the word woman out of my vocabulary, but would say "mooning women, and people" in order to acknowledge the non-binary people

247

present, someone else who would just say "mooning people" was asked to make the announcement instead. Is this what progressive feminism has come to?

If a girl with significant trauma looks around at the world and doesn't resonate with the overly-sexualized options she sees for what it means to be a woman, or with the socially accepted traumatic after-effects of medicalized birth, and the cultural marginalization of motherhood, or with the prevalence of rape and sexual assault (#MeToo), or with the fact that women still have not occupied the highest levels of political office in most countries, or that her body is not in fact actually hers because it can be legislated by the government, or she prefers sports to playing with dolls, getting her knees skinned and climbing trees to playing house, or for a variety of reasons, she just feels damn uncomfortable in her body, maybe she won't feel like she is or wants to be a woman. Obviously, being a man is still a more powerful position in today's society. Does that mean she should have surgery and take cross-sex hormones? Or does it mean we have some serious work to do in how we STILL, in 2024, treat women?

Similarly, if a boy does not resonate with superhero, businessman, politician, or warrior ideology, he could easily say that he doesn't feel like a boy. Again, does this automatically necessitate hormones and surgery? What if he's just gay? Maybe, instead, it requires us to make more space in the conversation about what the healthy masculine can look like and encompass. What does it actually mean when a young child, who cannot yet articulate complex internal emotional processes, says they don't "feel" like the sex they were born as?

Four decades of research shows that the vast majority of children that present with gender dysphoria, in some studies as many as 90%, will simply just end up becoming gay adults.[36] And the relatively new phenomenon of rapid-onset gender dysphoria, when seemingly out of nowhere, with no history of any kind of gender dysphoric expressions in childhood, a person (usually female) decides to change their pronouns and transition their gender *after* the completion of puberty, has been shown to have very real social contagion elements.[37] Essentially, peer pressure and influence, exacerbated by time spent online. This social contagion element is what concerns me the most, when we are talking about our children making irreversible changes to their bodies as a result. I'm not denying that gender dysphoria can be a very real and painful problem for some people, or even that some adults have been shown to benefit tremendously from undergoing transition surgery. That fact deserves space, too.

At the same time, however, in many places in the western world today, proper mental health screening before being prescribed hormones is being thrown out the window because the scientific and medical experts are afraid to speak up about what they know in the current political climate. They are concerned they will lose their careers and reputation, as they have seen happen to those who have been courageous enough to come forward. People in academia are losing their jobs and being silenced for telling the truth. This is actually happening, and it is happening now, in 2024. Because of this, a new precedent has been set: the "experts" advising the dispensing of medication have, in many places, been replaced by trans activists instead of trained scientists and medical doctors. While it is claimed that the effects of these drugs are "completely reversible", the evidence is to the contrary. Some effects, such as a lowered voice in

---

[36] The End of Gender: Debunking the myths about sex and identity in our society by Dr. Debra Soh

[37] https://journals.plos.org/plosone/article?id=10.1371/journal.pone.0202330

females who have taken cross-sex hormones, are lifelong. Others, like early onset osteoporosis, while reversible, are pretty damn serious. While more research is needed, it is also likely that the longer a person is on these drugs, the higher their chances are of getting cancer.[38]

The rates of "detransitioners" - people who transition back to their birth sex after socially or chemically and/or surgically altering their gender expression - is rapidly rising. Most detransitioners today were born female and are simply lesbians or struggling with sexual abuse trauma, or both, and didn't know how else to cope. Many are also on the autism spectrum.[39] Are pronouns, drugs, and surgery really the solution in this case?

After I came out as bisexual in 8th grade, I had about a year where the only people I was attracted to were female. This led me to believe that I must be a lesbian. So I came out again, this time as a "femme" lesbian (I liked wearing dresses and skirts too much to ever identify as "butch"). I do believe that some of this was due to social influence and my involvement with the gay community (whom I absolutely loved, btw). I also felt like maybe calling myself a full-on lesbian instead of just bi would somehow give me more "clout" in that community, and, therefore, social power. Or at least clarity. Or something. A year later, though, I recognized that the title of lesbian wasn't actually true for me. I was still also attracted to men. But I felt a little bit like I had backed myself into a corner identity-wise. This was all, thank god, before the advent of social media and smartphones. I have no idea what I would have done had I been raised in the current, gender-questioning climate.

---

[38] https://www.ncbi.nlm.nih.gov/pmc/articles/PMC5868281/

[39] The End of Gender: Debunking the myths about sex and identity in our society by Dr. Debra Soh

This experience led to my relatively young realization that identification based on sexual preference was inherently flawed, though I deeply understand and appreciate that we have a cultural problem with just accepting people for who they are, regardless of who they love. Instead, at 16, I gradually just stopped identifying as anything but myself and let people forget I had ever called myself a lesbian. Even though, in adulthood, I have still sometimes found myself attracted to women, I don't identify as any specific sexual orientation. I am just me. I am married to a man, so people just assume I am heterosexual, and I let people believe whatever they want.

Trans people are real and valid human beings who deserve all the human rights, just like everyone else. I don't begrudge anyone their sexual preferences, nor do I claim to know what it's like in another person's lived experience. But the aggressive political ideology surrounding the current trans movement gives me pause. The fact that anyone voicing any kind of alternative viewpoint is immediately shut down and blamed for "killing trans people" is bordering on authoritarianism and is, ironically, giving fuel to the fire of the very people being so goddamn awful to trans folx. I feel pretty clear that for me and *many* other women that I have talked to, the experience of being a woman specifically is centered primarily around being born with a womb and all of the amazingly sacred and sometimes challenging things that come along with that that we have discussed so far. Dresses, makeup, and nail polish have nothing to do with it. But we aren't allowed to say that anymore.

It seems like playing around with pronouns and gender identity is this generation's version of finding a way to express their individuality. At face value, I have no issues with that. I believe in pushing the bounds of reality, of exploring new realms, and, if not already obvious, challenging the status quo. I am definitely someone who has always felt "different", and there was a time where it felt important for me to be very loud and expressive about that. That can be a harmless and essential part of individuation in adolescence and early adulthood. If there was no tie to a potential money trail for big pharma, the whole thing would seem akin to the free love movement of the hippies in the 60s and the gay rights movement of the 90s. But there is a tie.

If you follow the money, the industry of body modification associated with the trans movement over the last 20 years financially serves the interests of the pharmaceutical and surgical industries, which is, in my estimation, why this social justice movement, far more than the women's or black liberation movements, not to mention the Missing and Murdered Indigenous Women's cause, has taken off with such aggressive fervor. There is A LOT of money behind it. I really struggle to trust a narrative or movement that has such a clear money trail. If we genuinely want to break down gender stereotypes, I don't believe it requires chemically or surgically altering our physiology in ways that tend to lead to profound, long-term, physical harm for the person undergoing the treatment. The obsessive need to continually modify our bodies, whether through dieting and exercise or revisionist surgery, is another perpetuation of misogynist thinking that denounces the sacred perfection of the body as it is; as it was designed. The body is the part of us that is earth, and it is not lost on me that here we have another movement devoted to pathologizing the body's inherent perfection.

The argument that Indigenous tribes recognized several different genders is incomplete at best. Indigenous communities are where I have encountered the most pronounced expressions of the gender binary. Many Indigenous cultures hold the binary as sacred, and there are rules and laws that are sacred that govern each sex, respectively. Some languages even have different words and phraseology they use when they are addressing men vs when they are addressing women. It is true that it has always been recognized in many of these societies that there are some people who embody more of an energetic that belongs to the opposite sex. These societies also tend to be kinder and more welcoming of everyone in their humanity, as we all should be. But the recognition that male and female bodies are different and, therefore, those inhabiting them receive different spiritual instructions exists in all the tribes I have ever encountered.

We have already discussed the ubiquitous nature of endocrine disrupting chemicals in our environment. It is also true that the use and strength of prenatal ultrasounds has skyrocketed over the last 30-40 years. Research from China has shown that prenatal ultrasounds can cause a whole host of health issues, including Autism, ADHD, genetic damage, allergies, and personality anomalies - issues that tend to appear as comorbidities in individuals with gender dysphoria and rapid onset gender dysphoria.[40] The EWG's downloadable PDF guide to endocrine disrupting chemicals starts with this question: "Have you heard about the male frog exposed to an herbicide found in tap water and how it ended up with female anatomy?" Who, exactly, do you think benefits from us not investigating the potential impact of ultrasounds and endocrine disrupting pollutants on intersex and gender questioning individuals, instead making it into a political movement that has us becoming vehement and aggressive with one another in a way that makes critical thinking and discussion impossible? I don't think it's us.

Part of the problem with this whole conversation and why it gets so heated so quickly stems from the use of the word identity. We are so much more than what can fit into the confines of a human body. Our spirits are vast and cannot be squashed into these little human forms. What biology we

---

[40] https://www.thehealthyhomeeconomist.com/50-in-utero-human-studies-confirm-risks-prenatal-ultrasound/

253

are born with and who we are as spiritual beings are two very different topics. In a sense, I do think that is what some people are trying to express when they call themselves "non-binary." In the ancient language of Aramaic, which is the language Jesus spoke, according to Aramaic scholar Neil Douglas-Klotz, the direct translation for the word God from Aramaic to English is "Birther, Father-Mother of the Cosmos." The divine is not gendered, and we are all precious children of the Creator, no matter how we identify. I often wonder, if more of us recognized that divinity as our true identity and the true identity of everyone else, would we even need to keep having conversations about gender ideology?

All that said, kindness rules in our house. Regardless of what someone is or isn't, says they are or says they aren't, the number one rule we follow is kindness. As I told my daughter the other day, everyone is fighting a struggle we can't see. We are all precious children of the Creator. If someone tells you that they use a certain pronoun or go by a certain name, call them that. That's a kind thing to do. If someone accidentally calls you something different from your preference, give them the benefit of the doubt and remind them. That's a kind thing to do. I don't think it has to be that complicated. Just don't be a jerk - whether someone agrees with your ideology or not. We are not all going to agree about everything. That's an important lesson too. How we treat one another, regardless, is what ultimately matters.

Exercise: Reparenting Our Pleasure

This exercise comes from my friend and Somatic Sex educator, Juliana Rose Goldstone. So grab your journal and dive in!

As we begin to shift our perspectives into a more pleasure positive approach to parenting, it will inevitably bring up the healing that we need to do for ourselves around all of the ways that our own big energy, our innocent curiosity, and our early expressions of sensuality or pleasure were shut down or shamed by adults that did not have this same understanding. With this work can come a lot of grief or anger, but this is where we heal our sexual lineage backwards and forwards, and resource ourselves to offer something different and better to our daughters.

Let these journal prompts be a reclamation, a reparenting, and a calling home of the innocent and curious parts that were exiled. Let your writing flush the wounds with your presence and let it be a manifesto for how you will do it differently.

1. What was the "pleasure climate" in your childhood home? Did your mother have "guilty pleasures" that were hidden or shameful? Did you witness your mother in enjoyment, fulfillment, or contentment very often?

2. What do you know about your pleasure as a baby? What kinds of stories did you hear about who you were and what you liked as a baby? Did your parents describe you as "hypersexual" or "shy"? Or as a baby who had to put everything in her mouth? Or as a stubborn or ornery child who wanted things her way? What is the energy behind the stories that were told to you? Frustration? Humor? Respect?

3. As a teen, how were your desires met by your caregivers? Were your fashion choices shamed or criticized? Were your crushes and desires for connection with others met with curiosity and support, or were they seen as a joke or an inconvenience? How were your first sexual encounters as a young woman?

4. As an adult, how comfortable do you feel with your own pleasure? Do you feel guilty about doing things for your own enjoyment? Do you feel guilty saying "no" when you don't want to do something? Do you feel guilty about resting or relaxing around your family?

5. How do you see your child currently expressing the 3 pillars of healthy sexual expression: curiosity, access to choice and voice (preference) and the ability to be seen in our authentic expression of who we are? How do you see them expressing curiosity about new sensations? How do you see them expressing their choice and voice and bodily autonomy? How do you see them asking to be seen and met in their authentic expression of themselves, and how do you meet it?

Exercise: Root

This is another one from somatic therapist Devorah Bry.

Root ~

1. Open Legs and Bend Knees - Bring attention and breath into the space just below your navel into the space between your inner thighs. Breathe for several minutes there, allowing energy to descend, making sure knees are, at least, slightly bent. Let your body settle into a powerful, grounded stance.

2. Using your mind's eyes/your inner vision, drop a cord-like tap root deep into the core of the earth. Utilizing the tap root, bring a flame up from the core of the earth into your sex organs. Allow it to enter in through your yoni, into your womb and low belly. Feel the heat and offer this flame, this ember, this heat of the earth some breath. Slowly, slowly, let it begin to move your body. Feed the sensations and the movements with your attention and breath.

3. Shake the body, inviting all tension and holding to loosen and drop into the earth. Shake by bouncing the knees, while you invite the vibration into the hips, pelvis and spine, and then into the shoulders, upper back, arms, and neck. Keep the jaw loose and relaxed, and allow the body to let go into the shaking for a while. Eventually, energy will begin to move through the feet into the legs and into the entire body. Feel into what this does for your sense of ground.

4. Rest into gravity. Lay on your back, with knees bent or some position that is relaxing for your lower back/belly. Slowly invite every point of contact with the ground to open as you melt all tension into the earth. Allow the earth to compost what is no longer needed. Let your awareness drop deeper down, and invite your body to let go and rest in the pull of gravity.

CHAPTER 6

WHAT TO DO WITH PERIODS

First off, I just want to congratulate you for coming this far on the journey with me. We've excavated limiting core beliefs, been to science class, rid our homes of environmental toxins, learned how to navigate tween tantrums, and tackle the subject of sex with our kids. We just walked through the heaviest and arguably the hardest part of this book. And you're still here! You are a fucking rockstar mom and I am beyond grateful to know that you are here on this planet, raising the next generation. If we were together, I would squeeze you.

In this chapter, we're getting bloody. And crafty! And then we are learning how to create ceremony and beauty. The most fun part is yet to come!

Our Blood is Positive, Powerful and Cleansing

I don't know about you, but I was definitely never taught this growing up. I had a fascination with menstrual blood, and its power was obvious to me - but nobody ever told me about it. Blood was to be hidden away; it was shameful, it was embarrassing, it was gross, and it smelled. There was nothing promoted as positive at all when it came to menstrual blood. They wouldn't even show it on TV in commercials for menstrual pads - instead, it was represented by the famous blue liquid (wtf was that stuff, anyway?).

Blood and gore are reserved for horror films and thrillers in our culture. Blood that comes from violent death or severe injury of another person is, for some reason, totally acceptable to show on television and in the media. But the blood that comes from our wombs - the only blood that requires no violence, incision, or killing to occur - is somehow grotesque and disgusting. Whether it be menstrual blood or blood from giving birth, the blood that comes from the power to give life is totally taboo to show anywhere. Maybe it's just me, but it seems we've got our priorities pretty messed up.

Years ago, I read a book that described in detail the process undergone by the women of the tribe in the book while on their menses. When the women would bleed, they would bring the clots of menstrual blood to the chief, who would put them in a long tube he carried at his waist that was lined with certain medicinal plants. At one point in the story, one of the tribal members falls and has a compound fracture in his leg. Laying there with the bone sticking out of his skin, the chief comes to the man, and this time, instead of opening the tube from the end in which he had placed the blood clots, he opens the other end of the tube. The blood, after sitting in the tube and mixing with the medicinal plants, had since turned into a paste. After singing the bone back into place (yes, with his voice), the chief applied the paste to the wound and it healed in a very short time.

I don't know if this ever happened in any tribe anywhere. The book has been discredited, and seriously angered the people it was written about so much that I won't even give the title, but I still love this image of the women's blood being used as a healing remedy in this way. It depicts very clearly the power in a woman's blood in a positive light - a way that can bring real healing to another. Even though the book is fictional, and this method may or may not have ever been used by anyone, it was the first book I ever read that depicted women's blood in a positive light.

Our blood is not disgusting. It does not deserve to be stopped up with tampons so that we never have to feel or see it and we can just power on, pretending that it's not there. Our blood is sacred and beautiful and life-giving. Our blood, when gathered intentionally, can be used as some of the most amazing fertilizer for houseplants, flowers, and food crops. Our blood allows us to cleanse and shed - both the lining of our uterus, and that which no longer serves us.

Ways to Promote a Positive View of Menstrual Blood

One of the best and easiest ways to promote a positive view of menstrual blood is to not hide your blood from your children. Ever since they were little, my children have been in the bathroom with me many times when I am changing my cloth pads. (I don't always want them in there, but, you know, motherhood). They see my blood. They've seen the soaking water for my cloth pads, and watched me give it to our plants and to the earth. They know this rhythm and process that happens with my body every month. It's not weird or gross to them. It's just "Mama's moontime."

We also get to openly talk about our blood with others in our life and not have it shamed or judged. Who in your life can you talk to about your blood with without it being a taboo subject or only a source of complaint? We need to shift how we have conversations about what happens in our bodies. Notice if the only time you ever talk about it with your girlfriends is when you are complaining about it. Can you find something positive to say about your own blood? If so, let your daughter overhear some of these positive and affirming conversations. If not - let's talk! There's some work to do.

This is where the rubber will meet the road for most moms. If you do not have anything nice to say about your period, where do you start? Every woman's journey will look different, but in this chapter, I will give you a few suggestions and hopefully by now in the book, you've already started to foster a bit of a different relationship with yourself.

Chances are, if you don't have anything nice to say about your blood, it's because you have some pretty uncomfortable, possibly even debilitating periods. If so, then the "Cramp Communication" exercise in this book is for you! When we have debilitating period cramps, our bodies are trying to get our attention about something. Often, there is an underlying health issue that also wants to be addressed and acknowledged. Our bodies are wise and are always communicating with us. Whether we are listening or not is another story.

The Vital Importance of Rest

In traditional cultures around the world it was - and still is in some places - understood that moontime was a time of ceremony and prayer. It was a time where the energy moved differently for women, things slowed down and, therefore, women were expected and encouraged to slow down, too.

Women's bodies are truly amazing. They give us an inherent period of rest and renewal - if we choose to take it. As we've already discussed, stress is the leading cause of nearly every major illness and disease. In our frenetic, fast-paced culture, a time to rest and slow down is *exactly* what we need. And as women, our bodies give it to us. How cool.

Often, this is interpreted as an inconvenience. And believe me - even I, who am writing this, have experienced my blood that way. Many times. But what we deem an inconvenience is all a matter of perspective. And once we start to work with our cycles in a more consistent and conscious way, we can actually craft our lives to be supportive of the natural rhythms that our body flows through.

It could be deemed a very anti-feminist mindset to think that we have to slow down every month just because of a physical experience that only we as women have. We have been deemed "the weaker sex" for centuries, in part because of this so-called "affliction." With the invention of tampons, Midol, and birth control, we no longer have to rest during our periods - or even have a period at all! We can just power through them and still do everything a man can do!

But at what cost?

Endometriosis, PCOS, fibroids, hysterectomies, cervical cancer, and breast cancer are at an all-time high. Hysterectomies are one of the most common surgeries performed today.[41] And while I'm not saying definitively that if we rest during our menses, we won't get cancer, I will take us back to the conversation around stress being the number one underlying cause for the majority of disease and illness.

For most people, cancer is a huge wake-up call. It forces people to face things in their lives and in themselves in a huge way, oftentimes calling them to make immense life changes - before it is too late. And sometimes those huge life changes in-and-of-themselves are what make the ultimate difference in a person beating cancer. Sometimes they aren't. Who lives and who dies and why is another one of those things that lives in the realm of the Great Mystery. I am a firm believer that death is not a failure. That said, I'm sure most of us are interested in acting in ways that give us the highest quality and longest life possible, especially if we've got kids.

As women, our bodies offer us a *monthly* moment to pause and reflect on our lives, to feel our feelings, to process what is up for us, to quietly create,

---

[41] https://www.hopkinsmedicine.org/health/treatment-tests-and-therapies/common-surgical-procedures

and to rest, release, and recalibrate. This is not an inconvenience. This is not a weakness. This is a tremendous gift and opportunity, if we use it.

There are currently 6 countries in the world that understand the significance of rest for a woman during her cycle. Spain, Japan, South Korea, Indonesia, Taiwan, Vietnam, and Zambia all have what is called a "menstrual leave" where a woman can take one day off - in some countries 3-5 - for each menstrual cycle.[42] Japan was the first to institute this law - in 1947. This has been legislated! Talk about countries that understand the value of a woman's life and blood! If you are starting to feel like the US is behind the times, it's because we are. Especially if you consider that in the US, in many jobs, women don't even get a maternity leave, much less a menstrual leave.

Christine Devlin Eck is the founder of the Center for Sacred Window Studies, a school that certifies professional postpartum caregivers through an Ayurvedic lens. Kayakulpa is a Sanskrit term used in Ayurveda that loosely translates to "body time." It is that "sacred window" time that Eck named her school after. According to Eck, there are several kayakalpa windows in a woman's life: menarche, postpartum and menopause. She says that from an Ayurvedic perspective, menarche is considered a very important time in life for establishing healthy tissues, and setting the trajectory for vibrancy in well being, on all levels.

She says that when appropriate support and care is provided during each of these 'sacred windows' of time, the body/mind/spirit will integrate each of these measures on an exponential level. Healing that takes place during a sacred window will be received at an elevated rate beyond what

---

[42] https://nation.africa/kenya/news/gender/why-kenya-needs-a-menstrual-leave-policy-4196290#

one might experience at a different time. In addition, the benefits provided by intentional care will last far beyond the window itself. When one is honored and well cared for during a kayakalpa, the impact will last decades into the future.

Eck says that as parents and caregivers of teens experiencing menarche, we have a very special opportunity in supporting tissue renewal, as well as fostering healthy mental and emotional skills and experiences that will be a guide for how they care for themselves in the future. How can we support our teens consciously during menarche and beyond in support of long term health and wellness? There are many ways! But here are some places Eck says to begin:

1. **Allow for Rest:** For many teens, the first years of bleeding can be especially painful with higher discomfort than they will experience later in adulthood. Most people will ignore this pain, suppress it and carry on with daily activity. As a parent, we can give our children the support and awareness that, when they are bleeding, it is a time for slowness. Activity can lessen, expectations can change, rest can be encouraged and facilitated. When we lose blood, our energy naturally lessens. We are in need of extra slowness in order to not deplete the tissues.

2. **Warmth**: During the resting period and increased slowness, applying warmth in various ways brings the body increased balance. Losing blood, and depletion in general increases coldness and instability. Providing warmth through baths, hot water bottles or pads, teas and soups offer the tissues an opportunity to release the constriction that comes with the cold quality.

3. **Love and Sensory Input**: Adolescence in itself is such a wide open canvas for creating patterns that will impact us for the rest of our lives. Love is medicine. Love from parents, love for self, love for our bodies - it all feeds into our ability to give and receive love in the future. What messages of love do our children receive from what they read, watch, hear and see? As we rest and rejuvenate during our bleeding, this is a perfect opportunity to increase love of self and others, through the intake of stories that inspire, that celebrate, and that connect with the heart. Talking to our children about sensory input, and how what we bring in can be either medicine or harmful, is an opportunity to learn a powerful awareness tool for life.

Rest as Nourishment

I am writing this right now on the first day of my moon. I am sitting on my deck, as the leaves are gently changing color and the air is getting crisper and cooler, announcing the presence of fall, listening to the water trickling down the rocks into the pond below. I am taking this pause from being with my family and the noise and the chaos first thing in the morning and making space for my creativity. Making space for aloneness and reflection. And I have crafted a life that allows me to do this. My husband knows how sacred this time is for me. He watched the girls so I could sleep in this morning, and asked no questions about me taking this time to write as inspiration hit me.

This morning, instead of coffee, I will make myself ceremonial cacao, because I can't think of a better ceremony to honor than this blood time, and cacao is chock-full of the minerals a bleeding woman needs (especially magnesium). It will give me the lift I like without the jitters I am prone to, specifically around my menses, if I drink coffee.

Today, I will take it easy. I will do what inspires me. That could be: go for a walk, dance slowly to my favorite music, sleep, write, make love, make music, make cookies. It helps that today is Sunday. But I also would do this if it were any other day of the week. I try not to schedule important things during the first day or two of my moon, when it is particularly strong for me.

That said, I'm also going to call a plumber because the water heater at the short-term rental property I own went out. Shit happens in life, and we don't have control over when it hits. Sometimes we have to move when we have our period. Sometimes we have to visit someone in the hospital or go to a birth or a funeral. Life happens.

It's less about WHAT we do during this time (though I am a 100% advocate of resting and doing what you feel inspired - or not - to do!) and more about the attitude and energy with which we do it. I can pack boxes in a stressed-out, hurried frenzy, or I can pack them while focusing on my breath, feeling the objects under my hands as I put them away, and making sure to take breaks - even just 1-5 mins - to sit still, close my eyes, and focus on my breathing. I can feel a ton of stress and overwhelm while calling the plumber and fall into victim mode about it, or I can dial a number, talk to a person or a voicemail, and do the thing because it's what needs to get done.

Moontime energy is amplifying energy. So, whatever space we are in internally is going to get magnified. If we are stressed, we turn into a raging tornado of "get the F out of my way." If we are in mindfulness, peace, and prayer, that is the energy that we emanate in a much larger way. A wake of gentleness follows us. We bring calm to a space. We have that kind of power. I do believe that it is this energetic amplification that is also why mooning women are not invited into certain ceremonies. If there is distortion in the field, a mooning woman can amplify that distortion. But don't we want to know what's off, so that we can correct it? It's not the mooning woman that needs to be removed - it's whatever is causing the distortion in the first place. From that vantage point, we could actually view her presence in the space as vital and welcome.

For me, especially on the first two days when my bleeding is particularly strong, meditation becomes automatically available to me. I close my eyes and I'm there - in the peace and the serenity of internal silence and quietude. If I'm not aligned or I'm forgetting my power, I can interpret this accessibility as feeling weak, feeling tired, etc. My body feels different. The energy in my veins is different. I don't feel like climbing mountains or running a marathon. I feel like sitting. I can make this a bad thing, or I can use it. Amazing inspiration can come through sitting in meditation. And the emanation of a vibration of peace is always of benefit - to ourselves and to the planet.

Our blood is life and our blood is death. Because we bleed we can hold and carry life. But it is also a small death every time. Feelings of sadness and grief are common around this time. Sometimes we are gifted insight into grief we may have been holding for quite a while and had buried. Moontime allows us to clear that grief, if we want to. Sometimes, it is merely grief that has no clear source. And while I don't think it's necessary to do a full-on grief ritual for every egg that was released that didn't become a baby (sometimes it's a celebratory "thank God I'm not pregnant" moment!), I do think that it's important to allow ourselves to come into a deeper relationship with what it means to hold death in our bodies, and how that affords us the opportunity to hold life even that much more sacred.

When we hold life as sacred, we become more conscious in our actions and in what we do with our bodies. We grow our desire to know when we are ovulating so that we can have more say in when we allow life into and through our bodies. As women, we truly do have the power - not to control life and death, as that is never really possible for humans to do, no matter how we try - but to dance in deeper concert with the forces of creation than those with male physiology are able to do. This is our feminine superpower. This is why we as a group have been subjugated and oppressed for millenia. We hold the ultimate power of life. And what an unstoppably powerful force that could be if we all knew and embodied that.

A woman who knows her power intimately in this way cannot be controlled. She is at one with the forces of life and death, and she knows a power larger than any individual human. She needs no intercessor for her divine connection. You'd better hope that she is kind and has done her inner work when she knows the power she wields. No wonder she was feared. A woman who knows her power in this way can definitely do some damage if she wants to. And I often find myself thinking that somewhere, historically, she must have in order for things to have played out the way they have.

Her First Bleed

Of course, when my daughter first found blood in her underwear, I was not at home with her. We had tickets as a family to go see the nutcracker, but my daughter was feeling sick with the annual winter crud that was going around. My husband was out of town, and I had been planning on taking the girls, along with my mother, to go see the performance. But since Sunna was sick, we decided that she would stay home and I would go solo with my mom and my youngest, Luna.

We silence our phones for performances, right? So I didn't hear it ring when my daughter, frightened at the sight of blood, called me in distress. It wasn't until after the show that I checked my phone and saw the missed calls. Of course it would happen this way, as I am in the midst of writing a book all about supporting your daughter through this very experience.

The guilt I felt at a) not physically being there, and b) not being able to answer the phone for her in her time of need was tremendous. Thankfully, her aunt and other grandmother live nearby and were available. Her grandma came over for the two hours between when she started and when I was able to get home, so she wasn't alone that whole time.

I made the quickest pit stop on the way home to grab a flourless chocolate cake and fresh berries to celebrate her (in the ways I was taught, berries are some of the most nourishing and healthful foods for the womb. And chocolate, well, do I even have to explain that one?). And even though she had been initially frightened and shared some tears as she related the moment to me, when we got home, there was a tremendous sweetness to the fact that there we were, 3 generations of women - my mother and mother-in-law, me and my two girls - as the ones there to celebrate and mark this moment.

Dancing with the Mystery

We never know exactly when the blood is going to come. We never know exactly when the baby will choose to come. We never know exactly when our last bleed will be our last bleed, or what our exact moment of death will be. This is part of why we call these "women's mysteries". Because as much as we want to calculate and quantify, we never know for certain when that moment is going to be. Surrendering to the mystery is one of the hardest, but also most satisfying, things we can learn to do.

My daughter was prepared - and she was still scared. Fear at seeing blood exiting our bodies is a normal response, especially when we have never seen it in our pants that way before. If your daughter experiences fear or trepidation upon the arrival of her first blood, this does not mean that you have somehow failed to adequately prepare her. Fear, like death, does not equal failure.

And this is also why preparation is so important. Because even though she had fear and I had guilt and sadness running as initial responses, I also felt SO GOOD knowing that she knew where to find her period products, and that she was prepared and knew what was happening, even if it was scary. I also felt, underneath the guilt, a certain stillness and solidity, knowing that I had prepared so much for this moment, and I was ready.

There was a palpable shift in my daughter that I noticed when I got home that night. Finding words for it is challenging, but I noticed that the way she held herself had suddenly, subtly changed. She had been through something scary by herself and had come through it. She also knew what that something was and the significance of it. She had crossed a threshold into a new way of being - and her carriage and bearing expressed the beauty and maturity of that passage. Something shone in her eyes in a different way. It was one of the most beautiful shifts in her I had ever seen. It was so slight that if I wasn't paying attention, I could have missed it. I am so glad I didn't.

I can't know for sure, but I strongly believe that if we hadn't had all the conversations, done all the preparation, and celebrated the moment in the way we did, that subtle shift might not have happened. There was a knowingness being expressed in her, through her, that had never been there before. The moment she had been waiting for, anticipating, worrying about, had come.

Only the Beginning

Remember when you were first pregnant? All the classes and energy and preparation was about the birth, right? You knew there was going to be a baby afterwards, but the main event was definitely going to be giving birth to that baby. And then the birth happened and it was like "oh, shit, now I have a BABY and there's all this life that is going to come after this, and I kinda wish I had prepared more for that part…" That's how it was for me anyway. Maybe your experience was different.

But I share this with you because, just like this preparation for birth as the main event, so it is with the first bleed. We can (and will) prepare, have the conversations, stock the cabinets, plan the ceremony, etc. And then the blood will come, and it will be a wonderful moment, and we will celebrate her. And then life as a cyclical, bleeding being will begin for your daughter.

When my daughter first started her bleed, it was the week of Christmas. Our whole household got sick and then it was Solstice and Christmas and New Years. There was no way I was going to try to plan her maidenhood ceremony in the midst of all that. So I planned it for the following month. We had our little cake and berries and sip of wine moment that evening, and she knew that something else would be coming down the road after that. She got her ears pierced, but not that day - not even that week. A couple of weeks later was the first appointment I could get. It doesn't all have to happen immediately. It's okay for it all to unfold in time.

We don't have to do it all for her the first time she bleeds. There will be another time. And another. And another. If you don't "get it right" the first time, you will be given plenty of opportunities to practice doing it differently. So go easy and gentle with yourself. This is a new stage we are celebrating and it's okay if it doesn't all happen in that one moment of her first blood. AND, how we respond to that first blood will, without a doubt, make an indelible imprint on her.

What is Normal?

I don't actually remember how long my first period was. I have no recollection of the amount of blood, or the length of time of my first cycle moment. I just remember that it happened and that, at the time, I knew something special had occurred - even if that wasn't necessarily reflected back by the people around me.

In terms of what is "normal" for a girl's first moontime, this is going to vary tremendously from person to person. Anywhere from 1 to 7 or 8 days can be considered "normal." As we discussed in Chapter 2, pretty much anything other than total hemorrhage or complete lack of blood at all before age 17 is within the range of normal. As her mother, it is your responsibility to start tracking her cycle - and help teach her how to track it - especially for the first two years. The amount, length, and rhythm of your daughter's cycle is important information for you to know, as it gives feedback about her overall state of health.

Don't expect that your daughter's cycle is going to mimic yours. Personally, I have a pretty light cycle that lasts about 5 days. The first two days are heavy, followed by a bit of a pause the third day, and spotting for the following two. This has been the consistent rhythm of my cycle as long as I can remember - though I do know it got lighter after I had children.

Sunna's first bleed was strange to me. She bled a little bit for a couple of hours and then stopped. I thought that was it for her first cycle and that we wouldn't meet her blood again until the following month, but then, a week later, she started bleeding in earnest and didn't stop for an entire week.

I'm not going to lie and say that I didn't have moments of concern and questioning whether or not this was normal. It was so different from my own cycle that it completely threw me. The amount of blood seemed considerable - more than I usually bleed. I found myself wanting to write stories that maybe there was something wrong with her. Should I be concerned? Should I take her to the doctor? She kept telling me that she was leaking through her pads and getting blood on her underwear. Was everything okay? But then I remembered my training - both in ceremony and in birth - and I picked my head up to look at the whole picture.

Here was my daughter, clearly healthy and happy (albeit a bit put out at times at the messiness of it all). She spent time with her friends, laughing and playing and scheming. She ate heartily. Her color looked good - she wasn't pale or flushed. She had some cramps at one point, but nothing unbearable - a dose or two of cramp bark tincture took care of them, no problem. She was clearly fine. And so was the amount of blood that was coming out of her. This was just what her first cycle looked like.

This does not mean that I am not going to track and pay attention to what happens for her moving forward. Quite the opposite, actually - I am paying close attention. I want to know what her normal is, and I want her to know what her normal is. And I want to make sure that if there is something outside the realm of normal, that I can help her address it early on. Many women who have endometriosis and fibroids later in life share that they had significantly heavy and painful cycles from the start of their first menses. So I am definitely paying attention. But with presence, not fear.

Because I also trust the process and the unfolding of it all. I trust the tools I have. I trust the health and wisdom in her body to lead the way. I trust myself to create an environment for her which makes that process easy for her body. That is the agreement I made when I became her mother. That is my job, until she is old enough to do that for herself.

How We Take Care of Our Blood Matters:
Diva Cup, Tampons, Pads, Period Underwear and
Free Bleeding

Tampons

In this section, we will go over the variety of ways you can deal with blood, teach your daughter to deal with her blood, and my thoughts on each one. I wanted to start this section, however, by outing my complete bias against using tampons - especially in young girls who are bleeding for the first time.

I am not here to tell you what to do with your body. You are a grown woman and have come to your choices and conclusions in life based on your experience. I am not here to minimize that at all. However, I will say that, in my experience, tampons are at the core of a lot of problems that arise with menstruation.

For one, tampons allow us to pretend and act as if we are not bleeding at all. This is why so many women love tampons and choose to use them. With tampons, we don't have to see or deal with our blood. But I don't see this as an advantage. Ignoring the fact that we are bleeding encourages us to completely override the signals that our body may be sending us about what its needs are during menstruation. When we don't look at or smell our blood, we may be missing some vital information as to our current state of health.

A quick google search will bring up the immense number of searches for "what do I do if I've left my tampon in too long" types of questions that have been anonymously asked. This mistake - common to make if you have completely disregarded and maybe even forgotten that you are bleeding - can have some pretty serious side effects. On the mild side, it can lead to an increased rate of various vaginal, uterine, and urinary infections. On the serious side, there is TSS or Toxic Shock Syndrome (yes, it still exists), which can be fatal. Tampons are also made of a variety of materials, some of which can shed small fibers which can accumulate and stay in the body and grow into who-knows-what over time. Yikes.

I don't know about you, but I don't trust that very many 10, 11, 12 year olds, etc, are necessarily going to remember to change their tampon regularly enough. If you are completely committed to using tampons for yourself or your daughter, PLEASE go with organic cotton ones! There are so many chemicals we are already exposed to in our world, we do not need to be additionally inserting them directly into our vaginas on a regular monthly basis.

Speaking of which, when it comes to using tampons with your daughter, there will also be the matter of insertion, which for a young girl can be scary, painful, unpleasant, and embarrassing. I remember reading one anecdote where a young girl thought she knew everything about tampons and how to use them because her mom had given her a book about menstruation. Only, she was completely unaware of how to insert them - or even that inserting them was necessary. She laid three out in her underwear and tried to sop up the blood that way, until a friend helped show her how to put one in effectively.

Tampons can also make cramps and other unpleasant period symptoms, like headaches, worse. When we have a tampon (or diva cup) inside our vaginas, there is a subtle and automatic tensing that our vaginal walls do to hold that inside our bodies. I have likened the sensation to a form of constipation, which, when prolonged, is usually accompanied by similar symptoms - abdominal cramping and headaches. When we stop using tampons, often these unpleasant symptoms go away, without us having to do anything else. There is a mirroring in the head and the pelvis, and often when we have tension in one of those areas, it presents in the other as well. Our blood is designed to exit our bodies during menstruation, not be held inside. When we let it flow, we can relax in a whole different way.

Last but not least, as with paper (or plastic) pads, tampons create an immense amount of waste, and have led to innumerable, costly plumbing backups, as indicated by the proliferation of "please don't flush your tampons" signs in bathrooms everywhere.

Diva Cup

There are other companies that make this kind of silicone cup nowadays, but Diva was the first one and the most commonly used, so that's the name I am using to refer to this device, for simplicity's sake. A silicone cup designed to be held inside the vagina like a tampon, the Diva Cup allows the user to catch her blood, wash, and reuse the cup. These cups come in two different sizes - those for women who have had babies and those for women who have not. I believe there are also companies now who have made a slightly smaller size for preteens. I know women who have had their same cup for over 10 years, so in terms of eliminating waste from tampon and pad use, this product has done an amazing job.

Waste from menstrual products, like with disposable diapers, is a real environmental problem. According to "An exploratory study of the impact and potential of menstrual hygiene management waste in the UK" authored in 2022, an estimated annual *28,114 tonnes* of menstrual products become trash every year - and that's just in the UK (that's British tonnes - a US ton is 2,000lbs, a British tonne is 2,240 lbs). That's a lot of trash! I think we are so blessed to have these alternatives, like the Diva Cup, to help us eliminate the unnecessary waste created from our monthly cycles.

Like a tampon, you will have to show your daughter how to insert this product and, as I mentioned before, insertion in young girls can bring up pain, feelings of discomfort, awkwardness, and embarrassment as she gets the hang of it. It can also be a great opportunity to open up a doorway into deeper conversations regarding her body and care for it; just be prepared for this aspect if a Diva Cup is the path you decide to go down.

Unlike a tampon, the risk of leaving it in too long is far less, as it will start to leak blood out if it becomes over-full. This can be annoying but also something to be grateful for, as it reminds us that we are bleeding and do need to tend to ourselves somewhat differently during this time (some women use a combo cup and pad, panty liner, or period underwear in case their cup does leak on particularly heavy flow days). Also, unlike a tampon, a Diva Cup is not made of a material that has the potential to release microfibers into your body. There is no risk of TSS with a Diva Cup, although improper storage and washing can lead to a potential for infection. This potential is still far smaller than with tampons, but proper hygiene and care for the cup is something you will have to go over in detail with your daughter (and probably to check in on at various intervals in at least the first 6 months of use).

I used a Diva cup for many years, until one day, during a particularly heavy and uncomfortable period, I had a very clear directive from my body to take it out and stop using it entirely. I had been having excruciating cramps and debilitating headaches often when I had my period. On this particular day during my cycle - I think I was in my early 20s - I was so miserable and crampy and needed to go to the bathroom to empty my Diva Cup. I pulled it out and immediately my cramping and my headache *went away entirely*. The contrast was so stark, it made me pause. I closed my eyes and tuned in, really listening to my body. I felt the blood flowing out of me into the toilet and I received a direct message from my womb - this blood wants to flow out. I was shown in a flash how keeping the blood held inside my body was creating a toxic buildup, like a dam in a stream. The cramping and headaches were a direct response to the stagnation that holding my blood inside me was creating.

I know tons of women who LOVE their Diva cups, and I think they are an incredible alternative to tampons, as they are far more sustainable, and we still have to be in relationship with our blood if we use one. For me, however, they are not the right choice. And if you are someone who usually suffers from extreme period discomfort and uses a Diva Cup or tampons, I HIGHLY suggest trying an alternative that allows your blood to exit your body as it is designed to do. It can be an adjustment if you are used to not interfacing with your blood this way (and likely there is an emotional component that you may have to face in the process), but the relief is SOOO worth it.

Pads

Pads come in many varieties, sizes, and heaviness of flow accommodations. They are made of a variety of materials, and if you choose to go the disposable pad route, it is important to know the ingredients that go into your pads. Many of them, especially some of the larger brand names, use plastics, scents, and chemicals that can disrupt the sensitive PH of our vaginas and lead to an increased rate of yeast infections and other issues. Choose organic cotton when you can and AVOID SCENTED PADS.

My go-to when it comes to pads are reusable cloth pads. Cloth pads, like Diva Cups, completely eliminate the waste-factor of period products. They are often made of really soft material like cotton flannel, which feels so nice when you wear them. I find that when I wear my cloth pads, I feel very held. They are comfortable and help me to let go, relax, and let my blood out, wherever I am. There is none of the bunching and weird twisting that can happen with disposable adhesive pads (not to mention accidental adhesive in places where you really don't want it). When I'm done with them, I throw my used cloth pads in a tub of cold water to soak, wring out the blood, and throw them in the wash. Easy peasy. I usually then use the soak water as fertilizer for my house plants - they love it! Sometimes I offer it back to the earth, at the base of a tree, with a prayer for peace.

Like with cloth diapers, you can bring a wet bag for your used pads if you are out and about, but I have also found that I can wear cloth pads for much longer than I can a regular disposable pad, depending on my flow and my attentiveness to my bleeding. I have also started practicing free bleeding more often these days, sometimes with a cloth pad as a back up, which I have found to be my favorite way by far to be in relation to my blood.

Period Underwear and Swimsuits

An incredible invention that has come out over the last several years is period underwear. Obviously, Thinx were the pioneers, but have also rightfully come under scrutiny lately because of their choice of chemically-treated fibers that they used in their product and the carcinogenic byproduct of regular contact with these materials. EDCs in the most unlikely places... So to be clear, not all period underwear was created equal!

I think period underwear can be great if you can find a brand that resonates with you. So far, Modibodi out of Australia is the only company I have found that uses merino wool as an absorptive pad in the underwear instead of some kind of weird technology that I don't fully understand. My biggest complaint overall with period underwear is the ubiquitous use of synthetic materials - see if you can find a brand that makes theirs out of cotton, as breathable underwear is really important! (I have listed some of my favorite brands in the resources.) I also don't love that most pairs are black, which makes seeing your blood very difficult. I'm sure this is intentional, and I clearly have strong feelings about being able to see and connect with your blood as a measure of health. I have had the eerie experience with my period underwear of recognizing that without being able to see my blood, I feel disconnected from the process of bleeding to a certain degree. There have been moments where, if I wanted to, I could almost pretend I wasn't bleeding at all.

As with cloth pads, having a wet bag and a change of undies in the event you leak through is always smart, but also as with cloth pads, period underwear is designed so that you can wear one pair for most of the day. In addition to Modibodi, I also like the Saalt brand for their use of cotton fibers instead of polyester, and I have purchased some from them for my daughter as well. That company also makes cups and a new thing called discs, which I have no experience with - but would be intrigued to hear yours if you try them!

My absolute favorite thing about period underwear technology, though, is that they now make period swimsuits! For girls who don't use tampons or cups, this is a game-changer. I know one young woman who is on the swim team and uses this option. It's made her passion for swimming feel accessible to her all the time, without any awkward and uncomfortable tampon moments. Having my own horrific memory of improperly inserting a tampon and having it come out while I was at morning swim with everyone at my coed summer camp, I love, love, love that this now exists!

Unlike cloth pads, period underwear should not be soaked, but instead rinsed thoroughly in cold water before washing and air drying. This level of care is something that you will need to go over with your daughter, as they can be pricey and they won't last long if you don't care for them properly. If you want to make a ritual of catching the blood water and feeding the plants, you can rinse them over a tub or basin that will catch the rinse water.

Free Bleeding

Free Bleeding is not for everyone, but I feel called to include it here because so many women don't even know that it's a thing, or that it is an option for them. Free bleeding, in essence, means not using any kind of product at all to catch or stop the blood and to just let your blood flow freely. This concept can come as a shock to many women, especially if we believe that we are just constantly bleeding all the time during our cycle. While it can feel that way, the truth is that our blood comes in gushes and fits and spurts. It is not a constant faucet running all the time (unless you have an imbalance such as endometriosis or fibroids).

When we start to become more in tune with our bodies, we can actually sense when we are about to release a flow of blood. When free bleeding, we catch those moments and tend to our blood in the moment. For me, the most practical thing often is to just sit on the toilet and let it flow. It means I am in the bathroom for longer than I would normally be, but it gives me a moment to pause, to slow down, to listen, and to feel my blood exit my body. This moment then also allows me to focus on what, if anything at the time, I am wanting to energetically release with my blood as it flows out of me. Whoever said prayer can't happen on the toilet never practiced free bleeding!

Some women, when free bleeding at their heaviest moments, will choose to sit on a beautiful blanket specifically designed to catch fluids, or on towels that they use specifically for this purpose. This can be a nice way to make yourself slow down and focus on a quiet, contemplative activity. I have also known women who wear skirts and no underwear during their moontime and carry a cloth around with them that they will use to soak up the blood when they feel it coming. But the absolute, ideal, and original way to free bleed - and my ultimate favorite of all time - is to sit directly on the earth.

It is hard to explain the power of this practice if it is something you have never done before. It is something that needs to be directly experienced to be truly understood. When we sit directly on the earth and let ourselves relax and let our blood flow out, there is a current and an exchange of information and energy between us and our original mother. There is no better remedy for cramps or fatigue that I have found. The surge of strength that is delivered to us from the earth in this practice is palpable. There is profound prayer and meditation accessible to us. We are brought directly into union and connection with the highest purpose of our moontime when we give ourselves the time to sit and bleed on the earth in this way. This is when we go within and harvest the wisdom and the intuition of moontime.

Traditionally, many cultures had moon huts or lodges where women went during their moontime. In some cultures, the lodge was larger and could accommodate several women at a time. Some were more solitary and were only large enough for one or two. Being under some sort of covering might feel better to you than being exposed for this practice. Weather will obviously have an impact on your experience, and for some, like myself, who live in places with particularly cold winters, this practice won't be practical to do year-round.

On a practical level, I have found moss to obviously be the most comfortable to sit my naked bottom on, but soft grass and leaves can work too. I make sure there are no little twigs or pebbles that are going to poke my flesh. I have also even folded a blanket underneath me in sort of v-shape, so my bottom and legs are on something soft but my blood has direct access to the bare ground. I make sure I'm not in a spot prone to muddiness, or where the water tends to pool when it rains, but somewhere with better drainage. I wear a skirt or a blanket wrapped around my waist. I sit cross-legged and upright. I will bring a cloth to wipe myself with before standing up to go inside. I have water or tea and maybe a few snacks and a journal with me, depending on how long I plan to be out for. I let myself pee and bleed directly into the earth and the spot where I'm sitting, and the earth soaks it all right up. The sense of freedom in this seemingly small and benign act is indescribable. The peace and stillness accessible to us in this action is beyond words.

If you have never sat directly on the earth to release your blood, I truly hope that at some point in your life, you will give yourself the experience. Forget your concerns of what someone will think of you, or what it might mean about you if you do something so "radical" and deemed disgusting or strange by society. Ours is a very sick society, and I for one am totally fine if I am not conforming to it. Forget whatever squeamishness around your own physicality or coming into direct and intimate connection with the physicality of Earth you might have. Give yourself this gift, as you give this gift of your blood to the earth.

Blood Offerings

I know many women who catch their blood, either from their Diva cups directly, or in water from soaking cloth pads or rinsing period underwear, and then use it to fertilize their plants or as an offering to the earth. Some women pick a special tree in their yard or have a specific place that they repeatedly offer their blood. I love this and think the ritual of offering our blood to the earth is so beautiful, and so needed at this time.

Menstrual blood is the only blood that can be obtained without violence or cutting, with the exception of the blood that flows when we birth our babies (which is, in essence, also menstrual blood). Offering our moon blood as a form of thanksgiving is a practice that has been known by cultures the world over for millenia, and one which I have engaged in for the past 20 years.

Indigenous cultures everywhere have understood that when we take from the earth, it is only rightful that we give something in return. In all Indigenous cultures I have encountered, the Earth is viewed as our first Mother, the one who provides us with everything we need in order to survive. Many elders say that part of the reason why we have fallen so out of balance as a species is because we have forgotten how to give and say thank you to the Earth for all that she gives us. (Side note - not all Indigenous or first nations cultures practice or promote a practice of women returning their moonblood to the earth, though some do. I have interfaced with several, especially central North American tribes, that have some pretty strict taboos regarding moon blood. I personally don't agree with all of these taboos, and I believe the way *some* of them are currently practiced can perpetuate misogyny, shame, and harm, but that's a whole other conversation. This is very important to know, though, especially if you are drawn to working more in these earth-based ways of prayer. Don't just assume everyone is welcoming to moon blood, Indigenous or no.)

Beyond what we can see with our eyes - the physical, tangible things that we see and extract from the earth - there are unseen forces operating that keep things in balance in the natural world. Every element, every plant, every body of water has a spirit that works alongside and within it, and when we leave offerings before taking from these elements, it is these unseen ones who reap the benefit and who use those offerings as food to continue to thrive and care for the places they inhabit. This reciprocity is at the core of maintaining harmony on this planet. This is, again, an understanding shared by cultures around the world who originated closely with the earth. This is not some new-age fluff or fantastical meandering of some random lady's mind. This is wisdom that has been closely held and kept and preserved. We don't have sophisticated enough tools and instruments to measure these kinds of things, so we write them off as non-existent. But ancient cultures know.

I remember learning many years ago that the price or offering for extracting metals from the ground was human blood. I find this fascinating if you think about how the primary original use for metals was weapons, and the incredible amount of unnecessary shedding of human blood that resulted. The machines of war are made of metal. We drive around in metal boxes that take hundreds of thousands of lives every year. Maybe this cost of extraction is true and maybe it's not. But it sure is fascinating to contemplate, and has made a lot of things make a lot of sense to me.

How we take care of our blood matters. It has been said that when the women return their blood to the earth, then peace will return to the earth. Returning our blood to the earth with love and reverence for all she gives us is such an easy and simple act. If such a simple act has the potential to have such a huge and dramatically positive impact, then why *not* do it? What if we really do hold the power to change the world?

Building Her Period Kit - The Fun Part!

What is a Period Kit?

Put simply, a period kit is a small bag of essentials that your daughter can carry with her in her school bag, gym bag, sleepover bag, etc., so that whenever her period hits, she has everything she needs with her and knows how to use it.

What goes in the period kit is entirely up to you! Just make sure that your daughter is well versed on how and why to use everything that is in it. I recommend making a period kit with your daughter and/or giving it to her a few months after she starts to develop breast buds, once her pubic hair has started to grow in. It might still be a year or so before she actually needs to use it, but these are telltale physical signs that puberty is well underway. It is highly unlikely that your daughter will bleed before those other two signs have occurred. Giving her this kit then plants the seed and starts the conversation. She will be prepared - and this itself is a huge ancestral rewrite for the majority of us.

The Fun Part!

This part is arguably the most fun aspect of this process of puberty preparation, especially for those of us with a crafty sensibility. You can decide if this is something you want to do on your own and gift to your daughter, or if it's a process you'd like to include her in. There are some pre-made kits out there if you are not the crafty type or feel that it is a task that will get dropped if you don't just buy it pre-made (no judgment either way! The important thing is to prepare our daughters).

My business coach got so excited about this idea of a period kit when I shared it with her that she went ahead and organized moms in her community and their daughters to come together and build the period kits as a community! I totally love this idea, as it has the added bonus of getting your daughter and her peers excited about menstruation together. Read this book together and then build the kits and have the ceremonies as part of building community. How fun and beautiful!

The power of community cannot be emphasized enough in this process! When I had a candid conversation with my daughter recently, she expressed sadness at not feeling able to freely share some of her knowledge about women's bodies with her female classmates. It was abundantly clear to her that what she knows about her body and how it works is not something that is shared by other girls in her class. She could tell by the negative projections they already have about themselves that either their parents haven't discussed much with them about these physical and emotional changes, or that the perspective in their households is not as body positive as it is in ours (or both).

What we are undertaking in bringing our daughters into puberty in this new way is revolutionary and goes against millenia of cultural programming. Making this kind of shift with a community not only helps provide support in the process, but also ensures a level of sustainability that trying to do alone makes that much more challenging. So get your daughter's friends' moms together for this!

The Main Components

By now, I'm hoping that you have come to some clarity within yourself about what kinds of products you want your daughter to use when she first starts her bleed. So, what do you need to make her period kit?

A bag - This is obviously so vast in terms of what it could be. It could be something you already have, something you buy especially for this purpose, something she picks out herself, something you make out of her favorite fabric. It all depends on how crafty you want to be! Make it as meaningful as you like, and make it something in her style that you know she will love.

Make sure it's big enough to fit the essentials - some pads, maybe some underwear changes, etc. - but not so big that it's going to be hard to carry around. Think clutch purse or travel toiletry bag size.

Period Products - I'm going vague with this title here, but it's probably obvious by now that I hope you don't include tampons in this kit. Period underwear, a teen-size diva cup, a few disposable and/or cloth pads - whatever you think would be best for her to have in an unexpected visit from her moontime. Whatever you put in her kit, make sure that you explain to her *in detail* how to use the product in question. This is crucial! Remember the tampons lined up in the underwear story? If you do put a Diva Cup or tampons in the kit, make sure you have shown her - a couple of times - how to insert it.

Extras - Chocolate, a beautifully scented oil she likes, tinctures, a womb balm - have fun with this part! Obviously, you don't want to over-stuff her kit, but this is where you can give her something that will help her feel how special and sacred she is during this time.

When I made Sunna hers, I felt time pressure to get it done quickly so she would have it before I went on a big trip and would be gone for two weeks. I really didn't want her getting her period while I was gone and being totally unprepared! The only bag I could find quickly and easily in the local stores that I liked, felt like her vibe, and was the right size was one that came with a bunch of samples of organic skin care in it. What a bonus! I was able to give her these skin care samples along with her period kit, which felt really good and like an extra way to love her up. In her kit, I included two pairs of period underwear, some organic disposable pads, two cloth pads, a bottle of Dragon Time essential oil blend, and a cramp bark tincture I had bought from a local herbalist.

She still has this kit, and it lives mostly in her school backpack. She is refining it with each cycle, clarifying what she actually uses and prefers to have on her for an unexpected arrival of blood. We refill supplies as needed, but she knows that she has her stuff with her at all times and that it has a designated home.

Exercise: Cramp Communication

Menstrual cramps are no fun. I encountered severe cramping in my earlier days when I suffered from PCOS, and have known women who have had cramps so bad that it's made them throw up. Some degree of mild cramping during your period is normal. But debilitating cramps that feel like labor contractions are not. Something else is going on if your cramps make you feel like you are going to turn inside out from the pain.

Please know that this exercise is not given from a place of wishing to diminish the reality of anyone's pain, but from the lens of knowing in my bones that healing is possible and our bodies talk to us. I used to liken my cramps to birthing contractions. Now I hardly get cramps at all.

This exercise will take you deep. That's what it is designed to do. And it's designed to be done while in the active stages of a cramping uterus. If you're really resistant, you will find some very creative (and sometimes legitimate) reasons to not do this exercise. You are probably the one who needs this exercise the most!

The next time you have cramps, try this:
Remove yourself from your immediate surroundings (unless you are already lying down alone in your bed).

Take yourself somewhere, preferably dark, where you can lie down and relax. This action alone may have already relieved the cramping somewhat. Mooning women are incredibly energetically sensitive, and it's possible the cramping is just your body's way of getting you to remove yourself from whatever is happening at that moment.

If you can't lie down (because you are at work or something), go to the bathroom and lock yourself in for the next 5-10 minutes. Sit down on the toilet, close your eyes, and relax.

Whether you are lying down or sitting on the toilet, if you have a tampon or Diva cup in, take it out. Let your blood flow freely out of you. Wait a few minutes. Breathe.

If the cramping is still loud and intense, see if you can observe where you are holding tension in your belly. (It helps if you have practiced the Soft Belly Exercise when you are not actively bleeding first). While bringing your attention to relaxing any place that is holding tension, breathe into your belly. Picture your womb, in her active stage of release. Ask her what she is trying to tell you.

This next part is the most important part: *listen for what she says.* It might be faint. It might not make any logical sense. It might not be words in your head, but the encouragement towards some kind of movement or sound or tears. Listen.

Ask her what she needs. *Listen for what she says.*
Tell her you love her. *Listen for what she says.*
Tell her you're sorry. *Listen for what she says.*
Tell her thank you. *Listen for what she says.*
Ask her for forgiveness. *Listen for what she says.*
Breathe.
Cry if you need to.
Relax.

You have now completed the exercise. Go easy with yourself.

Exercise: Yoni Steaming

Yoni steaming is something we can all practice and teach to our daughters, to great health benefits. This practice is found in a variety of different cultures around the world, from Mexico to Korea, but the way I learned it comes primarily from those who have been taught by Rosita Arvigo, who learned it in Belize. There is a fabulous free eBook on Yoni Steaming written by my friend, RN and Maya Abdominal Massage therapist Chaya Leia Aronson, that I will link to in the resources.

Note: Steaming, while mostly beneficial, is not for everyone and shouldn't be practiced all the time. When NOT to steam: when you have an IUD (steaming can eject the IUD), during menstruation, during an active vaginal infection, while pregnant, during the luteal phase if trying to conceive.

Materials:

- A pot or larger bowl that can hold several quarts of water
- A towel
- A blanket or long skirt
- Warm socks for your feet
- A yoni steaming stool (*Yoni steaming stools are something that can be made or purchased specifically for this purpose, but they can be expensive. You can also use the edge of a couch or bolster. I have even done a steam where a small clay pot was placed underneath me while I was in child's pose and my whole body was covered with a blanket. Chaya's eBook has great ways to get creative with this.*)
- Herbs for the steam. Some of my favorites are: mugwort, nettles, red raspberry leaf, rose, basil, calendula, lavender, rosemary, tulsi, sage, and motherwort. You can try a combination of some of these herbs, or just go with what you have or are guided to use. This, again, is a great opportunity to create a relationship with the plants and how your body responds to them.

Things that can be nice to have but are not required:

- Candles
- Peaceful music
- A journal
- Some water
- A mug of warm tea - could be the same herbs you put in the steam, or a nice tulsi rose
- A yoga block or extra blanket to adjust the height of the pot

The Process:

Set aside 30 mins where you can be undisturbed and quiet. Put a full kettle of water on to boil. You can also just put the water in the pot and bring it to a boil on the stovetop. As the water is boiling, get your stuff set up. If using a yoni steaming stool, all you will need to set up before-hand is having your blanket and towel nearby. If using the edge of a couch, you will want to put a towel down where you plan to sit, and have the blanket to wrap yourself in.

I like to do my steams by candlelight if I can, with beautiful music playing or just silence. It can be a nice time to meditate and some women like to journal. Personally, I prefer to just be present with myself and the process of the steam, but if you like journaling, this can be a nice time to do so.

Once your stuff is set up, place the herbs you will be using in the empty pot. (If you have decided to boil the water in the pot on the stove, wait to put the herbs in until after you have turned off the heat.) Bring the kettle and pot to your steaming station, along with a jar of cold water you can use to cool down the temp if the steam is too hot. Pour the water over the herbs and put the pot underneath where you will be sitting. (I like to put mine on top of a towel in case there are any spills.)

Remove all your clothing from the waist down, except for some warm socks, especially if your feet tend to get cold. Grab your blanket and sit down over the pot, wrapping the blanket around your waist and the whole stool. The point of the blanket is to trap the steam and heat in around you. You could also use a long flowy skirt, if it works with your set up. You just want to make sure that there is no fabric between your vulva and the steam and that the fabric is heavy enough to trap in the steam.

Sit over the steam and relax. If it gets too hot, you can add some cold water. Not hot enough, and you might need to adjust the height of the pot underneath you. Find the sweet spot and let yourself relax into the heat and the medicine of the plants. Breathe. Relax.

Generally you don't want to steam for longer than 30 mins. 20-30 mins is a great time length for a steam. You can do this alongside your daughter and/or with other women. It can be a lovely practice to share with others. Enjoy the magic of steaming!

CHAPTER 7

CREATING CEREMONY AND RITUAL TO CELEBRATE HER FIRST MOONTIME

We hear about cultures where rites of passage were a regular part of life and something deep within us awakens. We know in our bones the power of that, and we want something akin to it in our own lives. We want that for ourselves and for our daughters.

Ceremonies and rituals have been performed throughout the world, across cultures and time, for a variety of different significant life events. Many indigenous cultures have ceremonies and rites, for young women and young men alike, to mark the passage into puberty that are still performed to this day. There are a number of traditional elders who are passionate about preserving and passing on these very important ceremonies for the younger generations. A few of them you will get to hear from in this chapter, as we explore the ins and outs of creating meaningful menarche rites of passage for our daughters.

In our current, predominantly agnostic Western culture, there are very few significant ceremonial rites of passage that remain. Graduating from high school and college, buying your first house, and getting married are the few that stand out, but oftentimes they can feel kind of lacking - devoid of any real spiritual depth. This lack of ceremony and ritual has led many of us in the Western world into a spiritually bereft existence, seeking and reaching for meaning wherever we can find it. What has emerged is an undercurrent of people who are doing their best, taking what they can find and weaving it into some semblance of a ceremony, in order to mark and make meaning of certain significant moments.

What can be forgotten in the process, specifically in regards to rites of passage for young people, is that there was an entire culture and way of life to support not only those traditional rites of passage ceremonies, but their integration as well. Traditionally, in most cultures, puberty rites of passage took place around the age of 13-14. (13 is the age that Nana Vilma emphasizes as the perfect time for this kind of ceremony). This was also the time, historically, when young women became of marriageable age and young men would prepare to become husbands. Taking a young girl into the moonlodge when she started her moon to share what would be expected of her as a woman was necessary that young because, culturally, as soon as she started to bleed, she was ready to be wed. When she bled, she became a woman. In some cultures, that meant leaving her family home. It definitely meant a clear shifting of roles and power dynamics between mother and daughter. It meant sex and babies. She needed to know what came along with that.

Times are *so* different now - thankfully. So, the moonlodge or welcoming ceremony does not necessarily need to hold the same gravitas as it used to. In fact, what we have seen in our community with a number of the young girls who have gone through some of these attempted ceremonies is that the ceremonies have not worked for them. In many cases, it has backfired and actually been far too overwhelming for the youth receiving them. They came out of it feeling like they had been somehow harmed by the too-muchness of it all. In my study and contemplation of rites of passage, I feel I have come to greater understanding of why this has been so, which we will also explore here together.

Rites of passage are important to the development of an internal maturation. They are moments of significance in our lives, marked by being witnessed and held by the community that holds the person passing through. There are many elements that can be included in a ritual or ceremony to celebrate your young one coming into her first menses, and they can be as elaborate or as simple as you like.

Some of you will feel drawn to a larger, more elaborate ceremony for your daughter. Some of you might prefer something smaller, a simple way to mark the occasion in a positive way. One is not better than the other. If you are not currently living in or nearby a community of people who are all committed to holding rites of passage together for the youth, then I recommend keeping it on the simpler side.

The age when your daughter starts her period will have some bearing on how she receives her ceremony. Having age dictate some of the content of the ceremony seems appropriate. As we have seen, girls are starting their first moons earlier and earlier. We held my daughter's ceremony two months before her 12th birthday. While she wasn't as young as 9, she was still on the younger end of the age range of menarche. The community a child lives in, as well as the cultural context in which she is raised, will also have a significant impact, and should be taken into consideration.

Remember that we are doing this mostly fumbling around in the dark. We are, in essence, creating a new culture. So, while there are some incredible elders who are willing to share what they know with us, there aren't a lot of roadmaps for how to do this in the time and culture that we are currently in (unless you still live in a traditional culture that honors and carries these ways - in which case, you definitely don't need me giving you suggestions in this arena). Bridging the ancient ways with the now is part of the work of this time. I will share here with you the kernels that I have gleaned from different elders that I have worked with, as well as my own life experience, in the hopes that you can create something magical for your daughter and her peers that they remember, celebrate, share, and wish to replicate with their own daughters and community someday. That is how we create culture.

It is so easy to forget, as we age, the depth of the vulnerability and tenderness that exists in that time of early puberty. The sensitivity is turned up to the maximum, and how we interpret the world around us is magnified much more so than it is as we become adults. So when we design our rituals and ceremonies for these young girls, it is paramount that we keep that in mind. The bigness that our adult selves might crave from this kind of ritual can be too big and too much for the individual adolescent metabolism, especially if they have no other context within which to place the experience, or people that they feel they can share it with. Teens travel in packs, and so these ceremonies should happen that way too.

When I asked her to share with me about her cultural traditions, Nana Vilma - one of my elders I have mentioned a few times who is a Mayan lineage holder from Guatemala - spoke at length with me about the need for privacy at this stage of development. This is a point that she again mentioned to my daughter when we had her ceremony. This is a private time for most young girls, and it is important for us to respect that. The feeling of violation at sharing this information with others without her permission is huge, and is part of the backfiring that we have seen in our larger community with these ceremonies. Things that are seemingly small to us as grownups are a huge deal to our daughters at this age.

This is why I say: Keep it small. Keep it simple. Keep it light.

In retrospect, while I don't regret anything that happened with the ceremony we held for Sunna, or have a story that I "should have done it differently" (though I can identify many ways that I will do it differently the next time!), I can see how that moment with the chocolate cake and berries, and three generations of women the day she started her bleed would have been enough for my child - at least for a little while. What happened in her ceremony was immensely powerful, and is not something that any one of you reading this would be able to create - nor would I want you to try. Her ceremony was an expression of who she is, who we are as a family, the caliber of my sisterhood, and our family's ceremonial life path thus far. It also included not one but two indigenous elders (one Zooming in online from Guatemala). While small in numbers of people, energetically it was immense. And like all good ceremonies, it kind of lasted 4 days (even though the ceremony itself was about an hour and a half). The thing is, though, I don't think my daughter necessarily *needed* the particular ceremony that we made for her. I did.

I realized several years ago that, for whatever reason, I seem to have made some agreement with the universe (that I'm open to amending, btw, in case the right forces are listening!) that I will be the person to fuck up publicly in front of a whole bunch of people (especially in ceremonial space) so that everyone can learn something. Clearly, I really need to cultivate more humility. While understanding this can help me have more grace with myself when it happens - which, thankfully, is less and less as time goes by - it does not lessen the feelings of cringe and discomfort while I'm in the midst of it. My inner perfectionist does not like it at all. The aftermath of Sunna's ceremony - especially knowing that I was going to have to write about it - was kind of like this for me.

While I can recognize my mistakes, I am also so grateful that it happened the way it did because I don't think the depth of what this chapter gets to be would have happened without those mistakes. As usual, my mistakes are for your absolute benefit! They are what allowed all the wisdom in this chapter, including the inspiration to provide rites of passage for other groups of youth, to come through. Sunna is a golden warrior. When I look back at the conditions of her birth and her childhood thus far, I can see that she clearly had some contract with our family that she would come through my fumbling and mistakes with me, so that I could learn and do things better for the next one - for her sister - and for others. The depth of gratitude that I have for my daughter for this unspoken spiritual agreement is beyond words.

The Potential for Sabotage

Before you start designing something for your daughter, you've gotta ask yourself some important questions, the main one being - who is this ceremony for? I ask this because, so often, we create things for our children because we wish that we had those things for ourselves - without asking if that is what our unique child genuinely wants and needs. It pains me to say it, but this was totally a mistake I made with Sunna's ceremony, as you will see in a moment. I needed the elaborateness of it all. She did not.

That is not to say that there is anything wrong with having this experience also be a healing moment for you. Undoubtedly, for all women present who did not have some kind of rite of passage for their first menses, this will heal something deep within them. We need these moments as humans, and that ancient knowing awakens in each of us as we make the road for the next generation. These ceremonial ways heal backwards and forwards at the same time. That is the beautiful part of this work.

Obviously, I believe it is important for us to create some kind of ritual or ceremony for our young daughters to mark menarche as the passage from childhood into maidenhood. This is a huge event and deserves to be celebrated as such! But *how* that happens can sometimes be just as important as the actual ceremony itself - if not more so. It is quite possible - even likely - that you might have a need or desire in yourself for some kind of honoring, reclamation, initiation ceremony that you never received. That is so important to acknowledge, recognize, and then go about finding or creating for yourself. Your inner maiden is likely longing for some kind of initiation and acknowledgement of her sacredness.

Pause for a moment. Let's not bypass that if there is a very real need in you. How can you make space for that need to be met?

Can you gather with your local community of women and create that for one another? Is there someone near you or in your sphere of awareness offering something like this that you can participate in? I know a number of women doing this work. This is an important thing to honor in yourself. Tending to the elements of what would be nourishing for you in that way ahead of time allows for the experience to be centered around your daughter and what *she* needs at this time. Be mindful of any unprocessed desires of your own going into the creation of this rite of passage for her. Knowing that there has been or will be a dedicated moment for your inner maiden can help to quiet her so she doesn't inadvertently sabotage this moment for your child.

Sometimes it's not our inner maiden that sabotages it, though. For me, the sabotage moment came from needing to be the mother that provided this for her daughter, recognizing that I had wanted this for her since I first discovered that she was female. As one of my sisters who was present reminded me, for those of us that were in traditional circles before becoming mothers, a lot of responsibility gets passed on ceremonially to care for the next generation through these ways. While I don't think that is a bad thing at all - in fact, I believe it is correct and very needed, especially now - as I keep harping on, I am seeing now so clearly how essential proper preparation and peer involvement is in all of this.

Because we can also, if we aren't mindful of our shadows and lingering unprocessed desires trying to live themselves out vicariously through our children, do this so badly that we end up with the opposite result and embarrass the crap out of her, leading her far away from the sacred center we are trying to provide for her. I have seen this happen, too. I *almost* did that with my own child. The process is so, so delicate. This is why we think and talk about this well in advance. *This is why we prepare ourselves.*

Preparing for Ritual - Who Will Be There?

Part of the power of a rite of passage - part of what makes it a true rite of passage - is the element of being witnessed by our community. This means that if we are planning a ceremony to celebrate our daughter's first moontime, we are going to have to invite other people who she is close to be there.

When it comes to your daughter's first menses, this part is incredibly delicate and deserves to be done with total agency on your daughter's behalf. While we want to celebrate her, we also want to respect that this is her body and she may want to keep this detail of her life somewhat private. *A desire for privacy with our bodies does not have to be linked to a feeling of shame around our bodies.* I believe that a certain level of modesty can actually demonstrate a degree of self-respect, and doesn't need to itself be shamed. We can feel deep love and respect for our bodies without feeling a strong desire to constantly run around naked and shout our bleeding to the wind. Part of the teaching of maidenhood, of our blood as it relates to power, is the power in not always giving everything away. Nana Vilma was very clear with me when I spoke with her about this part. The desire for privacy itself is sacred and to be respected.

I *highly* recommend that she choose the guest list. In fact, this aspect feels non-negotiable to me in order for it to be a successful entrance into maidenhood that helps to foster her sense of dignity, self-respect, and a continued teaching of consent. She might want a lot of people there, she might not. She might not want ANYONE! *She might not want a big ceremony.* While this might be disappointing to you if this is in fact her truth and you were excited to throw her a big bash, it is of the utmost importance that you respect that for her. This is not your journey - it is hers. The differentiation from you as her mom is part of the process of growing up.

With my own daughter, I had a long list of women whom she had known for a long time - some her whole life - who were also ceremonial sisters or elders of mine that I wanted to be present for her when we had her maidenhood ceremony. These women I know and trust to hold a solid container for my child, to offer her wisdom and care and love in a way that I deeply desire for her. I also had friends of mine on my list who she is close with, but has only known for a few years.

I am a social person, so I have a lot of beloveds in my life. We talked about making it a hybrid event - in-person with folks who live far away being Zoomed in. The list quickly blossomed into something that felt totally overwhelming and unmanageable for her. She wasn't sure who, in my excitement, I was sharing this very special information about her with. She started to feel like she was not in control of this very important moment in her life and like her privacy was being violated.

I am so grateful that we have the relationship that we do that she was able to share her feelings with me on this before I took action and made the thing happen (even though, as you will see, I still managed to create some fallout). As soon as she shared her feelings with me, I immediately slowed down the process and took her lead on who should be there. While she didn't communicate her gratitude for my change of pace in words, the energetic shift in her being was palpable, and I am so glad that I listened to her. This was one moment where I could have easily energetically steamrolled over her desire and her no.

There might be women in your life that have hurt feelings about not being invited. Or she (or you) might be worried about that. Make sure you let your daughter know that this is not a time to care what others are going to think - including you. This is such a huge focus at this age - the desire to fit in, to not feel left out or make someone else feel left out. Some of us still haven't outgrown this as adults. This is not a time to give a crap about anyone else's feelings but your daughter's. She gets to be in complete control of what information gets shared about her, and to whom. It can be a powerful teaching moment.

In addition to older women being on the guest list, I would encourage you to have this be a ceremony not just for your daughter, but for other girls - friends of your daughter - who have also crossed the menarche threshold, and a few select women in their community as well. If younger girls or siblings who have not yet passed through menses are to be included in the ceremony, including them in a way that differentiates them from those who *have* crossed that threshold is crucial.

In my conversation with Nana, she also said that fathers could be welcome as well, to honor their place in their daughter's life and mark this passage and the change that comes with it for all the family. Considering the fact that there are very few places for men to find meaningful connection, I think including the dads in some way is beautiful. That said, women-only spaces have their own special magic too. Including the fathers in some part of the ceremony, while also making a time that is for women-only, would be my recommendation.

Key Ceremonial Elements

I was recently able to sit down with my teacher of many years and the founder of the Center for Sacred Studies (CSS), Jyoti Ma and co-founder and spiritual director of CSS Darlene Hunter, to ask about their vast knowledge and understanding of rites of passage ceremonies. For over 20 years, Jyoti and Darlene lived at the Kayumari community, which was a spiritual community they started with a few other individuals in the Sierra Nevada mountains in California back in 1995. You can read more about the founding of that community and the many elders and lineages that found them after its founding in Jyoti's book *An Angel Called My Name*.

Having been mentored by many Indigenous elders from a variety of different communities and lineages, Jyoti and Darlene shared with me that their community decided to have an annual rite of passage ceremony for all of the youth in the community. Once a year, this 4-day rite of passage for the teens would culminate in putting both the girls and the boys "up on the hill" as a part of their initiation. Leading up to the night on the hill, there would be breathworks, sweat lodges, talking circles, and fasting to prepare them. For the girls, the mothers, aunties, and grannies would make red dresses in the time leading up to ceremony. (Over time, that evolved to dresses with red, and then red shawls.)

Camped in a group, the boys were in one area and the girls in another - far enough away from one another that they were unable to see or hear each other (their community land was on 160 acres in the wilderness of California). They were put out there overnight with just their sleeping bags, under the stars. Each one was given enough space that, while they were together as a group, they each had their own separate spot that they were instructed not to leave until they were collected by someone from the community the next morning.

The community held an all-night fire for them, drumming and singing so they knew that they were being energetically held by everyone throughout this time. If they got cold, they could call on the energy of the fire for warmth. For the girls, inspired by Cherokee teachings the community was handed, they also had their own "Grandmother fire" that was kept by the elders and grandmothers of the community. Throughout the night, each girl would be brought one at a time to the Grandmother fire. Some years, this was actually held indoors, in a beautiful space that they would bring each girl into. There, the grandmothers would wash her feet and comb her hair and share with the girl stories of moontime and "secrets of womanhood" that were for women only. Then they would give her her dress or shawl to put on, making this initiation moment for her. When they were complete, they would "plant" her back on the hill, take the next girl, and do it all again, throughout the night.

In the morning, the entire community would be gathered in two lines with drums and rattles, ready to welcome the initiates back down the hill. The newly initiated youth would be collected by someone and led back down through this corridor of humans there to witness and celebrate the completion of their initiation. Parents would not be involved up until this final welcoming moment. The elders would then hold another sweat lodge for them to welcome them back and to hear what wisdom they had gathered in their time up there. In traditional cultures, this moment of listening to what the youth received would be taken quite seriously by the elders in the community, and used to inform how they would do things in the coming year.

Jyoti also shared a beautiful story with me of the first rite of passage for a young girl that she ever held, that was initiated by a direct request of her from the girl herself, when Jyoti was a student at the Jung Institute in Switzerland. Together, Jyoti and the girl decided who would come celebrate the moment her moon arrived and what they would do. When the girl's moon started, she summoned everyone on her list - friends, aunties, elders - and they had a chocolate party. Later, (I think maybe a few weeks or more) Jyoti "put her up on the hill." She found a spot in the mountains where the young girl could go to be alone with just her sleeping bag, and Jyoti held the fire a little further down the hill for her all night long. In the morning, she gathered the girl, who described her night with joy and reverence, having been given a name by the spirits of the place and her ancestors.

Obviously, not everyone will be able to have this exact kind of experience for their child (though I am currently in the process of finding land to be able to provide exactly this kind of thing for groups of youth - so stay tuned!). If you are creating your own version of ceremony for your daughter (and hopefully a few of her peers as well), there are a few things that I believe would be wise to include in every ceremony to celebrate the first menses:

- story sharing from elder women who have gone through it (elder in this sense means women at any stage of life past puberty. This could be teenagers, mothers, grandmothers, aunties - you get the picture)
- beauty
- celebration
- a moment for witnessing/questions from the young woman
- a moment of challenge for her to overcome
- peers who have also just crossed the threshold into menarche and are going through the ceremony with her at the same time and/or peers who will go through it soon
- LOVE

Story Sharing

Stories are powerful medicine. Throughout time and across cultures, women have gathered together to share their stories as a way of passing on crucial information, learning from one another, releasing their emotions, and growing together. Women are communally wired creatures, and gathering together in and of itself can be a sacred act.

It is important that the stories that are shared in this kind of first menses ceremony are positive ones. This moment can be virtual if people are unable to be present with you in person, but in-person is always better. A combo can work, too - zooming in folks who are far away and gathering in person with those who are local. That's what we did, though there were technical and audio challenges for those on the computer. Because of that, I don't think I would do it that way again. Instead, having folks who can't be present in real time give a pre-recorded video or write letters could be another way to weave them in without introducing the element of technology, which can make ceremonial space awkward. Letters then also provide a keepsake that your daughter can have for many years to come.

Make sure that everyone who will be attending knows that the mood is to be a positive one and that any horror stories will be redirected, unless they are shared in a way that brings humor and levity and culminates in growth or positive understanding. By the time she has her first bleed, with the help of the practices in this book, hopefully you will have already done some internal investigating and have clear anecdotes and answers that you can share with her. Being prepared ourselves is crucial to being able to properly support her in this very pivotal moment in her life.

If no one in your life or circle has positive menses stories, what are some ways you can project positivity into the experience for your daughter? What have you learned on the journey so far? What are you excited to provide for her that you didn't have? What do you wish had been done differently for you? If you don't have a positive story to share, what is a hope or blessing or kind and supportive words that you and others present can offer her? Make sure whatever hope for her is shared is not subtly imposed as an expectation.

Circles are one of the strongest shapes, and this is especially true when it comes to story sharing. Sitting together in a circle helps us to remember that no one is above or below us in importance. If you can, have the story sharing in a circle, or at least a format that allows everyone to see everyone else. If you feel called to formalize it, you can pass a talking object around the circle and have every person share a story, a blessing, a prayer, or their favorite thing about your daughter and what they see her blossoming into. I love talking circles this way, as they can minimize any awkwardness and talking over one another, and ensure that everyone present gets a chance to speak or share.

A basic talking circle format that was shared with me by my French Canadian, Algonquin and Innu elder Grandmother Nancy is to have a talking object - it could be anything, a special stone, a feather, a stick - that each person will hold as it is their turn to speak. In a traditional talking circle, the person leading the circle starts out with a question that is posed to the circle. In this case, it could be something like "what was your experience of your first moon" or "what is the most valuable thing you have learned about the power of being a woman?" The talking object is then passed, usually to the left in a sunwise motion, and each woman takes her time to answer the prompt.

While she is holding the talking object, no one else may talk. No responding, interjecting, or cross-talk is allowed. Only the person holding the talking object. Everyone else just listens. In our culture, where most people are just listening to respond, this is such a valuable tool and teaches us how to genuinely listen to one another. If you are holding a talking circle with people who have never sat in one before, make sure you clearly state this protocol at the beginning.

When the talking object returns to the person who is leading the circle, they can give their answer and/or pose another question or prompt. Then the object goes around again. It can be powerful to send it around several times, as sometimes we feel awkward to speak at first - especially if we are towards the beginning. Sending it around several times allows the fullness of what is in everyone's heart, as well as the expression of that circle - which is the constellation of everyone who shows up inside of it - to come to completion.

You might find that the talking circle, held in a beautiful space with a feast and celebration afterwards, is a perfect ceremony in and of itself.

Beauty

I like to think of beauty as a key spiritual principle. Beauty impacts our being in profound and subtle ways. Most people don't recognize the impact directly, but why do you think we have such curated Instagram feeds? We are wired to draw towards beauty, even if it's artificially created.

While beauty is, of course, subjective, we are wired as animals to feel most alive and in resonance in natural settings. Beauty has a beneficial impact on our psyche and the way we receive experiences. An abundance of fresh flowers, a clean space, and beautiful fabrics or objects can help set the tone for your ceremony. Have it outside if the weather and your space permits! You can even make a beautiful crown of flowers for her to wear to mark her special place in this ceremony. Crafting what would be meaningful for her with intention can bring a real purpose to the expressions of love and tending that go into creating a ritual space. One woman I know collected bunches of flowers for her daughter and made a special bouquet that they then hung upside down to dry afterwards as a special memento. Her daughter LOVED the flowers and that they were there specifically just for her. What do you think would feel beautiful to your daughter?

For Sunna, my sisters and I had a blast making my office into a gorgeous red tent for the ceremony. We gathered a bunch of red fabrics from around the house and got some more from the local second-hand store. The rug on the floor in my office is a Persian-style rug in primarily red tones. Covering the walls and doorway with red fabric made the whole space feel like a cozy womb. You can use the fabric to soften the corners in a space, making it feel even rounder and more womb-like. I brought out all of my goddess statues and gave them prominent places, emphasizing powerful feminine imagery. With those and the altars for the 4 directions and the flowers, it was absolutely beautiful in there. We even set up one of the fabrics over the doorway to be a threshold that she had to cross in order to enter the space.

Celebration

Make it fun! Throw on some of her favorite music and have a dance party. Make a special cake, food, or beverage. Have a feast afterwards! Let her choose what will be on the menu. Ask her what she wants. There are so many ways to celebrate.

One of my friends told me that when she first started her menses, she was at her aunt's house, along with her cousin who had started her bleed just a couple of years prior. Her aunt took out a bottle of wine, popped the cork, and poured each one of them a glass, as they settled into a casual and impromptu story share and celebration. It was simple and of-the-moment, and according to my friend, the absolute perfect thing.

I'm not suggesting you get your young daughter drunk, nor that alcohol has to be a part of the picture, but I love this story because it illustrates how sometimes ritual and ceremony doesn't have to be elaborate or contrived. Simplicity and authentic, in-the-moment sharing can be just as impactful.

Keep it small. Keep it simple. Keep it light.

My daughter knew that when she started her moon, she would get to have her ears pierced for the first time. This is something she had been looking forward to for years, ever since she asked me when she was 6 or 7 if she could get them pierced. Before getting them pierced, she already had her first pair of earrings that someone gave her sitting in waiting for the special event.

A Moment for Witnessing or Questions

It is also nice to create a space for her to share into the circle as well, if she would like to. Let her know at the beginning of the circle that there will be space for this, so that she can think about what she might want to ask. How is it for her? What does she feel like she needs or wants? What questions does she have of her elders, aunties and of you? It is possible that your daughter might be so overwhelmed with the moment, the people, and the new experience that she is unable to think of any questions at this time. That is totally fine.

Creating a pathway for your daughter to communicate with some of these women outside of the circle is crucial. Part of the intention of involving other women in this kind of circle to honor her first menses is to create a circle for your daughter of women who are committed to *her*. So considering ahead of time how you plan to back up those relationships in a real way that your child can count on - for years - is a worthy endeavor. She might have questions about someone's story after-the-fact. She might later have a fight with you, or be mad at you for some reason or another, but still need an older woman that she can lean into for advice. Intentionally creating relationships for your daughter with other women who aren't you, but that you trust to deliver wise advice that you yourself might give, is part of the secret sauce of successfully raising a confident and healthy daughter in this day and age.

Puberty and maturation bring a need for mentorship in a way you both might not have experienced yet. Moving away from you a bit is a healthy and normal shift that should be happening at this time. Knowing this can lessen the discomfort you might feel around this very natural process and help you to take it less personally. It's okay if you feel sad about it a bit, too! It's a totally normal and natural part of growing up. And don't worry - if you've built a solid foundation with her, she will circle back around later. But casting off into the world is a crucial part of our development. And it will start now that puberty is here in full force, if it hasn't already.

Challenge

After being a part of a few of these ceremonies for other young women, as well as my experience with my own daughter, I am now of the mind that a successful ritual for this age group would need to incorporate several elements that we did not have for Sunna. Those things are 1) some kind of challenge that the girl willingly takes on and rises to, and 2) other peers her age who are going through it at the same time. Ideally, each young maiden would have a chance for the focus to be on her and to ask her specific questions.

Puberty is an age where we are breaking away from having things done for us. We need to discover our own sense of self, and in order to do that effectively, it means we need to do challenging things on our own, without our parents. Historically, weaving this element of challenge into the ceremony has been a part of all coming of age rituals.

In an age where we can perceive challenge and struggle as lurking around every corner, we parents have a tendency to shield our children from experiences that they actually need in order to forge a sense of self and competency in the world. What this has led to is an epidemic of children going through adolescence and into what used to be adulthood having no idea how to care for themselves in the real world. They don't even know how to interact with conflicting opinions without feeling a direct threat to their personhood. In *The Coddling of the American Mind,* Jonathan Haidt and Greg Lukianoff do an incredible job of looking at this recent phenomenon across college campuses in the United States, and giving specific advice to parents as to what we can do to foster a greater sense of self in our youth. I believe that, if done well, these coming of age ceremonies have the potential to be a really powerful part of that process.

While it was before I started my menses, one of the most powerful rites of passage that I participated in as a young girl was a wilderness solo. This is not as scary as it sounds - I was not abandoned in the wilderness to fend for myself. It was the culminating part of a wilderness summer camp experience when I was 11. Similar to what was done in the Kayumari community rite of passage ceremony, the night before our final night at camp, the counselors took each one of us off to a separate place in the woods that was out of sight of the main camp. Our spots were all within a one-mile radius of the main camp, but we could not see or hear anyone around us. There was an all-night fire being kept for us, and we were told that if we really needed to come back to camp, we could. We were brought out at dusk with only our sleeping bags, some water, and if we wanted, a few snacks. No tents. Some chose to fast. We were instructed to stay in our spots, alone, for a full 24 hours, after which someone would come and collect us and bring us back to camp. Coming through this challenge at that age gave me a sense of security in myself and what I was capable of that nothing up until that point had done. My counselors even commented on how radiant and glowing I was after that experience. The feeling of successfully completing something that was very scary to me was beyond words.

While you may not be able to recreate a wilderness solo for your daughter (but you also maybe could…), having some element that is challenging and that she willingly engages in forges something in her. One of my friends shared her story with me about her menarche reclamation ceremony that she participated in in her early 20s. Part of the ceremony involved choosing to walk down a kind of long path through the woods that led to the red tent where the elders were waiting to receive her for her personalized ceremony. While she was in a group who did this together, each woman had an individualized portion of the ceremony. She had to walk this path alone and in the dark. She made the choice to walk it, and in doing so, her ability to receive the medicine that was waiting for her on the other side was amplified.

Whatever the challenge ends up being - whether it's as intense as a 24-hour wilderness solo, or a milder solo walk through the woods, or something in between - I do think that trying to incorporate something like this adds a layer that children of this age really need. The star nation, the earth, and the elements have things to teach us that no human can. Give her an opportunity to learn how to listen.

Peer Engagement

As I keep harping on, another key component in order for these ceremonies to actually be something that begins to change culture would be doing them in community with other young women who have also come through their menses. I cannot stress this enough. This is the biggest takeaway for me from Sunna's ceremony in terms of what we could have had in place but didn't that would have made the biggest positive difference for her. The community that surrounded her - while filled with sisters who love her deeply and have watched her grow, and whom she has beautiful and loving relationships with - was my adult community. It wasn't hers. Her peers were missing.

I recognize that this might not always be possible for everyone. Because of all of our moving around, it wasn't really easily possible for us, which is part of why it was missing. Now that I understand how important it is, if I were to do it again, I would have made an effort to collaborate with the mothers of her close girlfriends out east, even if it meant waiting and some extensive travel for us. Hopefully, if you have taken my suggestion at the beginning to heart and read this with a group of like-minded moms, then you already have started gathering your community around you. May it continue to grow and thrive through these years! Keep it going. After years of traveling around, searching for the perfect place to live with my family, the one thing that is abundantly clear to me is this: community is the most valuable resource there is. It takes time and commitment to grow deep roots together with others. Grow the trust together. Keep it sacred.

What I Didn't Expect

Actually, none of what happened for my daughter's ceremony did I expect. I did not expect people to fly and drive in from different parts of the country and descend upon our house for 4 days. I don't know why - I have some really incredible community folks in my life. We have moved a lot in recent years and have only been in our current home for a little over 2 years, so our most solid community connections are not currently local. It felt almost like a (really small) wedding celebration, with people flying in from all over, some of whom I hadn't seen in over 4 years. The recognition of the significance of this event by so many other dear sisters floored me.

I also did not expect that one of those people would be Grandmother Nancy, a traditional elder - which involves a very specific form of care that is different from just tending to someone who is older or elderly. I have benefited immensely from having traditional elders and their wisdom in my life. They are precious jewels, and I am beyond humbled and grateful that I have had - and continue to have - relationships with traditional Indigenous elders, the caliber of which most people will never get to encounter. And - it is no small feat to host an elder. There are protocols around caring for traditional elders and wisdom keepers that need to be adhered to when we call in this kind of ceremony. Those protocols involve tremendous attention, care, and often (and in this case) additional financial resources. It is wise to have someone specifically assigned to tend to that elder and their needs for the duration of their time with you.

It also meant that, due to custom and protocol, I made a significant amount of deference to this elder in terms of what would happen in the ceremony itself. What I originally thought we might do, and what ended up creating itself through the confluence of humans who showed up for this moment, were two totally different animals. What was created was beautiful beyond my wildest dreams - and it was also structured differently than I would have done on my own.

I didn't expect that this elder would receive a spiritual name for my daughter the night before the ceremony, which meant that the ceremony began with a naming. Spiritual names are gifted by the ancestors, and are given for us to grow into and embody throughout the rest of our lives. A spirit name is also something that, like menstruation, is often kept close and private - most people with a spiritual name do not share it with others outside of ceremonial contexts. In some cultures, people are given names at different points of maturation or rites of passage. So towards the end of their life a person will have many names, marking a path of the unfolding of their life journey. Some people walk this kind of spiritual path their whole lives without receiving a name. In and of itself, a naming could be its own ceremony and is incredibly significant. I think, because of this, I made a way bigger deal about her receiving a name than I should have.

I didn't expect the depth of wisdom that would pour forth from the mouths of my sisters when we sat in circle to honor my child, even though some other part of me knew that is exactly what would happen. I didn't expect the gifting and some of the other ceremonial elements that were present because of who gathered around her. I didn't expect that in the face of all these people that I loved and cherished that I would be as stressed out as I was!!!

And I definitely didn't expect that my daughter would find the ceremony itself way, way too much for her, so much so that she even got physically ill and vomited the following morning. I didn't expect the tears the following night (brought on by physical exhaustion from staying up way too late several nights in a row to drink in the goodness of all of our community, who traveled so far to be with us) and her expressions of how part of her didn't feel at choice with the ceremony. This shocked me, especially because, as I mentioned earlier, I thought I had done such a great job at crafting this along with her in a way that worked for her. I wanted her to love this experience so much. The possibility of her not loving it never even crossed my mind.

I didn't expect my own feelings of grief and confusion the day after Grandmother left, when my daughter seemed awkward and removed from me in a way I had never experienced before. This, perhaps more than any of it, floored me the most. I was not prepared for the possibility that, after this ceremony, my daughter would feel the need to pull away from me. It makes a lot of sense, if you think about it. A ceremony to initiate a young girl into the beginning stages of womanhood would naturally involve a pulling away and differentiation from her mother. But I foolishly did not anticipate this aspect, and energetically and emotionally, I was not ready for it at all.

After a good night's sleep (and the blessing of her fairy godmother remaining for a few days after everyone else flew back to their home places), my daughter's affect changed completely. My fears of her separating from me in a not-so-good way after the experience were shown to be clearly unfounded. In reality, the experience seems to have drawn us closer - though a differentiation is now clearer. I think by having some elements that felt like too much for her as a part of it, she can now start to identify more of her unique preferences that are distinct from my own. She is now, for the first time really, claiming her generational difference, which I don't see as a bad thing at all. As I was writing and reviewing this chapter with her, we also talked at length about how different it would have been had she had peers there, and she shared tears with me about how hard it was that she didn't have that. It made her feel like she had to compartmentalize the experience in order to go back to her regular life afterwards. So even though it didn't pull us apart, all of that not-knowingness and fear still came up for me - and I'm glad it did. What transpired during her ceremony was so immensely powerful that I expect both my daughter and I will be integrating this experience for many years to come.

One of the things she has shared with me that was confusing, and therefore challenging for her, was the use of the words woman and womanhood. She and I had had several conversations when she first started her moon about how she wasn't really a woman yet, even though she had definitely made a shift. We called it her shift from being a child into being a maiden - no longer a little kid, but not yet a woman either. This delineation seemed very satisfying and relieving for her. Before we knew Grandmother was coming, I even spoke with Maggie and Gia about making this part of the conversation in the circle.

But we didn't. And a number of the women in the circle, including Grandmother, used the verbiage of welcoming her into "womanhood." This was immensely confusing and overwhelming for my daughter. For her, she received a spiritual name along with a new title of woman, and what she was supposed to do with that, overall, felt like way too much. I'm sure it didn't help that I also made the mistake of welcoming her into the space flooded with emotion, sharing that ever since I found out she was a girl, I had been waiting for this ceremony, for this moment. No pressure, right? To be fair to myself, I also acknowledged at that moment that I had made so many mistakes with her and was certain I would make more (as I was in the process of making another one....oh, well. What can you do, right?).

Holding a long view can be so challenging with things like this. And yet, it is that long view that brings us to wanting to create these moments for our daughters. We look back and feel an emptiness in our own menarche journey, and we know it doesn't have to be that way.

It is very possible that no matter how hard you try to make this experience a beautiful occasion for your daughter, it will land as too much for her. I hope that after reading this chapter, that will not be the case, but we don't know what we don't know! Sometimes no matter how prepared we think we are, spirit has other plans for us. That is the way of things and part of the learning of being human. However it goes, here's the wisdom that Sunna's godmother Maggie so brilliantly shared after our ceremony: the experience of going from being a kid one day, to waking up bleeding, and now being on a path as a bleeding woman for the next 40 years or so, *is* too much. It doesn't feel like we are at choice with it - because we aren't. How we respond to that realization becomes our way of being with what is. In the words of my dear sister and elder, Marcella (who was also at Sunna's ceremony), these rites of passage ceremonies bring up that which normally lives hidden under the surface. Because of the murky depths that this stuff normally inhabits, we don't have the opportunity to engage with it. Ceremony provides us with that opportunity.

And so, having a ceremony to mark this occasion might very well just make that too much, not-at-choice feeling bigger. *But that doesn't mean that we shouldn't do it.* It just means that we need to be as intentional with crafting the integration as we are with the ceremony itself. How we work with what comes up matters so very much. Not bringing up what is lurking underneath is "easier," sure. But what's the trade-off? When I look at the ceremonies that have happened for the young women I know that have backfired, this integration alongside community is the part that I think has been missing.

Integration

Integration is such a crucial component to this kind of culture shifting work. Whether it's a major ceremony, a spiritual workshop, or a personal development seminar, without proper integration these kinds of big experiences can blow out all of our systems - and it can actually register as a kind of trauma. Integration helps us to understand the experience, to digest and metabolize it, and to give opportunity for us to look at and hold it from a variety of different angles, while applying its medicine to our lives.

Often attributed to Krishnamurti, I have always loved the phrase "it is no measure of health to be well adjusted to a sick society." This rings true for me. These kinds of ceremonies are a beautiful way of doing something new and different - and yet if our daughters are somewhat adjusted already to our totally bizarre cultural norms and we don't have the in-person, day-to-day community to support this kind of work, then going back out into consensus reality afterwards could feel jarring. Considering how your daughter feels about having peers present, it might be valuable to offer this perspective that inviting at least one friend that she maintains regular connection with afterward would be a good idea. Obviously, I am of the mind at this point that doing this kind of thing at this age alongside peers is the only way it works.

If you have started a group through the process of reading this book with other moms, then you are well on your way to having a built-in format for integration for your young one (I really hope you have. If you haven't, read this book again and do that part this time). Having a commitment from the older women in attendance that they will be there for your daughter over the years cannot be overstated. Grow your relationship and communication skills to increase the likelihood of this happening! This is not a performative ceremony - this is a way of life. Faulty or half-hearted mentorship can cause all sorts of heartbreak on its own. In my conversation with Darlene Hunter about rites of passage for young people, she said this: "The witnessing by the community *is* the integration." The committed community is what makes integration possible.

Having regular mother-daughter circles that start well before the menarche ceremony can be a beautiful way to create a natural container for integration. Even if the kids just go off and play while the moms connect, coming together regularly with intention is in-and-of-itself a dramatic culture shift. If you haven't been cultivating adult women friends for your daughter until now, or find yourself at the beginning stages of wanting to change and grow alongside others, you are not alone. We are all in different stages and phases of personal and community growth. It's okay if you haven't really started that yet. You can start now.

Creating the kind of lasting community that allows for healthy integration necessitates longevity of relationships. When I started out in my ministry training at CSS, this was something that Jyoti and Darlene spoke about often. Many times, Jyoti would talk about how we live in a throw-away culture. If you don't like something someone did, you cancel them. If you don't like something someone said, you get rid of them in your life. It's so much easier to throw a person away, to shut them out of your life, than it is to have the hard conversations that lead to sustained, healthy relationships over time. When discussing their Kayumari community experience, the importance of committing to longevity of relationships was something she emphasized regularly.

I have been intentionally curating relationships for my daughter with other powerful and beloved women in my life since she was a little girl. They have not been forced, but she knows that there are people that she can reach out to if she ever needs them. She has their contact info and knows how to get a hold of them. She knows and loves them. And they are wise to the point that they understand that they should not wait for her to contact them. They reach out to her often as well. I trust these people.

Trust can be tricky for adults. Especially if we have been hurt in the past (who hasn't, right?), growing trust with others can feel scary. But trust is essential if we want the longevity of relationships. In my experience, cultivating trust with others takes a few things. It takes a willingness to be vulnerable and open about how I am feeling, especially when I'm feeling uncomfortable. It takes doing what I say I am going to do - and if for some reason I can't, communicating openly about that. It takes acknowledging where I may have misstepped, and being willing to apologize without caveat or excuse. And it takes being willing to be confrontational in a loving way that allows things to be aired and cleared so that they don't fester in the shadows. It takes commitment to maintaining the relationship - which sometimes means having scary and hard conversations that make us feel shaky inside and like we are going to puke. And it takes being met by the other person with a willingness to do the same. Without trust, we cannot have true community. And without community, we cannot have successful integration.

When we come through a transformative experience and are witnessed by our community in the process, it allows for the change to register in a whole different way. We know we have changed - we can feel that something is different. Having ceremony and being witnessed by those closest to us in that change allows our community to also know that we have changed, and adjust accordingly. One thing I hear a lot in the personal and spiritual growth spaces is how when people grow and change, their family, friends, spouses, etc., keep relating to them as how they were before. This can inhibit both sustaining the growth for that person, as well as the longevity of the relationship. Oftentimes, people feel like they are forced to choose one or the other. When we can be witnessed and celebrated in our growth by those important to us during our threshold moments, we minimize the likelihood that someday we will have to make that excruciating choice.

Exercise: Cedar Baths

This is an Algonquin tradition that was passed on to me by Grandmother Nancy Andry, and is shared here with her blessing.

The plant we use for this bath is called Flat Leaf Cedar, or Northern White Cedar (Thuja Occidentalis). This plant grows in the Northeastern part of the North American continent, extending through to parts of the Midwest as well. Western Red Cedar, found on the west coast, can also be used.

There are many teachings around this plant, and different tribes hold it differently. Cedar has been taught to me as the women's herb, and cedar baths are traditionally used as part of the moonlodge ceremony. Cedar is especially helpful for us around our moontime, as it helps us to cleanse and purify ourselves energetically, and moontime is a time when we tend to be more sensitive to energy and more energetically porous and absorbent. It clears away that which is no longer serving us, helps to remove stuck or stagnant energy, and brings in a clarity and sweetness with it in the process. Cedar is a magnificent clearing herb. Anyone who has had a cedar bath will attest to it - you can feel the results immediately.

To Prepare a Cedar Bath:

For this bath, you will need the fresh plant, not dried. When harvesting cedar, there are a few things to keep in mind:

1. The plant you are harvesting is a living, conscious being. You are asking something from it. It is always right before asking for something to make an offering first. Tobacco, cornmeal, or a bit of your hair can all be appropriate offerings.
2. Come humbly. Listen to the plant's answer to your request - whether you like it or not. Sometimes it is not the right season, or there might be one branch or tree that is happy to offer themselves

and another that is working on making berries, or for some other reason unknown to us, is not willing. NEVER TAKE FROM A PLANT THAT HAS SAID NO. You don't want that kind of medicine.

3. Only take what you need. It shouldn't be clear to an outside observer that you were there harvesting after the fact.

Harvest enough cedar to loosely fill the pot you will be using. Cover with enough water just to cover the plant material and set on a high flame. Cover, bring to just before a boil, and turn off the heat. (The phrase "a watched pot never boils" actually comes from herbalism - you don't *want* the water to fully boil, as that can destroy many of the beneficial plant constituents.) Let it sit for at least 15 minutes. It's best when it is still warm but cool enough to touch without burning yourself.

This cedar water is what will be used for the bath. You can pour the water directly over a person (or yourself), or you can do what we sometimes call "brushing off" with the water. To do this, I like to use the branches of the cedar that are still in the water. Making sure plenty of water is still clinging to them, I brush them over a person - usually starting with their head, then down their back, arms, chest, buttocks, belly, thighs, legs, and feet.

You can use cedar water to lovingly wash someone's feet, but I always prefer a full-body cleansing - especially on my head (to help clear out those ruminating thoughts!) and over my heart and belly/womb. Cedar water made this way is intended for external use only (unless you make it in a glass or ceramic vessel, as metal renders the cedar water toxic for internal use).

If there is any cedar water left over, lovingly offer it to the earth.

THE PERIOD AT THE END OF THE SENTENCE: YOUR INTEGRATION - BRINGING ALL THE PIECES TOGETHER

So, what changes after menarche? Well, in many ways, nothing. Your daughter will still go through her daily life as she did before she started her bleed. She'll brush her teeth, eat her meals, play with her friends, sass you sometimes. Except now, also, *everything* has changed. Because now she is a bleeding maiden and will be for many, many years to come. And so, the integration of that reality looks like a rhythmic adjustment that will ebb and flow as she settles into her cycle and what it means to eventually mature into a woman. Hopefully, she has peers that she can share this positive experience with. Everything we have discussed in this book now starts to get applied - little by little, day by day.

I have given you everything I could around this topic that I have been steeped in for over 20 years - and yet I'm sure once it's out in the world, I will wish I had added that one other thing. Life, and creating, is like that. We do our best, and it's imperfect and messy most of the time.

We've gone on such a journey together! We've investigated the cultural and historical contexts for our self-limiting beliefs. Hopefully, a practice of self-awareness and re-writing those beliefs has started to happen - if it wasn't already underway for you. We've walked into the tenderness of befriending the body. This is a life-long process - if you're not besties with her already by the time you finish this, it's okay. Cultivating true friendship takes time. We've learned some skills to help navigate relational challenges with our kiddo - and others in our life, too. We've challenged the mainstream approaches to just about everything when it comes to women's health. We've detoxed our homes from endocrine disrupting chemicals - yay!!! We dug into the scariest and most uncomfortable underbelly topics of sex. And we've explored what's possible in the realm of creating powerful rites of passage for our young ones.

And now the journey continues. What will *your* integration look like? Who is the community that you have gathered around you? Who have you yet to call in to walk this kind of path alongside you? How do you plan to take what's been uncovered here and implement it in your daily life? What do *you* want to come next?

I hope this book has led to a journey that has been as expansive and meaningful for you as a reader as it has been for me to write it all down. So much has been revealed to me about the next unfoldings of my own journey as it relates to this work. Make sure you stay in touch over at pathtopuberty.com so you, too, can be a woven part of it. Follow along with how it is evolving, and come share your own story on the podcast. This is more than just a book. As evidenced by the extensive number of contributors and supporters of this book coming into being, Path to Puberty is a collective movement. It is my prayer that this book serve as a catalyst for a complete culture shift in the way we relate to our wombs and our daughters.

I may not get to see all the ways the threads of this work weave into place in the tapestry of our culture moving forward. And yet I still place the threads, cast the seeds, and do the work. Thank you for being a part of it.

ACKNOWLEDGEMENTS

Oh, man, I had better not leave anyone out...

First and foremost, I want to say thank you to this abundant Earth Mother and all she provides for all of us. Thank you to the sacred waters of life and to all of my relations - the two-winged, one-legged, four-legged, swimming and creepy crawly relatives, without which there is no life for any of us. To that Grandpa sun, who shines and gives life and light to us all, serving as a reminder of where we come from, I give great thanks.

As far as my two-legged relatives go, there are many, many for whom I am grateful - for their contributions not only to this book, but to my life as a whole. To my mother, who had the grace, courage, and surrender to birth me in full conscious awareness and imprint me with the orgasmic love of Creator upon my arrival here, I say thank you. To my brother Laszlo and father Ion, and to all my ancestors in the spirit world whose hands have ushered me to this path, I say thank you. To my husband who said yes to a truly wild woman, thank you for your prayers, for your dance, for your music, for supporting our family for all these years, and for sticking with me on this journey. Thank you for giving me incredible children. To my children, Sunna and Luna, my Sun and my Moon - this work would not exist for me without you. Sunna, thank you for walking this journey with me, for letting me tell the world about it, and for giving me feedback when I screw up. Also, thank you for seeing how important putting the mistakes I made with you in a book for others was. You are such a cool kid.

To my elders and teachers - Nana Vilma Cholac Chicol, Grandmother Nancy Andry, Natem Anank Nunkai, Jyoti Ma, Darlene Hunter, Jon Delson, Rashani Rea, Cindy Delcourt, Ron Anderson, Gene Delcourt, Tom Thompson, Robert Jacobo and the entire Sundance family - your teachings and wisdom have deeply altered the fabric of my life in the best possible way. Thank you from the depths of my heart for sharing these gifts of ceremony, healing, and prayer with me. I am forever a changed and better person because of what I have learned from you.

To Emilee Saldayya and Yolande Norris Clark - for opening the floodgates for the return of sovereign birth, thank you for being my mentors and teachers on this path. To the April 2023 RBK cohort - you women give me hope and inspiration for the future. Thank you for witnessing me at a critical time in my life, for supporting my writing, and for doing the work of encouraging more sovereign births. The world needs you!

For the women of the womb who contributed their brilliance and offerings for this book: Nikki Ananda, Juliana Rose Goldstone, Chaya Leia Aronson, Mangala Holland, Devorah Bry - my deepest gratitude for your work in the world and for offering a taste of it into this space. Christiane Anna Rodriguez, from one queen to another, thanks for cheering me on from go. This is just the beginning, sister! Andrea Olsen - thank you for being the best fucking business midwife ever. This book would absolutely not exist in any way, shape, or form without your clear, grounded, and loving guidance. Thank you for showing me how to get organized in virtual space so I could write this thing. As far as writing a book goes, this was way less painful than everyone says it is, and I am convinced it's because of your help. And to all the mompreneurs in the Accelerator program, thank you for your continued support and cheerleading!

To my sisters Maggie White, Marcella Eversole, Gia Neswald, and Suzette Pena - thank you for walking this beauty way with me, for your love and encouragement, and for checking a sister when she needs it - in the most gracious and loving way! Thank you for being the best aunties ever to Sunna, and for continuously getting me in and out of trouble.

Glenn Drapeau, thank you for entrusting your nation's origin story into this work. Nick Jorgenson - thank you for being my brother on this spiritual path, for introducing me to the MN prayer family and for giving me Glenn's phone number. Joni Little Owl - thank you for letting me include your father's wisdom in here. May it serve many.

To the Madison Waldorf School community - thank you for being a landing place for us in a time of craziness and great change. Rozeskes - you've been like family to us and we are forever grateful for your love and support. Thanks Heidi for introducing me to *everyone* and for being my sister in charcuterie and wild European ancestral adventures. Here's to more! To Team Women, thank you for holding me up so I can share this out far and wide!

RECOMMENDED READING

Menstruation and Women's Health:

- *Her Blood is Gold* - Lara Owen
- *Wild Feminine* - Tami Kent
- *Everything Below the Waist: Why Healthcare Needs a Feminist Revolution* - Jennifer Block
- *Taking Charge of Your Fertility* - Toni Weschler MPH
- *The Fifth Vital Sign* - Lisa Hendrickson-Jack
- *In the Flo* - Alisa Vitti
- *Healing Wise* - Susun S. Weed
- *Hygeia: A Woman's Herbal* - Jeannine Parvati
- *New Menopausal Years The Wise Woman Way: Alternative Approaches for Women 30-90* - Susun S. Weed
- *Wise Woman Herbal for the Childbearing Year* - Susun S. Weed

Sexuality:

- *Sex, Love & Health: A Self-Help Health Guide to Love & Sex* - Brigitte Mars
- *Women's Anatomy of Arousal* - Sheri Winston
- *Sexual Secrets: The Alchemy of Ecstasy* - Penny Slinger and Nik Douglas
- *Healing Love Through the Tao: Cultivating Female Sexual Energy* - Mantak and Maneewan Chia
- *Orgasms Made Easy: The No-Nonsense Guide to Self-Pleasure, Sexual Confidence and Female Orgasms* - Mangala Holland

Trauma:

- *Call of the Wild* - Kimberly Ann Johnson
- *Waking the Tiger* - Peter Levine
- *The Body Keeps the Score* - Bessel Van Der Kolk
- *Dreambody* - Arnold Mindell
- *The Aroma Freedom Technique: Using Essential Oils to Transform Your Emotions and Realize Your Heart's Desire* - Dr. Benjamin Perkus
- *The Tapping Solution: A Revolutionary System for Stress-Free Living* - Nick Ortner

Women's Spirituality and Feminism:

- *Women Who Run With the Wolves* - Clarissa Pinkola Estes
- *A Woman's Journey to God: Finding the Feminine Path* - Joan Borysenko
- *Barefoot on Holy Ground* - Gloria Karpinski
- *Sacred Woman* - Queen Afua
- *Portal: The Art of Choosing Orgasmic, Blissful, Pain-Free Birth* - Yolande Norris Clark
- *The Beauty Myth: How Images of Beauty are Used Against Women* - Naomi Wolf
- *An Angel Called My Name: A Story of a Transformational Energy That Lives in the Body* - Jyoti

Parenting:

- *Hunt, Gather, Parent: What Ancient Cultures Can Teach Us About the Lost Art of Raising Happy, Helpful Little Humans* - Michaeleen Doucleff, PhD
- *The Coddling of the American Mind* - Greg Lukianoff and Johnathan Haidt

- *Girls and Sex* - Peggy Orenstein
- *The Seven Spiritual Laws for Parents* - Deepak Chopra

Books to give to your daughter:

- *Cycle Savvy: The Smart Teens Guide to the Mysteries of Her Body* - Toni Weschler MPH
- *Celebrate Your Period: The ultimate puberty book for preteen and teen girls* - Amanda d'Almeida

Conscious Communication, Healing and Personal Growth:

- *The Power of Humility: Choosing Peace Over Conflict in Relationships* - Charles L. Whitfield, Barbara H. Whitfield, Russell Park and Jeneane Prevett
- *Your Wish is Your Command Audio Series* - Kevin Trudeau
- *Sitting in the Fire* - Arnold Mindell
- *Ask and It Is Given* - Abraham Hicks
- *The 15 Commitments of Conscious Leadership: A New Paradigm for Sustainable Success* - Jim Dethmer, Diana Chapman and Kaley Warner Klemp
- *Getting the Love You Want: A Guide for Couples* - Harville Hendrix PhD
- *The Genius Zone: The Breakthrough Process to End Negative Thinking and Live in True Creativity* - Gay Hendricks
- *Learning to Love Yourself* - Gay Hendricks
- *Loving What Is* - Byron Katie
- *Becoming Supernatural: How Common People are Doing the Uncommon* - Joe Dispenza
- *You Are the Placebo: Making Your Mind Matter* - Joe Dispenza

RESOURCES

For the most up-to-date links on the best resources mentioned throughout this book, go to the resources section of the website: pathtopuberty.com

REFERENCES

https://www.hopkinsmedicine.org/health/wellness-and-prevention/anatomy-of-the-endocrine-system

https://www.betterhealth.vic.gov.au/health/conditionsandtreatments/parathyroid-glands

https://www.anoptimalyou.com/estrogen-hormone-balancing/

https://www.ncbi.nlm.nih.gov/pmc/articles/PMC6433066/#:~:text=Preclinical%20studies%20have%20shown%20that,relieves%20symptoms%20of%20mood%20disorder.

https://www.harpalclinic.co.uk/blog/dhea-pregnenolone-and-human-growth-hormone-the-mystery-hormones/#:~:text=DHEA%20and%20Pregnenolone%20are%20precursor,hormones%20(cortisol%2C%20aldosterone).

https://my.clevelandclinic.org/health/body/22525-gonadotropin-releasing-hormone

https://www.hopkinsmedicine.org/health/conditions-and-diseases/hormones-and-the-endocrine-system

https://www.ncbi.nlm.nih.gov/pmc/articles/PMC7566378/

https://www.ncbi.nlm.nih.gov/pmc/articles/PMC6074149/#:~:text=A%20relationship%20between%20estrogen%20and,steroids%20in%20the%20human%20ovary.

https://www.ncbi.nlm.nih.gov/pmc/articles/PMC5192018/

Puberty
Richard E. Jones PhD, Kristin H. Lopez PhD, in Human Reproductive Biology (Fourth Edition), 2014

Female Reproduction
Jacqueline Y. Maher, Howard A. Zacur, in Encyclopedia of Reproduction (Second Edition), 2018
https://pubmed.ncbi.nlm.nih.gov/31792807/

https://www.niehs.nih.gov/health/topics/agents/endocrine

https://www.ncbi.nlm.nih.gov/pmc/articles/PMC2726844/#:~:text=The%20group%20of%20molecules%20identified,%2C%20plasticizers%20(phthalates)%2C%20pesticides

https://www.ewg.org/skindeep/browse/ingredients/706622-TRICLOCARBAN/

https://factor.niehs.nih.gov/2023/5/science-highlights/phthalates-and-beauty-justice

Londonclinicofnutrition.co.uk

https://www.ncbi.nlm.nih.gov/pmc/articles/PMC5087699/#:~:text=More%20than%2090%25%20of%20men,2001%3B%20Kontula%2C%202009).

https://www.commonsensemedia.org/press-releases/new-report-reveals-truths-about-how-teens-engage-with-pornography#:~:text=The%20report%27s%20key%20findings%20highlight,first%20viewing%20pornography%20is%2012.

https://open.spotify.com/episode/1wRKmg6NnfZoOlnuOyhUCA?si=i3GirnnOQ7KcyTE1dXFXGA

https://open.spotify.com/episode/0jbltlhQbaFfDb5lDV8vD7?si=cUFW1DEvS42sfTncqrtqiA

https://journals.plos.org/plosone/article?id=10.1371/journal.pone.0202330

https://www.medicalnewstoday.com/articles/265215#:~:text=BMI%20(body%20mass%20index)%2C,of%20Medicine%2C%20University%20of%20Pennsylvania.

https://www.ncbi.nlm.nih.gov/pmc/articles/PMC5868281/

https://naturalwomanhood.org/pill-cause-infertility-yes-no/

https://www.factsaboutfertility.org/wp-content/uploads/2018/08/Odeblad_Discovery-Cervical-Mucus_1994.pdf

https://www.cdc.gov/std/chlamydia/stdfact-chlamydia.htm

https://www.cdc.gov/nchhstp/newsroom/docs/factsheets/std-trends-508.pdf

https://www.ncbi.nlm.nih.gov/pmc/articles/PMC2820578/#:~:text=According%20to%20this%20model%2C%20human,in%20the%20morning%20%5B8%5D.

https://www.cdc.gov/nchs/data/hestat/maternal-mortality/2021/maternal-mortality-rates-2021.htm
lecture given on March 7th at the 2024 WALC conference by Kajsa Brimdyr PhD, CLC

Portal: The Art of Choosing Orgasmic, Pain-Free, Blissful Birth by Yolande Norris-Clark

Spiritual Midwifery by Ina May Gaskin

https://www.bbc.com/travel/article/20210107-kintsugi-japans-ancient-art-of-embracing-imperfection#

Everything Below the Waist: Why healthcare needs a feminist revolution by Jennifer Block

The Coddling of the American Mind - Greg Lukianoff and Johnathan Haidt

Girls & Sex: Navigating the Complicated New Landscape by Peggy Orenstein

Taking Charge of Your Fertility by Toni Weschler, MPH

Sex, Love and Health: A Self-Help Sex Guide to Love & Health by Brigitte Mars

https://www.plannedparenthood.org/learn/stds-hiv-safer-sex/hiv-aids/what-are-symptoms-hivaids#:~:text=You%20may%20not%20have%20any,that%27s%20when%20HIV%20becomes%20AIDs.

https://childsafety.losangelescriminallawyer.pro/children-and-grooming-online-predators.html

https://www.nspcc.org.uk/about-us/news-opinion/2023/2023-08-14-82-rise-in-online-grooming-crimes-against-children-in-the-last-5-years/

https://legaljobs.io/blog/online-predators-statistics#:~:text=66.7%25%20of%20online%20predators%27%20victims%20are%20female.,-(Screen%20and%20Reveal&text=Similarly%2C%2077%25%20of%20offenders%20target,based%20sexual%20abuse%20(60%25)

https://www.thetrevorproject.org/resources/article/facts-about-lgbtq-youth-suicide/

https://segm.org/segm-summary-sweden-prioritizes-therapy-curbs-hormones-for-gender-dysphoric-youth

The End of Gender: Debunking the myths about sex and identity in our society by Dr. Debra Soh

https://journals.plos.org/plosone/article?id=10.1371/journal.pone.0202330

https://www.ncbi.nlm.nih.gov/pmc/articles/PMC5868281/

https://www.thehealthyhomeeconomist.com/50-in-utero-human-studies-confirm-risks-prenatal-ultrasound/

https://nation.africa/kenya/news/gender/why-kenya-needs-a-menstrual-leave-policy-4196290#

AUTHOR BIO

Author, podcaster, ceremonialist and singer, Tatiana Berindei is a mother of two girls. While she currently resides in Wisconsin, any place where she can touch the wild earth she considers her home. A perpetual student of life and the Great Mystery, Tatiana loves traveling, getting her hands in the dirt, making and eating good food with her community, sitting in prayer and ceremony with her friends and family, dancing and singing: in circle with others, and from stages, living rooms, and mountaintops. Tatiana's mission is to bring as many people as possible into harmony and union with themselves, each other, and the natural world around them, and to restore the original place of birth as a sacred entrance into the world. Her workshops and retreats are beloved by all who participate. Find out more at pathtopuberty.com.

Made in the USA
Monee, IL
26 May 2024

58790773R00193